Lucille Clifton

Lucille Clifton with her children. From left to right, top row: Frederica, Lucille herself, and Channing. Second row: Gillian, Alexia, Sidney, and Graham. Photograph by Rollie McKerna.

WOMEN WRITERS OF COLOR

Lucille Clifton

Her Life and Letters

Mary Jane Lupton

Joanne M. Braxton, Series Editor

Westport, Connecticut
London

818.5409
C63L

Library of Congress Cataloging-in-Publication Data

Lupton, Mary Jane.
  Lucille Clifton : her life and letters / Mary Jane Lupton.
     p. cm.—(Women writers of color, ISSN 1559–7172)
  Includes bibliographical references and index.
  ISBN 0–275–98469–9 (alk. paper)
  1. Clifton, Lucille, 1936– 2. African American poets—Biography. 3. African American women
educators—Biography. I. Title. II. Series.
  PS3553.L45Z75 2006
  818'.5409—dc22   2006008237

British Library Cataloguing in Publication Data is available.

This book is included in the African American Experience database from Greenwood Electronic
Media. For more information, visit www.africanamericanexperience.com.

Library of Congress Catalog Card Number: 2006008237
ISBN: 0–275–98469–9
ISSN: 1559–7172

First published in 2006

Praeger Publishers, 88 Post Road West, Westport, CT 06881
An imprint of Greenwood Publishing Group, Inc.
www.praeger.com

Printed in the United States of America

The paper used in this book complies with the
Permanent Paper Standard issued by the National
Information Standards Organization (Z39.48–1984).

10 9 8 7 6 5 4 3 2 1

Copyright Acknowledgments

The author and the publisher gratefully acknowledge permission for use of the following material:

Glaser, Michael S. "A Poet for Our Time." Writer's Center, Bethesda, Maryland. National Poetry
Month (April 1999, updated), 1–6.

An earlier version of the Crazy Horse section of Chapter Five was published as "Remember My
Name: Lucille Clifton's Crazy Horse Poems," *Zora Neale Hurston Forum* (XVIII 2004): 77–83.

To Ken again

Contents

Acknowledgments

I owe a great debt to Lucille Clifton for generously sharing so much of her life with me. Without her deep involvement, this biography could not have been written. I thank Alexia Clifton, Eugenia Collier, Freeman Habrowski, Margaret Reid, and Elaine Philip for their insightful interviews as well.

I am especially grateful to my friend and former colleague, Margaret Reid of Morgan State University, for sharing archival materials on Lucille Clifton from her private collection. These materials are indicated in the Selected Bibliography as "From the collection of Professor Margaret Reid."

I thank Hilary Holladay and Joanne Gabbin for making available a transcript of Holladay's interview with Lucille Clifton, videotaped on Thursday September 23, 2004, at the Furious Flowering Conference. Joanne Gabbin granted permission to quote from this interview, which will be part of a DVD to be released in 2006.

Linda Myers, my friend and former graduate student at Morgan State University, emailed her reminiscences of Fredonia, the university that Lucille attended in 1955. Caroline Maun helped download my files and lift up my spirits. Michael Glaser and Edgar Silex, two of Lucille's colleagues at St. Mary's College, provided me with statements of appreciation of her and her poetry.

The following people helped me discover more about Fred Clifton: Donald Patterson, William Sullivan, Martin Dyer, Whitney LeBlanc, and Elaine Philip. Sullivan sent me a tape of Fred Clifton reading his poetry, which Alan Wonnenberger, audio technician at the University of Maryland at Baltimore County (UMBC), enhanced so that I was able to hear it. My husband Kenneth, who has a better ear than I, transcribed it.

In addition I wish to acknowledge the following: Johnny Fields and Reggie Harris of the Enoch Pratt Library; Clarinda Harriss Lott of Towson State University; Thom Ward, Clifton's publisher at BOA Editions; Ken Reinhard of UCLA; Meena Khorana, editor of *Sankofa*, a journal of children's literature of the African Diaspora; Julie Caran, editorial assistant for the Furious Flower

Poetry Center; Aimee Wiest of Lewes, Delaware; Annette Palmer, professor of history at Morgan State University; Dolan Hubbard, chair of the English Department at Morgan State; and Ruthe T. Sheffey, editor of the *Zora Neale Hurston Forum*, who invited me to submit an essay on Lucille Clifton and Crazy Horse for volume VIII, published in 2004.

I also wish to thank Piotr Gwiazda, my friend at UMBC, who sent me his excellent essay on Amiri Baraka; William Hankin, M.D., of Cape May Court House, New Jersey, who taught me about commitment; and Jack and Carol Ann Hohman, who for Christmas 1991 gave us the *Mayo Clinic Family Health Book*, which has remained useful in writing about Lucille Clifton.

My lifelong friends and collaborators Emily Toth and Janice Delaney are responsible for our shared research on menstruation, first conducted in 1976 and updated in 1988. Our work together has been invaluable in examining Lucille Clifton's poetry about menstruation. I also thank anyone else who has encouraged this project and whose name I have unintentionally omitted.

I thank my twin daughters, Ellen and Julia Lupton, for their love, for their incredible and continuous energy in design/writing/research, and for mothering our six grandchildren while keeping spaces for their own work, as I did for mine.

I thank Joanne Braxton, editor of the Women Writers of Color Biography Series, and Suzanne Staszak-Silva, senior editor of Praeger Publishers, for their contributions to my proposal for this project and for their meticulous editing of the manuscript, as well as for answering questions regarding margins, word count, bibliography, permissions, and other matters large and small.

I am grateful to my students at Morgan State University for having stimulated my interest in poetry, in biography, and in the way the two intersect, with special thanks to Mary Beth Hansen, who first introduced me to the poetry of Sharon Olds.

As always, I thank my husband Kenneth Huntress Baldwin for his generosity of time and love, for listening to my constant retelling of episodes from Lucille Clifton's life, and for listening as I read to him some of her most disturbing poems. I appreciate his intelligent critiques of this project at its various stages, especially during the copyediting. I also thank him profusely for my sixty-sixth birthday present: an almost perfect first edition of *Good Times*.

Series Foreword

I ntended to include biographies of women writers of Hispanic, Asian, and Native American descent, the "Women Writers of Color Series" begins with a focus on African-American women writers. Overlooked for too long, these women, like other women of color writers, deserve a place in our libraries and on our bookshelves.

Among women of color writers in the United States, women of African descent have been preeminent, setting high standards, and opening doors for women writers from other ethnic groups. Beginning in the eighteenth century, the tradition of black women writers in these United States has been one of long struggle, or perhaps of a series of interrelated struggles. For the earliest writers, there was the struggle to achieve freedom from enslavement and physical abuse. Literacy, self-definition, autonomy, and self-respect are some of the goals that eighteenth- and nineteenth-century poets, orators, novelists, and essayists promoted among the general black population. But first and foremost, they were concerned with physical survival—the survival of their families, loved ones, and themselves; survival is something that no black woman writer has ever taken for granted.

Graced with few weapons other than what they could carry with them, Africans new to the Americas brought with them a rich cultural heritage that included a vibrant oral tradition. Having endured the dreaded Middle Passage to the New World, the first Africans in America had still to survive its harsh climate and the cruel conditions they would suffer as enslaved men and women without legal rights with which to resist rape, disfigurement, starvation, or the separation of their families. Not only would they endure, but—to borrow Faulkner's phrase—they would prevail.

Contemporary women writers of color, including those women of color who are not of African descent, have looked to these foremothers as heroes and miracle makers. It is because of such women that this series exists. It exists for every woman writer of color whose work we will never know. It exists for everyone of any race who can read these words and appreciate them, and for every little girl of any race who ever wrote a poem and hid it. This general audience series is intended to be enjoyable reading for an enlightened multiethnic audience that knows both the cost and the necessity of creativity, for poets, writers, schoolboys, and librarians who will read with their eyes wide open. Naturally there will be something new and refreshing for the scholar and the critic, but this series is also for the daughters of those mothers whose creativity and intelligence were suppressed, hidden, targeted, and denied—women like June Jordan, whose mother, Mildred Maude Fisher Jordan, might have been an artist, but instead succumbed to madness and suicide; and Lucille Clifton, whose mother, Thelma Moore Sayles, burned her poems because her husband didn't approve. Audre Lorde's mother also wrote, and she hid the poems that she wrote in secret.

Therefore this series exists. It exists so that girls and women of all races everywhere and in all layers of society will know that that there were those who went before them who survived beatings, sexual violation, and all manner of psychological and emotional abuse, as well as various other attempts to degrade and silence them. Instead of becoming silent victims, these women of the word went on to become poets, novelists, poets, and essayists. Inspired by the models offered by the brave literary women who are the subjects of these biographies, the coming generations will refuse to write their poems and novels in secret; and those who have written in secret, and without the affirmation of friends, family, and loved ones, will come out of the literary closet, bravely bringing their once hidden works into the light of day. Each volume is published with a user-friendly bibliography so that the readers of the Life and Letters Series can pursue original readings by these writers and find existing literary criticism more easily.

Lucille Clifton: Her Life and Letters by Mary Jane Lupton is the first biography of a most influential black and female poet. Clifton's superbly crafted poetry and children's books have won many literary prizes and awards, including the YM-YWHA Center Discovery Award, the Juniper Prize, and the National Book Award, among others. She has been Poet Laureate of the state of Maryland and is currently Distinguished Professor of the Humanities at St. Mary's College of Maryland and a Chancellor of the Academy of American Poets. Therefore, as Clifton has been an influential poet over the past quarter century, her life and work are of great interest to readers of American poetry.

Biographer Mary Jane Lupton, Professor Emeritus from Morgan State University, was first introduced to the poetry of Lucille Clifton while teaching her graduate seminar in poetry at Morgan. Herself widely published, Lupton was drawn to Clifton's work because of the poet's fluid interweaving of style and structure and her extraordinary openness when writing about the female body; she found some of these poems reminiscent of the work of Sylvia Plath and Anne Sexton. Lupton further observes that being a black woman in white America gives Clifton an acute awareness of history—the slave ships of the Middle Passage; the auction block in New Orleans; the church bombings of children in Birmingham, Alabama; the murder of Civil Rights leader Medgar Evers; the murder of a black man dragged along the highway in Jasper, Texas. In her poems about these atrocities, Lucille Clifton identifies herself with the victims as one of them in spirit, and through immersion the reader vicariously endures the same experience.

Clifton's poems about grief and her poems about living with cancer also have a universal appeal, connecting the reader with the infinite and unanswerable, "Why?" As readers of all races and ages are drawn to this profoundly human poet and her work, the publication of this biography is an event of great literary and cultural significance.

Joanne M. Braxton
College of William and Mary
Series Editor

Introduction

L ucille Clifton is a major figure in contemporary American poetry, a woman whose intense exploration of her body and psyche has helped make possible a new honesty, a new perspective. Her poetry and her children's books have been reviewed and honored widely, beginning with her very favorable review by the *New York Times*, which called *Good Times* one of the ten best books of 1969, and continuing with each new publication. Lucille, as she has asked me to call her in this biography, is the author of eleven books of poetry, one prose memoir, and nineteen books for children. Her memoir, *Generations*, published in 1976, traces her ancestry from her paternal great-great-grandmother Caroline through her grandparents, her parents, her children, and her future grandchildren. In *Generations* she writes, "Lines connect in thin ways that last and last and lives become generations made out of pictures and words just kept" (275).

Lucille Clifton makes words into pictures through her unforgettable characters, from Everett Anderson and Miss Rosie in her early writings to the violated Leda in her 2000 book, *Blessing the Boats*. Her characters range from family members like her father to biblical heroes like King David; to women from Greek mythology like Leda; and to contemporary heroes like the real Malcolm X and the fictional Clark Kent, the Superman who failed her ("if i should," *Book of Light* 41). In many of these poems Lucille transcends the racial limitations of the Black Arts Movement (BAM), which reportedly began in 1965 when LeRoi Jones (Amiri Baraka) and other activists formed the Black Repertory Theater, established the *Journal of Black Poetry*, and adopted the term "black power" as a means of self-definition.[1] Although she espoused many of the principles of the Black Arts Movement, Clifton ultimately has chosen to weave her meanings into a rich tapestry of ideas that places the human condition above issues of race and gender.

Writing the biography of this extraordinary and generous woman has not been a simple matter. The first difficulty in reconstructing the life of Lucille Clifton is that biographical accounts are filled with inaccuracies. One person credits her with the authorship of *Things Fall Apart* in 1959, confusing her with Nigerian novelist Chinua Achebe.[2] In addition, information on her marriage and immediate family has been difficult to uncover. An unidentified staff writer for a Baltimore newspaper claims that her husband, Fred, was head of African-American Studies at Howard, not at Harvard, whereas Hilary Holladay, the foremost Clifton scholar, in a 1999 essay calls Fred a "job consultant," rather than a professor and political activist.[3] In some Internet sources on the history of the Civil Rights Movement and the Black Arts Movement, Fred Clifton is not listed except as Lucille's husband. I am grateful to his former friends and neighbors for helping me get a far better sense of the man, who with Lucille parented six children and shared her interest in poetry and politics.

The second problem for a biographer is that many of the people Clifton mentioned in interviews or dedications are almost impossible to identify, even with the assistance of Internet sources. People in her life—Dr. Joyce Johnson from her childhood and Annette Baldwin from her days at Howard are only two examples—have eluded my detection. One reason, perhaps, is that when Lucille was growing up, African-Americans, even those with law degrees or with doctorates, were less likely to achieve recognition in mainstream society. Until Lucille was eighteen there was a strict separate-and-unequal policy, legally overthrown in the 1954 Supreme Court decision of *Brown versus the Board of Education*, which claimed that racial discrimination "violates the 14th amendment to the U.S. Constitution, which guarantees all citizens equal protection of the laws."[4] To avoid being misled by inadequate or inaccurate sources, I have verified persons and events mentioned in this biography through personal interviews with Lucille Clifton, with her sister Elaine Philip, and with her youngest daughter Alexia Clifton, as well as with friends and colleagues who are familiar with her life and achievements. I had the pleasure of interviewing Alexia in July 2004. In a telephone interview a year later, I talked with Elaine Philip, who told me many wonderful stories about Lucille as a child. Without them the biography could never have come alive. Whenever possible, I have also tried to connect her poetry to her extraordinary life rather than to have one engulf the other.

Clifton's life as a mother and sister, both now and then, has enabled her to explore a variety of familial roles in her poetry and her children's fiction. She also possesses an intimate awareness of black history—the slave ships during the Middle Passage; the auction block in New Orleans; the church bombings of children in Birmingham, Alabama; the murder of civil rights leader Medgar Evers; the murder of James Byrd, Jr., a black man dragged along the highway in Jasper, Texas. In her poetry she identifies herself with the victims, sharing their humanity. As she has said on numerous occasions, she believes that a poet's job is to tell the truth. Although much of her poetry is private, her compassion goes beyond personal, familial, national, and racial boundaries, and most certainly beyond the strictures of the profession. "Academics take the music out of poetry," she said, adding, "I think I was born a poet."[5]

One of her most moving volumes, *Next* (1987), includes poems on the death of her mother and her husband and a series of poems on the death of Sioux warrior Crazy Horse. She also examines other large-scale historical moments: the incarceration of South African freedom fighter Nelson Mandela, the bombing of Nagasaki at the end of World War II, and the mass suicides of more than 900 people from drinking poison in the village of Jonestown in Guyana in 1978. Her poems reach out to the people of South Korea, to the Cherokee Indians of Georgia, to those who were persecuted as witches in Salem, Massachusetts, to the victims of Hurricane Katrina in 2005. One can only imagine her thoughts on the tsunamis and hurricanes that claimed so many lives in 2004 and 2005.

As a poet, Clifton believes that she has a personal obligation to discuss these horrific events with her students and to require that they do research on issues that might otherwise go unexplored. "I try to talk with the students about things that have happened, for instance, offenses against humanness," she said in our interview of March 5, 2004. "We talk about My Lai and the Trail of Tears and the Salem Witch trials. Not just African-Americans. There are all kinds of things."[6] Still, she remains hopeful. Assuming the familiar posture of the witch or old hag she writes, "but when I wake to the heat of morning / galloping down the highway of my life / something hopeful rises in me" ("hag riding," *The Terrible Stories* 26). This hope has touched her students, her family, and her friends.

In "the making of poems" Clifton writes, "the reason why I do it / though I fail and fail / in the giving of true names / is I am adam and his mother / and these failures are my job" ("Two-Headed Woman," *Good Woman* 186). Within the grand scheme of poetic production she sees her poems, her "namings," as failures. In a moment of irony, one of many in her poetry, her failures become her "job," a word that, when, capitalized and pronounced with a long *o*, would refer to Job, the Old Testament hero whose endurance was his redemption and whom she cites in the epigraph to her memoir, *Generations*. Yet she is unique in her androgynous presentation of herself as Eve: "i am adam and his mother." In dialectical fashion Clifton sees the good and the bad within herself: the failure and endurance, the mother and son, the weakness and strength. As this biography will show, her strengths are many and her failures few.

Lucille Clifton, poet and educator, has challenged stereotypes about blacks and women, and in so doing, her humanism has transcended issues of race and gender. In her early volumes of poetry and in her children's books about her best-known character, Everett Anderson, she primarily explored the lives of men. In the poetry of her middle stage she began to focus on women. Yet she has evidenced in all of her works a compassion for both men and women. Nor does she see being black as a reason for critics to categorize her poetry as an echo of established black poets, such as Langston Hughes or Gwendolyn Brooks. "I am not a sub-genre," she has insisted.[7] Clifton aims her writing at a universal readership: "What I hope is to write poetry that my Aunt Temmie can understand on one level; the cab driver can understand on another; and the

Ph.D. can understand on yet another. And that's good enough."[8] In this way, her poetry has reached a large audience and has won a significant number of awards and the affection of friends and colleagues throughout the world.

Clifton served as Poet Laureate for Maryland from 1979 to 1982. Her official function was to write occasional commemorative verse, for which she was paid $1,000 a year. In these "official" poems it was important for the poet to relate her personal history to the broader political vision. Often these two were in conflict. In an interview in the journal *Callaloo* she remarked that when she was asked to write an anniversary poem about "Our Happy Colonial Days," she faced an immediate problem. "Well, people who look like me didn't have a lot of happy colonial days, you know," she said, laughing.[9]

A proponent of peace and nonviolence, Clifton was one of the fifty poets and writers to sign the "Statement for Peace," published in the February 13, 2003, issue of the *New York Review of Books*. This statement urged President George W. Bush and his administration not to make a first strike against Iraq and to support the formation of a Palestinian state in the Middle East. She signed the "Statement for Peace" in her position as Chancellor of the Academy of American Poets, one of the most distinguished positions in American letters, to which she was appointed in 1999.

In 1976 Clifton received an Emmy for her participation in writing the screenplay of the television special, *Free to Be You and Me*. She has also won the Juniper Prize for Poetry (1980), the Distinguished Writers Award from the Mid-Atlantic Writers' Association (1981), the Shelley Memorial Prize (1992), a Lifetime Achievement Award from the Lannan Foundation (1996), two National Endowment for the Arts Fellowships, and a number of honorary doctorates—from the University of Maryland, from Towson State University, and from Dartmouth College, among others. She told Susan Somers-Willett, tongue in cheek, that although she never earned a college degree, she was inducted into the prestigious honorary society Phi Beta Kappa in 1998.[10] In 1999 she became a Fellow of the American Academy of Arts and Sciences. The following year, she received the National Book Award for her volume *Blessing the Boats*, along with $10,000 and a trophy.[11] Although she has not won the Pulitzer Prize, Lucille is the only American poet to be a finalist for the Pulitzer for two books in the same year—for *Good Woman: Poems and a Memoir, 1969–1980* and for *Next: New Poems* in 1987.

A gifted teacher of poetry and creative writing, Lucille Clifton is in demand as a visiting professor. She has taught at Coppin State College, Columbia University, the University of California at Santa Cruz, and St. Mary's College in Southern Maryland. Ironically, St. Mary's College is built on the shores of the Saint Mary's River, an upper branch of the Chesapeake Bay that once served as "a gateway for the first blacks brought to the colonies from Africa."[12]

At St. Mary's she has taught for a number of years as Distinguished Professor of Humanities. She also held the Hilda G. Landers Endowed Chair in Liberal Arts. Dr. Maggie O'Brien, president of St. Mary's College, was quoted in the *Baltimore Times* as saying, "Throughout her career, Professor Clifton has received countless acclaim for her work. ... Her accomplishment comes as no surprise to the St. Mary's community. She continues to inspire us with her presence as a professor, poet, and a human being."[13] Although she retired from St. Mary's in 2005, Lucille has agreed to continue her affiliation by teaching for one week during each semester.[14]

Referring to her laureateship, her honorary degrees, her endowed chair, her Phi Beta Kappa key, and her other honors with her typical humor, she remarked, "I've gotten the National Book Award, and I've got awards hanging from my bedpost at home. I have the honorary degrees arranged because I like the colors and the last one I got, I was so excited because I wanted blue. I had a lot of red."

However, driving an automobile is not one of Lucille Clifton's many achievements. She does not drive, nor has she ever taken lessons. Once the former president of St. Mary's told her he would grant her an honorary doctorate if she would learn how to drive. She has many other interests, though, not all of them having to do with poetry. For example, she has a penchant for slot machines. She likes to play the slots in Atlantic City with her close friends, Sonia Sanchez and Joanne Gabbin.[15] When the three friends play the slots, Lucille often comes up a winner on the "Fire and Ice" machine because she simultaneously pulls the lever and recites Robert Frost's apocalyptic poem, "Fire and Ice": "SOME say the world will end in fire, / Some say in ice."[16] For Christmas in 2003, her daughters gave her a slot machine imported from Japan.[17] She also loves going to Disney World and Universal Studios with her grandchildren.[18]

During the last four decades our paths have crossed in a number of ways. When Lucille was poet in residence at Coppin State College in the early 1970s, I was teaching at Morgan State College; both of these colleges are historically black institutions of higher learning in Baltimore. For a brief period of time two of the Clifton children attended the Baltimore Free School, of which I was co-founder. One night Lucille read her poetry at the Angel Tavern, a beer and wine bar of which I was part-owner. Although I had taught some of her poetry at Morgan State, her reading at the Angel was my first exposure to the real "Lucille." Finally, we have both examined the menstrual process in our writings.

I first interviewed Lucille Clifton on March 5, 2004, at Saint Mary's College in Saint Mary's City, Maryland, a tranquil academic community on the shoreline of Saint Mary's River at the edge of the Chesapeake Bay. As my husband Ken and I entered the student dining hall in anticipation of the interview, we were told that to get snack food we should go upstairs to the second floor. There, on the two-story wall that was at least twenty feet high, I recognized the title poem to *Blessing the Boats* inscribed in silver lettering. One needed no greater sign of the regard with which St. Mary's College holds Lucille Clifton.

Lucille is a large-framed African-American woman who walked slowly toward her office as I, early as usual, sat tensely on a bench waiting for our one o'clock appointment, which was to be our first interview. When she arrived she immediately hugged me and introduced me to her friend, Kathy Glaser. Later, after we were seated in her small office, I asked her what she preferred to be called in the biography. She decided that since her students call her Lucille, that is what I should call her in this book. "Some of my students call me Professor Lucille," she joked. "One student said if her grandmother knew she was calling me by my first name she would turn over in her grave."

The poet pushed aside her carry-out shrimp salad sandwich so that she could answer my questions. During the entire interview her door was open to visitors, including students, staff, and fellow writers. Edgar Silex, a young colleague and a poet, came in to say hello.[19] A technician arrived to deliver a set of three videotapes of internationally known poets from sixteen countries who had participated in a conference in Jerusalem; the American representatives were Lucille Clifton and Galway Kinnell.[20] She took these interruptions in stride.

I was initially curious about one of her most famous poems, "wishes for sons," published in *Quilting* in 1991, twenty years after *Ms. Magazine* became the first national journal to advocate abortion rights and gender equality.[21] I still remember a remark attributed to Flo Kennedy that turned sexual assumptions upside down and became a touchstone for *Ms*: "If men could have babies, then abortion would be a sacrament."[22]

In "wishes for sons," an ironic poem about menstruation, Clifton turns the sexual worldview upside down, cursing men with periods. Like Flo Kennedy's reversal, she reverses the biology-is-destiny cliché, assuming the role of the Wicked Witch of the Grimm's fairy tale, *Sleeping Beauty*.[23] The witch is a frequent figure in her poetry, representing candor and spirit. In the Grimm's version she is the angry, uninvited guest at the christening of the baby princess Briar Rose, much as the menstruating woman is the uninvited guest in a society run by men. In a 1976 book called *The Curse: A Cultural History of Menstruation*, Janice Delaney, Emily Toth, and I connected the menstrual bleeding of the pubescent princess with the punishment placed by God on the first mother, Eve. This punishment is known popularly as "Eve's curse" or more simply, "the curse."[24]

Clifton obviously knows the story of Sleeping Beauty and of the twelve guests at her christening who wished her joy, grace, happiness, and nine other feminine virtues. Her 1993 poem, "sleeping beauty," is not about the princess's christening but rather about her startled reawakening, after a century of sleep, to the presence of a strange man: "he was the first thing she saw / and she blamed him" (*Quilting* 32). In "wishes for sons" the poet also blames men—not just her own sons but sons everywhere—for their treatment of womankind. She structures the poem as a series of curses disguised as wishes: "i wish them cramps. / ...." "i wish them a strange town / and the last tampon. / i wish them no 7–11" (*Quilting* 60). Other wishes for sons run the gamut of menstrual ailments, from clots to hot flashes to unanticipated menstrual periods. In their directness about the female body and its functions, Clifton's poems epitomize the new and quite serious exploration of women's biology that peaked in the 1980s and 1990s and that remains a significant aspect of contemporary women's poetry.

Like menstruation, abortion was another hush-hush topic during the emerging women's movement. Between 1963 and 1972 American feminists, most of them white and middle class, challenged male control over women's reproduction through private discussions, petitions, and legal actions.[25] Gwendolyn Brooks and Anne Sexton also addressed these issues in their poetry. Gwendolyn Brooks, in her 1945 poem "The Mother," focuses on the impact of abortion on the memory: "Abortions will not let you forget. / You remember the children you got that you did not get."[26] In June 2000 Lucille told Hilary Holladay that her own poem on abortion could never have been written without Brooks' precedent.[27]

In fairy-tale format, Sexton's poem "The Abortion" records the painful memory of losing her unborn child. She drives through the coal regions of central Pennsylvania to see a doctor who is "not Rumpelstilskin, at all, at all... / he took the fullness that love began."[28] In the transformational format that characterizes Sexton's technique, she converts the fairy-tale gnome who exchanged babies for gold into an abortionist.[29]

Lucille Clifton describes the physical and psychological pain of abortion in "the lost baby poem," a work that begins with the horrific line, "the time i dropped your almost body down," a line that suggests a protagonist who has aborted her fetus into a toilet (*Good Woman* 60). Like the Brooks poem, "the lost baby poem" dwells on the unfinished nature of potential motherhood, on the emptiness that abortion brings as the "almost body" drops into the waters and runs "one with the sewage to the sea." Clifton's equation of baby and sewage is even more severe than the image in Brooks's "The Mother"; the baby's final resting place is with the garbage swept under the city. In all three poems of Brooks, Sexton, and Clifton the ache of thwarted motherhood is felt in the remembrance of the unborn child and in the cold silence of the landscape.

Ironically, Lucille Clifton's most painful poem concerning abortion is not the ambivalent "lost baby poem," but the unmistakably autobiographical poem, "donor," published in 2000 in *Blessing the Boats*. Dedicated to her youngest daughter Alexia, "donor" begins with Lucille's unsuccessful attempt, thirty years earlier, to abort her with coat hangers and pills, only to have the child "refusing my refusal" (17). Alexia Clifton is the insistent and "stubborn baby child" whose kidney was successfully transplanted into her mother's body three decades later, giving her new life.

In the late years of the twentieth century, when so many formalist poets were writing abstractly about their craft, Lucille Clifton, Gwendolyn Brooks, Anne Sexton, Sylvia Plath, and other women were charting forbidden territory, describing menstruation, kidney failure, childbirth, dialysis, madness, abortion, and breast cancer. Lucille Clifton has become a major surveyor in this expedition; she speaks for the common woman but also for the survivor, for the courageous self within. Like Maya Angelou and Margaret Walker, her poems "all hit at the heart," says Eugenia Collier, a Baltimore native and the author of a brilliant collection of fiction, *Breeder and Other Stories*. When compared to other black women poets, "Lucille's work operates on a different level. You have to read and reread her poems. Her poems can get inside of you. The voice is familiar and accurate. The mystery goes down inside."[30]

During our first scheduled interview at St. Mary's College we talked about some of these issues and about some of her poet-friends. After the hour was over, my husband Ken, by prior agreement, drove us back to the poet's home in Columbia, Maryland. The car interview was different in tone, more intimate perhaps because it was uninterrupted. She spoke frankly about the deaths of her husband Fred and of two of her children, Frederica and Channing. She spoke of the horrors of dialysis and showed me the scars in her arm and neck where the needles had been inserted. During the ride I continued to record our conversation until the tape ran out.

By the time we arrived at her home we were all exhilarated but exhausted. Always generous, she invited us in. A letter sent Priority Mail was on her doorstep; her editor from BOA Editions was on the phone within minutes of our arrival. We said goodbye, assuring each other that this would not be the last meeting. Later that year, I was privileged to see Lucille Clifton from a distance when, on November 18, 2004, the Poetry Society of America sponsored "A Tribute to Lucille Clifton" at Hunter College in New York City. This major event in her life is discussed in chapter 7.

On June 21, 2005, more than one year after our first meeting, we had a follow-up interview to establish priorities in the book's content and to deal with possible objections from her family to material in the biography. Lucille was in the process of having new carpeting installed. She was dressed in loose-fitting clothing and was wearing no shoes. Although we sat in the front room, I could see the shelves in the adjacent room that housed her African-American dolls, some of them new, some of them dating back to the plantations, and most of them gifts from admirers around the world. She thanked me for having sent her a cardboard cut-out of a slave child that was designed as a pencil holder. On this occasion there was time to observe the splendid African figures sculpted by the late Fred Clifton—large statues using the techniques of Congo woodcarvers but in a more contemporary style. Lucille pointed to a photograph of Fred Clifton, a splendid image that occupied a special place on the wall and, obviously, in her heart.

Lucille Clifton is a richly complex woman. She can be warmly compassionate; she can be intensely angry. She refuses to accept general statements about her character, for she "learned a long time ago not to buy other people's definitions of who I am and what I'm supposed to be like."[31] Given her warning, I will do my best not to paint any definitive one-dimensional portrait either of Lucille Clifton or of what she is "supposed to be like." While approaching her life in an intimate way, I hope to offer multiple views of this incredible artist.

ONE

An Early Dreamer

A Northern child with Southern and African roots, Lucille Clifton was born Thelma Lucille Sayles in Depew, New York, on June 27, 1936. Her great-great-grandmother on her father's side, Caroline Donald Sale, was an enslaved Dahomey woman "born free in Afrika in 1822 / died free in America in 1910."[1] Her father, Samuel Louis Sayles, was born in Bedford, Virginia, in 1902; he had been married to Edna Sayles, who died young and was the mother of Lucille's half-sister, Josie. Lucille's mother, Thelma Moore Sayles, Samuel's second wife, was born in Rome, Georgia, in 1914. Neither of her parents finished elementary school. Her immediate family consisted of two half-sisters by her father's previous relationships, Josie by his wife Edna and Elaine by Ophelia, his girlfriend. Lucille's brother Sammy, called "Hon," born to Thelma and Samuel in 1938, was two years her junior. Thelma raised all of these children. Lucille was delivered by Dr. Terrell, the doctor who sixteen years later performed her college physical examination before she left for Howard University.

Clifton remembers Depew as a small town that was mainly Polish. Other than for her extended family and the small Southern Baptist church, there was virtually no black community. Depew has not grown much since she was a child. The 2000 U.S. Census shows that the town has about 16,000 inhabitants, half men and half women, with the majority of people being of Polish or German descent. Only a small percentage of the current population of Depew is African-American.[2]

An exceptional fact about Lucille's birth is that she was born with twelve fingers, six on one hand and six on the other, as were her mother and one of her daughters. She associates this congenital difference with European witch-craft and with Egyptian royalty. One poem begins, "I was born with twelve fingers / like my mother and my daughter / each of us / born wearing strange black gloves." She describes these hands as having "invisible fingers" connecting the three generations through "our terrible shadowy hands" (*Good Woman* 166). When she was a newborn, the doctor wrapped string around her extra digits, cutting off the circulation until they fell off.[3] Her nephew, the son of her deceased brother Sammy, was also born with twelve fingers.[4]

Another congenital distinction that Clifton addresses throughout her poetry is her one bad eye; she had poor vision in her left eye from birth. Over the years her right eye has compensated for the left eye's weakness. In an untitled poem from *An Ordinary Woman*, reprinted in the 1987 collection, *Good Woman*, she refers to herself in the first line as "lucy one-eye" (*Good Woman* 145). In "the light that came to lucille clifton" she observes that she was not "mistress even / of her own off eye" (*Good Woman* 209). The poet views her weak eye as enhancing her spirituality, intensifying the power of her visionary experience. In "the gift" she describes such a woman: "there was a woman who hit her head / and ever after she could see the sharp / wings of things" (*Mercy* 11).

Lucille's childhood was not easy; the family had little money and no convenient means of transportation. In an early poem, she retells the story about her father, who walked one day more than twelve miles from Depew to Buffalo to order the first dining-room set ever owned by a black family in her town: "first colored man in town / to own a dining room suit / things was changing" (*Good Times* 50). When she was a child her family lived on Muskingum Street, several blocks from her mother's family, the Moores, who had a "big frame house on Laverack Street with one toilet" (*Generations* 265). There were a lot of people, young and old, living with her maternal grandparents, who had a goat in the back yard; the economic foundations of the extended family were shaky (*Generations* 266). In the celebrated poem "Good times" she describes their joy when her Uncle Bud hit the numbers. The rent got paid, the insurance man left, "the lights is back on," and everyone is singing, dancing, and getting drunk (*Good Times* 10).

The poem "imagining bear," written for her maternal grandfather, Alonzo Moore, Sr., compares this gruff-hided man to a bear who lumbers along and growls in the wind. "imagining bear" is a very simple poem constructed of seven couplets, six of which begin with the word "imagine"; the central couplet rejects this form, ordering the listener to "give him an old guitar / give him a bottle of booze" (*The Book of Light* 17). In a telephone conversation with Lucille's sister Elaine Philip on July 6, 2005, I learned that Grandmother Moore is the "Georgia" of Lucille's well-known poem, "Miss Rosie."

When Lucille was seven the Sayles family moved from the town of Depew to the city of Buffalo, New York, where they lived in a rented house on Purdy

Street in the black community. The number of black people living in Buffalo, a city of more than 350,000, was much higher than in Depew. Several of her relatives also moved to Buffalo and joined the Southern Baptist church that had formerly been located in Depew. Clifton remembers her Aunt Blanche, who rolled her "basketball of a body" into a street in Buffalo one Sunday morning (*Blessing the Boats* 23). She also remembers her Aunt Timmie, who used to iron the sheets for a famous male poet, even though under her breath Timmie composed poetry of her own, part Indian and part African. In her uneducated way Timmie understood "form and line / and discipline and order and / america" ("study the masters," *Blessing the Boats* 25). However, it was to her parents, her brother, and her sisters that Lucille devoted most of her early attention.

LUCILLE'S FATHER, SAMUEL SAYLES

During his lifetime her father, Samuel Sayles, held a number of jobs. He had been a coal miner, but he moved to Buffalo to work in the steel mills and struggled through several illnesses, including emphysema and a brain tumor. He was injured on the job and had to have his leg amputated. In *Generations* Clifton tells how her sisters, Elaine and Josie, were at his side when he lost his leg. "Jo had cursed the nurses and made them clean up the mess in the hospital and Punkin [Elaine] had held his hand and they had bought him his wheelchair" (241). In one of her poems, "the killing of the trees," the reference to the photograph of an "old warrior" with brown wrinkled skin and "one good leg" reminds the reader of an older Samuel Sayles.

The snapshot of Samuel Sayles in *Generations* presents a contrasting image—a young, dapper man, right hand in pocket, tall and casually dressed as he looks with assurance into the camera. Critic Cheryl Wall describes the picture as a "snapshot, rather than a studio portrait," unlike the earlier studio portraits of Lucille's family. "Suavely dressed, replete with vest, suspenders, tie, and sharply creased trousers, he looks like his father's son."[5] In "album" the poet playfully imagines her father's survival as a lucky old man on his ninetieth birthday (*The Terrible Stories* 51).

When they were young Samuel used to read to them the poetry of Paul Laurence Dunbar and Langston Hughes; Elaine Philip said that Lucille mastered black dialect by the time she was eleven or twelve.[6] He also told his children ghost tales. They sat on his bed while he made up scary stories, stories that Elaine thought were far scarier than the ones they listened to on the popular radio program, *Inner Sanctum.*[7]

Although Samuel Sayles was an avid reader, he never learned to write. It became Lucille's responsibility to deliver notes to school and to go for money orders. She recalls that one day when she was twelve she took a note to school from her father that said, "She do not have to pledge the flag, When it means to her what it means to a white girl, then she may stand." However, embarrassed at being considered rebellious, Lucille jumped to her feet when the Pledge of Allegiance began.[8]

According to Clifton's surviving half-sister, Elaine Philip, who moved in with the Sayles family at age ten, Samuel Sayles had an enormous appeal to women. "He was a lady's man with many girlfriends, even when he was married to Thelma. He verbally abused his wife and evidently was not interested in her. They had separate bedrooms. He was not a nice man," Elaine told me. As a husband and a son, Samuel clearly withheld his affection. Clifton told Michael Glaser that the only time she had ever seen Samuel kiss his mother on the mouth was when he went to Virginia to visit her when she was dying.[9]

Generally detached from the household, Elaine recalls him as always reading newspapers or the Bible or listening to sports on the radio. He outlived Thelma and fathered another daughter before dying at the age of sixty-seven. His funeral was to become the centerpiece for Clifton's 1976 memoir, *Generations*. Reynolds Price, who reviewed *Generations* for the *New York Times*, reads the memoir as both elegy and funeral oration; in the latter form Clifton alters "the style and language of America's greatest orators, Negro preachers."[10] The poet's funeral orations are formal responses to the deaths of her mother, her father, her husband, her sister Josie, her brother Sammy, her husband, and two of her six children.

According to literary critics, textual evidence supports the idea that Samuel Sayles sexually abused Lucille. According to Hilary Holladay, "the abuse was clearly a defining component of her youth and has been a continuing source of melancholy."[11] In her insightful essay on *Generations*, Cheryl Wall interprets the memoir as a "meditation on the meaning of his life" and a veiled exploration of the incest taboo. "The lingering compulsion to keep the family secret," claims Wall "may well explain the silence surrounding incest in *Generations*."[12] Linton Weeks of the *Washington Post* commented on the critics' preoccupation with incest when in 2000 he wrote, "In the past, she had talked openly, and written about sexual abuse at the hands of her father. Today, she doesn't mention it."[13]

Indeed, in "moonchild" (*Blessing the Boats* 2000) Clifton is specific about her incestuous relationship with her father. The poem begins with her birth, "roundheaded and unsmiling," having emerged from her mother's womb. Her father cradles her in the moonlight. Years later she and her sister giggle and pad their bras. Then the verse takes a dreadful downward turn as one of their friends, Ella, brags about learning to French kiss and asks Lucille who is teaching her. In "moonchild" the poet silently answers: "how do you say: my father?" (*Blessing the Boats* 15) In "forgiving my father" she calls her father "daddy, daddy old lecher / old liar" (*Good Woman* 178).[14]

In *Mercy*, she is open, almost outspoken, about the abuse. Not published until 2004, the title poem "mercy" leaves little doubt that if she was not technically raped she was surely sexually abused. Although Samuel Sayles never had intercourse with Lucille, she told me that he did "everything else but that."[15]

In "mercy" she claims she is grateful that "he" did not "replace his fingers with his thing." She was both "sick" and "mad" and "grateful" when he decided "maybe I shouldn't do that" (*Mercy* 30). Another poem, "what did she know, when did she know it," suggests that her mother may have been aware of Samuel's "soft tap tap / into the room" and may have known "why the little girl never smiled" (*The Terrible Stories* 52). Like many abused children, Lucille remained silent for many years, wanting to protect herself and her father even though her accusations were true.[16]

Samuel's love for sharing stories represented his good side, but scary things happened when he went out with friends, came home at two in the morning, and went into his daughters' room pretending to be a ghost. Elaine remembered him wail, "I'm a spooky wooky spook."[17] Lucille's sister suspects that these late-night incursions may have been alcohol related, although she never saw him drink any liquor at home except for the Thanksgiving and Christmas punch. Elaine says she never knew of the abuse until about ten years ago, long after her father died, and claims that she had escaped Lucille's fate because her father knew she would tell on him, just as she stood up to him when he unleashed verbal tirades against Thelma.

As an abused child Clifton responds sympathetically to the silence that Maya Angelou embraces in *I Know Why the Caged Bird Sings*.[18] When Marguerite, the victim of a childhood rape by her mother's boyfriend, hears that her attacker has been murdered, she refuses to speak for five years. "I've never put this together," Clifton once said in an interview, "that Maya has a thing about when she was raped. She was mute for a couple of years. And I think that the way you try to deal with not being able to talk about it is to write."[19] It is possible that the young Lucille, who began in earnest to write poetry when she was nearing the age of twelve, found in writing a way not to talk about her father's betrayal.

LUCILLE'S MOTHER, THELMA SAYLES

Clifton's mother, Thelma Sayles, a launderer and a poet, was her daughter's major source of inspiration. She was a capable and imaginative woman and a practitioner of "very traditional iambic verse."[20] She obviously disapproved of Lucille' less poetic conventional style; in our conversation of June 21, 2005, Lucille mimicked her mother, saying "Baby, that ain't no poem. Let me show you how to write a poem." Clifton's sister remembers Thelma as a very beautiful woman, slightly plump and with thick hair, who sat by the window smiling.[21]

One of her earliest memories is of her mother's support. When she was five, little Lucille was supposed to recite a poem at the annual Christmas program at her church. But she couldn't remember the lines, and to hide her deep humiliation and embarrassment, she became sullen and angry. She stood there in her new dress in front of the congregation, unable to speak. "Then, like a great tidal wave from the ocean of God, my sanctified mother poured down the Baptist aisle, huge as love, her hand outstretched toward mine." Her mother said, "Come on, baby." Turning towards the congregation, Thelma announced, "She don't have to do nothing she don't want to do." At this moment the young Lucille felt "empowered and made free."[22]

Lucille remembers her first real job working at the beauty salon next door. She also remembers sitting on her porch while Thelma greased and braided her hair. She had a photograph of this intimate moment in her life, but the moment is disappearing from memory.[23]

She clearly remembers the day she watched her "sanctified mother" burn her own poetic efforts, an event that she was later to record in her poem "fury: *for mama*": "remember this. ... / the coals glisten like rubies. / her hand is crying. / her hand is clutching / a sheaf of papers. / poems. / she gives them up." The crying hand is central to the poem, which is replete with images involving survival, religion, and memory. The mother's eyes are "animals." She is a "serpent's obedient / wife," the serpent being her husband, Samuel Sayles. She will "never recover" (*The Book of Light* 44).

Clifton claimed that her mother burned her poems because her husband Samuel didn't want her to publish them; "a lot of people now might not understand that, but then a wife obeyed." Her father once said, "Ain't no wife of mine going to be no poetry writer."[24] His prohibition, which had a tremendous effect on the young Lucille, is perhaps the reason she kept on writing. She resented the way he treated Thelma. Clifton said, "I can forgive my father for driving us crazy. He was driven crazy, you know. *But* I cannot forgive him for driving my mother mad. And she was probably always on the edge."[25]

Thelma's madness was not solely the result of her husband's abuse, however; Lucille's mother was an epileptic. Prone to seizures, Thelma kept to her room during much of the time when her daughters were growing up. Over the years the girls watched their mother's health deteriorate. After the birth of Lucille's brother, Sam, Thelma said to her daughter, "Get away, get away. I have not had a normal life. I want you to have a normal life. I want you to get away" (*Generations* 272). Elaine remembers her mother's radiant smile at her wedding reception at which Thelma wore a silk dress and danced. Elaine recalls it was the only time she had ever seen her mother have a good time.[26]

Lucille's mother, Thelma Sayles, a powerful presence in each of the Sayles daughters' lives, died in 1959, a month before the Cliftons' first child, Sidney, was born. Sadly, Elaine was living with her husband in Tacoma, Washington, at that time and learned about her mother's death in a telephone call from Lucille.[27] Thelma's death was a great loss for all three sisters and for "Hon," Lucille's younger brother.

When writing about her mother's death Clifton frequently takes the point of view of her subject, a technique she uses in her memoir *Generations* and in many of her poems. Ancestors both speak to and through her mother, Thelma, with the poet possessing the voice of the departed spirit. In "the death of thelma sayles" (*Next* 51) her mother's voice claims: "I leave no tracks so my live loves / can't follow." This metaphor reveals a mother who slides in and out of time and space, visiting the living and making their souls tremble, much as in the earliest elegy, "My Mama moved among the days," she had been a "dreamwalker in the fields." The image stresses the ephemeral nature of Thelma Sayles as a "dreamwalker" who floats through Lucille's dreams and becomes a ghostly reality.

Several critics of Clifton's poetry have commented on her re-birthing of her mother through poems written in her memory, poems that establish a symbiotic relationship between the death of Thelma Sayles and the someday death of Lucille Clifton.[28] Thelma's passing instilled in Lucille the fragile bond among herself, Thelma, and her ancestors. She gained an enormous respect for all mothers and for their sacrifices.

Reliving the life and death of her mother occupied much of Clifton's emotional life during the 1960s. An innovative piece of research by Hilary Holladay connects Lucille's barely disguised feelings for her mother to two pieces published a decade after Thelma's death in *Redbook* and *House & Garden*.[29] In the mid-1970s the deceased Thelma started to speak to her daughter in visions. This "unsought, unexpected supernatural contact" was the beginning of Lucille's spiritual awareness.[30] In "the death of thelma sayles" her mother's voice claims: "I leave no tracks so my live loves / can't follow" (*Next* 51). In a rather grotesque image Thelma throws her heart to the "little girl" standing by the river; she catches it and runs home to her children. "i whisper in her ear," the dead and heart-less Thelma states at the end of the poem; at times Clifton whispers back in a supernatural exchange of call and response.

The poem, "to thelma who worried because i couldn't cook," is based on an extended metaphor of cooking, feeding, and kneading (*Good Woman* 175). The poem reveals Clifton's frequent joy at punning—"kneading/needing." It is also one of the few poems to address masturbation: "because no man would taste you / you tried to feed yourself / kneading your body / with your own fists." Two other elegiac poems immediately follow in *Good Woman*. "poem on my fortieth birthday to my mother who died young" uses the conceit of life as a race in which Thelma tripped "on the forty-fourth lap." There is a physical sense of perseverance in this poem, which ends with the affirmation, "i'm trying for the long one mama, / running like hell and if i fall / i fall" (*Good Woman* 176).

"february 13, 1980" marks the twenty-one years in which Thelma has been gone from Lucille's life. Twenty-one years is an unusual date to commemorate, but as her daughter explains in the poem, "even your absence comes of age" during the years between Thelma's death in 1959 and the publication of *Good Woman* in 1980. Fabian C. Worsham comments that "february 13, 1980" marks a major moment in Clifton's life. "Having rescued her mother from death by living for her, she now faces the death which swallowed up her mother."[31]

LUCILLE'S RELATIONSHIP WITH HER SIBLINGS

Elaine is just six months younger than Lucille; Lucille was born in June and Elaine in January. Elaine says her half-sister was then, and still is, "funny, smart, and caring; she hasn't changed a bit."[32] When they were children, Lucille's stories were so much in demand that the others used to wash the dishes so that their talented sibling could recite to them. In their house was a small empty room that the three children used as a playroom. They called it "Candy Land."[33] There were drawings on the walls of the playroom and stacks and stacks of paper on the floor. The children, under Lucille's imaginative leadership, would fly to "Candy Land" and live there. Even then she had her brother and sisters believing in the world of the imagination. According to Elaine, "Everybody loved Lucille. She is the kindest person I have ever known. I always wanted to be like Lucille."[34]

Often, when Elaine and Lucille were falling asleep, they heard mice in the dresser drawer. Lucille sang so that Elaine wouldn't be afraid. Clifton's funny poem, "this is for the mice that live / behind the baseboard," humorously captures a similar scene. As "she," presumably Elaine, lies whispering with cheese on her fingers, the poet calls to them, mimicking their voices but making no promises. "this is for the mice that live" is a duet written in two voices, with Lucille's voice confidently assuring Elaine's (*Quilting* 32).

Sometimes, when they went to the library together, Lucille read books while Elaine looked out of the window. When they were of drinking age they would go to the bar on the corner on Friday nights where Lucille would have a draft beer and Elaine a glass of Mogen David wine. Elaine was devastated when her sister went off to Howard University. Elaine was married at eighteen, but her marriage dissolved after only four years. The sisters still see each other from time to time, especially when Lucille returns to Buffalo to do readings. Elaine, who stayed with Lucille when they attended the Columbia Jazz Festival in 2005, claims that "everything she learned she learned from Lucille."[35]

Clifton captures a few of these intimate moments with her siblings in her poetry. "sisters: for elaine philip on her birthday" begins in black English: "me and you be sisters, / we be the same." It announces their sisterly affinities, which began in their childhoods, when Mama Sayles would laugh as her girls stepped on roaches or ran along Purdy Street. The sameness still remains as they mature; they get older, they have babies, they get black. In the last two lines Clifton interrupts these similarities in a marvelous comparison: "only where you sing / i poet" (*Good Woman* 112).[36]

Another poem for her sister is "lane is the pretty one," which begins: "her veins run mogen david / and her mind just runs" (*Good Times* in *Good Woman* 18). The poem creates a set of parallels between Lucille, with her "crooked nose" and her "too wide mouth," and Elaine, "the best looking colored girl in town." In the center of the poem there is a set of rhyming couplets: town, brown: glass, class. The strongest couplet, which appears at the end of the poem, is based on repetition, with the sisters joined by the word "love": "dear sister love dear sister." Each of these simple structures reinforces the closeness between the two young women.

Clifton had a more distant relationship with her brother, Sammy, which might be attributed to a difference in age and gender, as Sammy was two years younger than Lucille. Sammy, called "Hon," was very smart, but he was also very spoiled by his mother and by his three sisters, as only the youngest boy among all of those women would be. "Hon" eventually became a heavy user of drugs and alcohol because "he simply couldn't deal with the world."[37] With no steady job, he was supported by those who loved him, including his sister Lucille. He eventually gave up the drugs but not the alcohol and died from heart failure at the age of fifty-five.[38]

The Terrible Stories has four poems that refer to Sammy. One is an elegy, "in the same week," written for Samuel Sayles, Jr., 1938–1993. Images of burning and shells of fire suggest that Sammy had been cremated. He died in the same week that "stafford folded his tongue / and was gone, nothing / innocent is safe" (53). The phrasing is reminiscent of Robert Frost's famous poem about the impermanence of nature, "Nothing Gold Can Stay."[39] The reference to Stafford is one of several allusions in Clifton's poetry that are almost too obscure for the general reader to trace. Like the better known poet, Robert Lowell, William Stafford (1914–1993) was a conscientious objector during World War II. He did not publish his first book of poems until he was forty-six. According to Donald Hall, Stafford "has referred to an unspoken tongue that lives underneath the words of poetry."[40] The folded "tongue" in Clifton's elegy to her brother is an emblem of her own unspoken art as well.

This rather impersonal elegy is followed by an ironic glimpse of her brother looking down from the edge of heaven with some friends and laughing at Lucille, who, "even when she was right, she was wrong" ("heaven," *The Terrible Stories* 54). The messages that Clifton, in her various practices with the Ouija board and with automatic writing, had received from her mother and her other dead relatives tended to be far more considerate than this one from "Hon" Sayles.[41]

Her brother is also mentioned briefly in her poem "Memphis": "my mother had one son / he died gently near lake erie." Sammy's gentle passing is offered as a contrast to the violent deaths of "schwerner / and chaney / and goodman / and medgar," all who died in the struggle for human rights (*The Terrible Stories* 42).

Her most emotional elegy to her brother is "august." Addressed to Elaine, it uses the recurrent phrase, "what would we give," to express their regret that they can no longer "fuss with him again." In a strange metaphor she asks "what / would we give / to smile and staple him / back into our arms," imply-ing that Sammy needed a physical attachment stronger than love to keep him with his sisters. The dilemma is resolved with the idea that "honey boy," although he had not been sober, had been "at least, alive!" (*Blessing the Boats*

24). Lucille rarely uses an exclamation point, as she does in "august," to emphasize her emotions.

Her older sister, Josephine, or Josie, as she was called, was the daughter of Samuel and his first wife, Edna. Seven years older than Lucille and Elaine, Josie was too old to share their pranks or step on roaches. Judging from the biographical information Clifton provides in "here rests" (*Mercy* 31), Josie was born in 1929 and died in 1989 and was a prostitute with a "heart of gold."

"Here rests" combines two of Clifton's favorite genres, the elegy and the birthday poem. It describes the loving way in which Josephine and her pimp, "Diamond Dick," came in from the streets to care for their dying father, reading to him from the Bible and reminding Lucille that "when you poem this" she should remember the Book of Job. Even though Josephine had already been dead for fifteen years by the time the poem was written, the poet wishes her a happy birthday. In the poem, Clifton's prayer for her sister Josie is that "heaven be filled / with literate men / may they bed you / with respect."

Clifton is inconsistent in her use of capitalization in this poem. The name, Diamond Dick, Josephine's pimp, is capitalized, as is the Book of Job and Josephine, whereas "july," "the bible," and "heaven" are in lower case. Although these alterations in style call attention to the major actors in the poem, they nonetheless seem somewhat arbitrary.

LUCILLE'S TEENAGE AND YOUNG ADULT YEARS

Young Lucille loved her siblings and had an enormous appreciation for her mother's and father's gifts of poetry and storytelling. At the same time she revealed a noticeable fear of her dashing father coupled with a qualified love for her fragile mother. "Poems to and about her mother proliferate, and spin through yearning, rue, rivalry, and passionate identification. Her father is adored, pitied, rebuked."[42] She always saw "something deeper" in what her father said and found herself asking many questions. A willing listener, she also paid close attention to the stories told by her grandmother and her aunts. Clifton acknowledges Reverend Merriweather from the Macedonia Baptist Church as her greatest childhood influence after her parents; his orations stimulated her interest in the spoken word.[43]

Simultaneously, young Lucille was engaged in her own writing, an early interest cultivated and encouraged by her mother. Lucille loved writing and the music of poetry. After she began writing when she was about ten, her name "began to take on metaphoric meaning," referring to the clear associations between Lucille and light.[44]

The first piece of writing that Clifton remembers was a story she wrote called "The Gypsy." She had a crush on a classmate, Ivan Askew. Elaine, "the pretty one," liked him and thought she could impress him; however, Lucille was the smart one. She wrote about the "Gypsy," who was the best kisser in the world, on the planet even, and left the story on Ivan's desk. He took it home to his mother because he couldn't read cursive. His mother thought Lucille was so mature that she was allowed to walk him to school; this was in Buffalo, with its bleak and terrible winters. Ivan would wear clumsy buffalo-front boots, and she would have to help him unbuckle them. When she tells young people this story, Clifton always warns young people that once you know how to unbuckle a man's boots you don't like him anymore.[45]

After writing "The Gypsy," the adolescent Lucille began to write poems in imitation of established women poets. Clifton recalls her youthful attraction to the sonnet form, and she wrote a number of sonnets in the style of Edna St. Vincent Millay; she also modeled some of her poetry after Emily Dickinson, committing to heart a number of Dickinson's crisp lyrics. Clifton remembers writing sonnets in high school, although she didn't turn them in as English assignments.

However, Clifton had no expectations of ever joining the ranks of women poets or of making a career of writing poetry. In her own words, she says, "As a child I never dreamed of having a career as a poet."[46] She told one interviewer, "What you want to understand is that 50 years ago, one never saw a person who looked like me as a published poet. I certainly didn't in the schools in Buffalo, New York, where I grew up."[47]

Lucille was a bright but quiet and shy teenager who got straight A's in school and was always on the Honor Roll. Because of these achievements at Fosdick-Masten High School in Buffalo, she received a full scholarship to college. Her church was very proud of her when she earned one of the nine annual scholarships awarded by Howard University in Washington, D.C. "I was scared and proud and happy to get away," she wrote in *Generations*. "I had begun thinking of myself as special" (249). Clifton says that her parents thought she was going to Harvard, because they didn't know the difference between Howard and Harvard and the names sounded the same.

Howard University is one of the 117 historically black colleges and universities in the United States. It was founded in 1866 by white preachers as an educational seminary, and most of its early students and administrators were white.[48] "Its goal was to duplicate the curriculum of northern white schools and produce black students who could compete in the same arenas."[49] Its early African-American professors and students were light-skinned and conservative and came only from the best families. In its first sixty years, to avoid a "strong black image," the school appointed white male presidents and commissioners.[50] It was not until 1926 that Dr. Mordecai Johnson became the first black president. During his thirty-four years as president of Howard, he pushed for Congressional funding and accreditation for its programs and the hiring of distinguished faculty.[51] Mordecai Johnson was the chief administrator during the short period when Lucille was at Howard, from 1953 to 1954, and it was not until after he retired in 1960 that Howard changed its conservative image.

When Lucille arrived in Washington, she and some friends from Buffalo were met in the train station by Howard sophomores and juniors assigned to welcome the freshmen. One of the Howard men was very friendly to an "awfully cute" freshman. Then he said to Lucille, "You must be her mother." Humiliated, she realized that "I knew I wouldn't last" (*Generations* 268).

Lucille was very nervous and uncomfortable in the dorm. Surrounded by classmates more light-skinned and affluent than she, Lucille would deliberately try to hide where she lived. She would tell them that she was from New York, which was acceptable. Her classmates assumed she meant she lived near New York City, not realizing that the closest big town to Buffalo was Toronto. She kept her belongings in an old trunk that her grandmother had given her. Because she was embarrassed by its condition, she kept it stored in the basement, tied with a rope. She remembered how she would steal down at night for clothing or tuna fish so nobody would see the trunk or associate it with her poverty.

Intellectually, however, her friends at Howard constituted a who's who of the black intellectual elite. She was overjoyed when the famed Sterling A. Brown asked her to join a group of writers that included James Baldwin, Owen Dodson, and Joe Walker. These authors, now so well known, were then, with the exception of Brown and Dodson, struggling young writers. Brown, who had an intense interest in the roots of African-American music, wrote poems such as "Memphis Blues" (1931) and "Ma Rainey" (1932). It was at one of Brown's seminars that she first heard a recording by the great blues singer Billie Holiday. Owen Dodson, who had a long career as a poet and a playwright, was in the theater department at Howard.[52] But Joe Walker, author of the play *River Niger*, was the adult Lucille's "first crush."[53]

Through her mentor Sterling A. Brown and her young friend from Buffalo, LeRoi Jones, she was able to affirm her identity as a black woman. A drama major, she appeared on stage, playing the part of the sister in the first American performance of James Baldwin's *Amen Corner*. Although the Howard Players were world-famous at the time, she never traveled with them. She was in several plays and she loved to act, but she was awkward in her movements and could not dance. Showing contempt for the required curriculum, she engaged herself in drama and neglected her other studies. She told Frederic Kelly, "I dreamed so much that I forgot to study."[54] Although she enjoyed theater, it was the writing group conducted by Sterling A. Brown that had the greater impact on the impressionable young student.

At Howard Lucille numbered among her friends two young women who would later skyrocket to fame: Roberta Flack, who was to become a major vocalist, and Chloe Wofford, later to be known as Toni Morison, winner of the Nobel Prize for literature. Other women, less widely known in the media, were also at Howard. She met Patricia Roberts Harris (1934–1985), a 1945 graduate who later went to Howard Law School. Harris became the first African-American woman to be an ambassador and a member of the presidential cabinet, and she became the first female dean of Howard's Law School in 1969.[55]

After the initial excitement of Howard, it was time to go back to Buffalo for Thanksgiving vacation. The first time she went home on the train from Washington to Buffalo her father and her older sister, Josie, met the train. Everything in Buffalo suddenly seemed so small. Her father admonished her, saying "Girl, you'd better get yourself together." [56]

Following her freshman year, in 1955 Lucille left Howard altogether and entered Fredonia State College, now the State University of New York at Fredonia. Again she had a scholarship. Her change of school put her closer to home and to her family, as Fredonia is located in western New York State, only 45 miles from Buffalo. At Fredonia she became part of a group of young intellectuals who had formerly been at Howard. They wrote poems and acted in the theater. Lucille was one of three people of color on the Fredonia campus; white people driving by would see her and stare in disbelief. [57]

LUCILLE'S MARRIAGE AND CHILDREN

While she was at Fredonia, Ishmael Reed introduced her to her future husband, Fred Clifton. [58] Ishmael, who was thirteen or fifteen when he and Lucille met, lived not far from Buffalo and was attending the University of Buffalo. Ishmael told Lucille, "There's this guy, all the women are running after him, and he likes *you*." Lucille thought that Fred Clifton was one of the best-looking men she had ever seen.

Fred was born in Dunham, Kentucky, and served as a Marine in the Korean War before attending graduate school at the University of Buffalo as a John Hay Fellow and a New York State Regents Fellow. He taught at the University of Buffalo and later at Harvard, where in the early 1960s he helped found the Department of African American Studies. [59]

Being a steelworker, Samuel thought that Fred spent far too much time in the useless occupations of academic life; in short, that he was wasting his time. [60] Because Samuel Sayles disliked Fred intensely and was strongly opposed to the marriage, Lucille and Fred eloped on May 10, 1958, when she was 21 and he was 23.

The editor of *Essence* described their marriage as "a perfect coming together of like minds and spirits. They shared an enduring love of words, of family, and, most of all, of each other." [61] In his wife's eyes, Fred was an amazing and beautiful man whose good looks she celebrates in "the kind of man he is." She praises "the look of him / the beauty of the man," his darkness, "the sound of him" (*Good Woman* 87).

They soon shared the responsibility for raising six children, born one after the other. The oldest girl was Sidney, born in 1960. Frederica soon followed in 1961. Their first son, Channing, was born in 1962 and a third daughter, Gillian, in 1963. A second son, Graham, was born in 1964 and their last child, Alexia, was born in 1965.

When her children were infants, the young mother stayed at home caring for them. She enjoyed being with them while she was writing. Because of that early experience of writing with their noise ever present, she now likes to write with the television on in the background. "I learned to work in my head a lot. Because I had the kids. I would never put aside kids for a poem."[62]

But, as is true for many young poets, the creative act of writing poetry did not produce an income. Getting help with the children, Clifton took other jobs to help support her family. As a newlywed she worked as a claims clerk in the New York State Division of Employment in Buffalo from 1958 to 1960. When she worked for that government agency, she did not discriminate racially among her clients, who would sometimes say, "We want to speak to the Polish colored girl."[63]

Meanwhile, Fred was teaching philosophy and African-American studies at the University of Buffalo. A very spiritual man, Fred Clifton was a vegetarian and practiced yoga. From his studies in Eastern philosophy Fred had achieved a sense of center and balance and a need for order. According to his wife, he believed that "the job of an artist is not to add to the chaos in the world."[64]

It was after attending a philosophy conference in Cincinnati that Fred was radically transformed; he became committed to a life of helping others. Hospitals would call him to sit and meditate with leukemia patients in crisis. Lucille believed in Fred's conversion and in the possibility of receiving messages from the ones who had already passed, although, as Akasha Hull has demonstrated, her earliest and most lasting spiritual contact was with her mother.[65]

Fred encouraged Lucille's ventures into poetry and children's books. He was pleased by her winning the Discovery Award, and he supported her literary judgments.

In her "Letter to Fred," written five years after his death, Lucille recalls living with the family on $150 a month, which is what the GI bill provided. "You and me and six babies coming one right after another," she wrote. She remembered that Fred was the one to bathe the babies, because she was too nervous. "I remember how you would take off your shoes and socks and walk in the bathtub filled with diapers and soap." She remembers when people warned her not to marry Fred because he was too dark. "'That boy is too black,' some folks would say. 'Baby, he's so dark, think of the children.' 'Girl, we got to think about lightening the race.'"[66]

In 1967 the couple moved from Buffalo to Baltimore, Maryland, because Fred was hired as director of the Baltimore Model Cities program. They began to search for a house large enough for a family of eight in West Baltimore and found one in Windsor Hills, a house on the edge of Gwynns Falls Park. One of their neighbors was Freeman Habrowski, the current president of the University of Maryland Baltimore County. When Lucille was poet in residence at Coppin State College, he was a dean there. "There was a lot of love and a lot of children," Harbrowski said.[67] Her younger son, Baggy [Graham] used to "highjack"

Habrowski into mowing his lawn. Baggy would mow the lawn first and then tell Habrowski what he owed him.

Another neighbor, Eugenia Collier, had a son, Phillip, who was a close friend of Channing Clifton. Collier remarks that Philip, Channing, and Marc Chapelle were inseparable when they were teenagers. She also knew two of the Clifton daughters from activities at Windsor Hills School Number 87.[68] Unfortunately, the Clifton family was evicted from the house in Windsor Hills because they could not afford the payments, and it was sold at auction. Lucille, who made the financial decisions, hated telling Fred, but her primary concern was that her children would not feel displaced or frightened.[69]

In the early '70s, when Lucille was teaching at Coppin State College, their two oldest daughters were enrolled briefly in the Baltimore Free School, a progressive institution based primarily on the ideas of Jonathan Kozol, whose writings presented alternatives to public education and gave instructions on how to set up what was then called a "free school." Jonathan Kozol and other educators of the decade argued that public schools disregarded the needs of students and offered little opportunity for their personal growth.[70]

During one of the first weeks of school a Clifton child reportedly came close to drowning in the neighborhood public pool that the free school had been given permission to use. Fred Clifton stormed into the Baltimore Free School the next day, condemning the staff for their irresponsibility, and he immediately withdrew his children. Years later Alexia explained that the safety of his children always came first for her father.[71]

As parents the Cliftons insisted that their children receive an education free of prejudice. More than once they kept their children out of school and risked being arrested in order to guarantee that their children would not lose their sense of racial pride. Lucille thought that if you don't do go to jail for your kids, for whom else are you going to risk arrest? They had learning tools and toys all around the house. Their children were literate and understood a lot of things. Lucille had little sympathy for mothers who looked for excuses to avoid child-rearing. She liked to tell the story of a neighbor whose husband asked her to hurry over and take care of his wife's two children because the woman was "catatonic." Clifton told her to get off the floor and get "uncatatonic."[72]

A vital and respected civil rights leader and educator, Fred Clifton was responsible for helping create a national black political agenda. He was an officer of the Black National Political Party and co-chaired the Maryland delegation to the National Black Political Party Convention in Gary, Indiana, where 4,000 delegates gathered to write platforms on race for both the Republican and Democratic presidential conventions.[73] Lucille attended some political gatherings with Fred.

As a neighbor, though, Fred Clifton was fairly inconspicuous. Neither Eugenia Collier nor Freeman Habrowski, who knew the children, ever met him. Fred occasionally attended community meetings and was once at the traditional

New Year's party of a neighbor, Martin Dyer.[74] But his wife was a more active, more visible presence in the community.

Fred, despite his political activism, was basically a quiet person, devoted to yoga, to mediation, and to family. The subject of some of Lucille's most passionate poetry, Fred loved his wife and his six children. Above all, he loved his people. "I could not have married anyone else," Lucille tells Fred in her posthumous letter to him. "I could not have lived with a man who could not feel and could not cry about our people's need."[75]

And like his wife, Fred Clifton was also a poet. According to Dyer, Fred "recited poetry in a small theater group at a church. Lucille read regularly. Fred read once, that I can recall, and both my wife and I attended. He read a series of poems."[76] Another Windsor Hills resident, William Sullivan, remembered Fred's reading at the community theater in Windsor Hills under the direction of Whitney LeBlanc, who has since moved to California. Sullivan made a recording that he sent to me. The recording arrived in the mail in April 2005, beautifully wrapped but damaged. Through the efforts of Alan Wonnenberger of the UMBC music laboratory, Fred Clifton's voice, silent since the recording was made in 1969, was again audible.

He is introduced by Lucille, who says, "Fred Clifton is a man, a man who is, I think, the only real artist that I know. He is a poet, educator, and sculptor who is just a magnificent human being. I like him! He is a very honest man, Fred is. He is the most honest man I have ever known, and he makes me honest, forces me to be honest in ways that I am not courageous enough to be by myself. I have been much, much increased by being Fred's wife."

At the beginning of his reading, Fred called his collection of words a "set of etchings," a good image to describe his acerbic style, like an acid pen cutting out images on glass. His tape-recorded poems are interspersed with remarks and commentary, no longer totally distinct after the passage of nearly forty years since Bill Sullivan first recorded his words. He told the audience not to be "cowards," but to let their feelings come out. His poems, he says, are written with "sighs, moans, screams, blood, and piss."

With that kind of self-evaluation, Fred's first poem is surprisingly tranquil. Its controlling image, the boat, cannot help but remind the listener of Lucille's "blessing the boats," although the tone of the two poems is very different. Using the collective first-person pronoun, he compares the "destitute" navigators to "great blackened pirate vessels" and, in an obvious racial metaphor, laments that "we," his people, are "conceding our masterful contentions." Other poems are studies in racial contrast as he attempts to "simplify the complex psycho-sexual dynamics that always mediate between blacks and whites." In "Where We At?" he writes that black people "always walk slightly to the left" as they take their "long journey to slow change."

One of his most interesting poems is a description of the Baltimore fire of 1904. In this poem, Fred's *persona* is sitting in a restaurant, the House of Welch, one of the only buildings in the block left standing. Portraits of dead presidents are on the walls, and black waiters serve the clientele. A "precious white woman" brushes past the observer, "with her hip against my shoulder and her odor as she passed." In this ambivalent and angry poem, the white woman, who has evidently called him by a racist name, is also somewhat tantalizing. But hers is an "odor" and not a fragrance.

Fred has other enigmatic poems about women, including "On Viewing a Seasoned Secretary through Too-Clear Glass," a portrait of a secretary in which he explores her view of reality. The language is lush, with descriptions of the woman's "over-exposed neck and invisible necklace space" and the "high spot" on her belly. The poem ends with the image of the woman taking vengeance on her "electric machine," explaining in his commentary, "Her efficiency is the only glory that she has; in fact, it's the only morality she has." The "electric machine," like many of his images, is ambiguous; it suggests the typewriter but also the vibrator.

One of his best pieces is "The Wall," addressed to Lucille. In his remarks he says, "In a way it's a poem about marriage and about what happened when people commit themselves to each other unconditionally or conditionally and one of those conditions is unconditionally. The intention is to create the feeling of a wall, and yet things are always leaking through." He uses an elongated structure to represent this wall—or so it seems from listening to the poem. References to the ivy, to secrets, and to truth indicate that the poem was written for his wife, who, like Fred, was always concerned with the truth: "Your secrets are my truth." Later, in *Generations* Lucille tells about how she and Fred would "fuss" about the issue of the truth. He "told me one day not to worry, that even the lies are true. In history, even the lies are true" (245). This concern for the truth is a major philosophical theme that Lucille and Fred shared equally.

Fred Clifton's poetry conveyed an intense interest in the differences between blacks and whites, as well as men and women. Had he lived longer and had he not been so engaged in political action, he might have become a major poet in the African-American tradition. As it was, his short lifetime and his commitment to a nationalist agenda left him with little time for self-reflection or for the careful editing that he needed to perfect his style. When he died of lung cancer at the age of 49, the brief obituary from the *Baltimore Sun* identified him as "Activist wed poet laureate." Fred would have found this dependency on Lucille distasteful, being so much of a person in his own right.

Although she had already lost both parents, it was the loss of Fred that most affected Lucille Clifton's middle years. With Fred gone, she was left a widow with six children, the youngest being Alexia, who was almost nineteen when her father died. The blow was somewhat softened by the fact that Lucille was by then a fairly well-known poet and educator, with a job waiting for her at the University of California at Santa Cruz. Still, if it is hard under normal circumstances to pack one's belongings and move from one coast to another, how much more difficult must that be when one's helpmate of twenty-six years is gone, if not in spirit at least in fact. As we shall see in a later chapter, Fred Clifton's death from cancer at such a relatively young age triggered for his widow not only successive stages of grief but also deep feelings of abandonment. Later, when she develops the same disease that killed her beloved, she experiences intense feelings of anger. Not surprisingly, Fred Clifton's early passing affected Lucille's immediate circumstances, her poetry, and the rest of her everyday life.

TWO

Children and Other Good News

During the intense years of child-bearing, marriage, and early mother-hood, Lucille Clifton continued to shape her craft, even though she had few models to go by and little awareness of how to make public an art that she had been practicing privately since childhood. She was at that time unfamiliar with the work of black writer Gwendolyn Brooks, who had won the Pulitzer Prize for her poetry collection *Annie Allen* in 1950 when Lucille was fourteen, and who would later become a close friend. "I was just a housewife with four babies in diapers and no washing machine," she has told several interviewers, noting that Pampers disposable diapers were unknown until the birth of her sixth and last child, Alexia.[1]

Wishing to share her work with an audience, Clifton sent several poems to the well-known poet Langston Hughes. In 1969 she sent some poems to Robert Hayden, past president of the National Endowment for the Arts and a prolific poet who had been published in the *Negro Digest* and elsewhere. Hayden in turn showed her poems to Carolyn Kizer. An influential poet and administrator, Kizer was director of the literature program at the National Endowment for the Arts from 1966 to 1970.[2] As luck would have it, Kizer showed the poems to colleagues at the 92nd Street Y, a community center in Manhattan known for its support of the arts. In fact, the 92nd Street Y was, at that time, reportedly the poetry capital of the country. This extraordinary cycle of discovery and support led to Clifton's winning the New York Young

Women's and Young Men's Poetry Center Discovery Award in 1969, sponsored by the Y.

With their six children safely under the care of a baby-sitter, Fred and Lucille drove to Manhattan to receive the award. Lucille changed her clothes in the car.[3] At the Y she read some of her winning poems, and later she and Fred attended a dinner in her honor, held at Claudette Colbert's apartment in New York City. At the dinner, "Ishmael [Reed] broke a chair," she recalled. She remembered thinking, "Do I have to pay for this chair?" For Lucille, the "housewife," the event was very exciting.

An editor from Random House, Natalie Robbins, was in the audience. After the reading she asked the young poet if she had a manuscript of her poetry. Clifton recollects, "Yes, I had some poems. I had always been very careful about how poems went together, how they flowed together, in smaller terms how a line follows another line and a poem follows another poem. Random House accepted the manuscript. I was pretty shocked."[4]

The slim manuscript was published in 1969, almost immediately after she won the award, under the title *Good Times*. It was chosen by the *New York Times* as one of the ten best books of the year. Chad Walsh of *Book World* argued that in "affirming blackness more than it denounces whiteness, the book somehow reveals joy in the midst of misery."[5]

In this volume of thirty-seven poems she begins to apply two of the techniques she is to use consistently throughout her later works. First, she frequently uses a grammatical structure that has come to be known as "black English."[6] Second, she generally avoids capitalization and punctuation, preferring to use them only when they seem to have significance.[7] This second technique enhances the first, giving her poems their stunning oral quality, as if they were spoken rather than printed. In *Good Times* she infrequently capitalizes the first-person singular pronoun, giving her voice a muted effect.

The title poem "Good times" appears on page 10 of the original edition. It reflects Clifton's joy in the economic survival of her family, after the rent had been paid and "the lights is back on." "Oh these is good times / good times / good times" (reprinted in *Good Woman* 24). In *Good Times* she unveils her skills at creating characters who suvive the circumstances of the black neighborhood; she values their lives and lifestyles.

The untitled first poem, "in the inner city / or / like we call it / home," sets the tone for the book, which contains family poems to her father, her mother, and her great-great- grandmother Caroline. "My Mama moved among the days / like a dreamwalker in a field," she writes in the second poem. The poem that immediately follows is about her father and his fingers, "grotesque as monkey wrenches" from chipping steel. This is Lucille's first reference in her poetry to twisted or deformed fingers, a motif that stems from her own birth and that recurs throughout her works.

Many of the poems in *Good Times* are about men. The most moving is "robert." Robert's first name is uncapitalized in the 1987 edition but capitalized in the original. He has no last name, no further affirmation of his existence. He was "born obedient / without questions" (*Good Woman* 20). The lines—"until he died / the color of his life / was nigger"—end the poem. In these concluding lines the reader immediately recognizes the absence of any form of punctuation or capitalization, a form that reflects robert's lowly place in society. The poem's structure also offers clue about his status. From his birth in the first line of the poem until his death in the tenth, one gets the sense of robert's unbearably short life from the shortness of the lines devoted to him. The most surprising touch, though, is the play on color ("the color of his life"), a description that concludes with the shocking word *nigger*.

Most readers know that *nigger* is an offensive term that designates a black person or person of color, derived from the Latin *negro* or black. The 1997 edition of *Webster's New World Collegiate Dictionary* offers virtually a sermon in its definition of *nigger:* "USAGE: originally simply a dialect version of *Negro,* the term nigger is today acceptable only in black English; in all other contexts it is now generally regarded as virtually taboo because of the legacy of racial hatred that underlies the history of its use among whites, and its continuing use among a minority of speakers as a viciously hostile epithet."

What happens, then, when a black poet such as Lucille Clifton, fully aware of the word's vicious hostility, uses the tabooed *nigger,* "acceptable only in black English," as racial self-epithet—much as Dick Gregory did in his infamous 1964 autobiography, *Nigger,* published five years before *Good Times?*[8] Clifton's anger becomes apparent through the beaten figure of Robert and through the use of the word *nigger,* which is applied sparingly in her later poetry, in an untitled poem from *Mercy,* for example (68).

Eight of the poems in *Good Times* concern young men much younger than Robert, again with no last names: "tyrone (1 to 4)" and "willie b (1 to 4)." Their futures, like Robert's before them, are bleak. In the series of related tyrone/willie b poems, the poet displays what is to be another trademark, her compilation of similar material into a sequence; it is an organizational tool that is essential to her later poetry. The language of these poems is harsh, the action violent:

- "and my daddy was / a white man / [line skipped] the mother fucker" ("willie b (1)")
- "today is mama's birthday / and I'm gone get her that tv / out of old steinhart's store" ("willie b (2)")
- "i'm the one / what burned down the dew drop inn" ("willie b (4)")
- "the spirit of the buffalo soldiers / is beautiful / how we fight on down to main street" ("tyrone (2)")

The theme of spirited children at play links the poems about willie b and tyrone. The sequence shows children "laughing and shouting / we happy together" ("tyrone (2)"). The happy children coincide with Clifton's second career as a children's book author, also begun in 1969, with the publication of her first book in the Everett Anderson series. The theme bears comparison to William Blake's brief book of deceptively simple poems, *Songs of Innocence* (1789). Clifton's slim volume *Good Times* takes on some of the innate concepts one finds in Blake, especially the idea that children are innocent until society exploits them and denies them freedom. "flowers," for example, supports a Blakean reading: "here we are / flourishing for the field / and the name of the place / is Love" (*Good Woman* 33). The capitalization of *Love*, with capitalization so spare a device in Clifton's' poetry, tends to evoke Blake and his abundant use of capital letters in such poems as "The Blossom," which opens with the line, "Merry Merry Sparrow" (*Songs of Innocence* 10). In her 1996 poem, "Blake," Clifton identifies openly with Blake's poetry and his visionary experiences (*The Terrible Stories* 44).[9]

Typical of most young American children, tyrone and willie are playing war, playing at being soldiers. Although some victorious black athletes are mentioned—the baseball player Jackie Robinson in "tyrone (3)" and the boxer Muhammad Ali in "willie b (3)"—the dominant reference is to the buffalo soldier, a figure from post–Civil War history.[10] The Cheyenne and the Comanche Indians nicknamed the black members of the Ninth and Tenth Cavalries "buffalo soldiers." Ostensibly assigned to harness the Indian population, buffalo soldiers also explored and mapped huge sections of the country, protecting settlers living on the frontier and railroad crews at work.[11] Descendants of these famous but nameless ancestors, tyrone and willie b take to the streets, charting maps of their neighborhood and knowing exactly where to find a television set for willie b's mama's birthday.

Directly following the eight-poem sequence is a bleak poem that describes the end of any war, any time and anywhere: "war over / everybody gone home / nobody dead / everybody dying" ("buffalo war," *Good Woman* 46). Perhaps Clifton is recalling the end of World War II in the summer of 1945, when she was nine years old and her fictional willie b was twelve: "mama say / I got no business out here / in the army / caused I ain't but twelve" (25). More likely the poet is foreshadowing the end of the war games as the boys grow up and become dissolute teenagers, a sad event commemorated in the untitled poem, "those boys that ran together / at tillman's / and the poolroom" (*Good Woman* 28).

Her depiction of those "fine boys" who are now remembered as "a shame" will surely remind the reader of Gwendolyn Brooks' "We Real Cool," her almost legendary poem about "seven at the Golden Shovel."[12] "We Real Cool" was published in 1960, nine years before Lucille Clifton's "those boys that ran together." One remarkable aspect of both poems is the women poets' ability to present the young male's point of view, as Brooks did in several of her works and as Clifton was to do in many of her children's books, especially in the Everett Anderson series.

Of the women in *Good Times*, the most meaningful is her mother, Thelma Sayles, to whom the book is dedicated. She also writes about her sister ("lane

[Elaine] is the pretty one," *Good Woman* 18) in a poem that reveals the poet's insecurity about her own appearance. In "for deLawd" she reaffirms her African heritage: "i come from a line / of black and going on women." These women fry chickens, do the ironing, sweep the stairs, and grieve "for their still alive sons / for their sons coming / for their sons gone / just pushing" (*Good Woman* 32). The vision in "for deLawd" is more secular than religious, with the last word, *pushing*, suggesting survival through the mother's birthing or "pushing" forth of new generations of sons. This succession of sons will be crucial to the structure of her 1976 memoir, *Generations*.

Clifton's lineage is the subject of "ca'line's prayer," a marvelous poem in two stanzas that contrasts the blighted "desert country" of her great-great-grandmother's old age with being a child "running across Dahomey / black as ripe papaya" (*Good Woman* 33). Using similar images of vegetation in "generations" (*Good Woman* 36), she laments the "people who are going to be / in a few years / bottoms of trees," arguing that the present generation bears responsibility for those who follow. In the poem "generations," as in the willie b and tyrone sequence, the themes of war and death are prominent. Various references to rice, grasshoppers, and invisibility suggest the invasion of Southeast Asia during the Korean War from 1950 to 1953 and America's extended involvement in the Vietnam War, which peaked in 1969, the year in which *Good Times* was published.[13]

As for the women in *Good Times*, they produce sons. The sons go to war, either in the street or in the pool hall or on the battlefield. The issue of gender is not of prime importance in *Good Times*, as it will later be in *Two-Headed Woman*, published eleven years after *Good Times*. And yet, by some act of magic, Clifton conjures up in *Good Times* one of her most memorable female sketches, "miss rosie." Like "ca'line's prayer," the poem is based on the contrast between youth and age. When we first meet her through Lucille's gaze, "miss rosie" is "wrapped up like garbage." She wears "old man's shoes / with the little toe cut out," an image that suggests both the derelict and the circus clown. These are not shoes fit for a lady. Yet this "wet brown bag of a woman" was once "the best looking gal in georgia / used to be called the Georgia Rose."

Although the state of georgia goes uncapitalized in the 1987 version, miss rosie's former state of glory is by contrast accentuated: she used to be the "Georgia Rose." In her tattered attire, miss rosie is the female counterpart of robert. But although in "robert" the subject is reduced to the word *nigger*, in "miss rosie" the poet who silently gazes at her finally rises in protest: "i stand up / through your destruction / i stand up" (*Good Woman* 19). According to the poet's sister, Elaine Philip, Miss Rosie is none other than Georgia Moore, Lucille's maternal grandmother.[14]

"miss rosie" is probably Clifton's most widely anthologized poem. Charles H. Rowell once told Clifton, "I have carried Miss Rosie in my head all of these years. She personally represents our ancestors, our common past."[15] Maya Angelou begins one of her autobiographical musings, "Art for the Sake of

Soul," with praise of "miss rosie."[16] Alicia Ostriker compares the poem's structure to the triple quatrains of Shakespeare's sonnet 64. "Only what time destroys for Shakespeare is for Clifton destroyed by time and poverty joined."[17] Most critics of Clifton's poetry single out "miss rosie" as representing a new *persona* in contemporary African-American poetry. She sets the stage for the women's voices that will come later: Kali, Leda, Mary, and Lucille herself.

Good Times ends, fittingly, with a humorous poem in which the poet as mother advises her girls that the first time a white man "opens his fly / like a good thing" they should laugh: "when they ask you / why is your mama so funny / say / she is a poet / she don't have no sense" ("admonitions," 37). As Hilary Holladay has noted, "The double negative in the last line of "admonitions" captures black vernacular speech but also asserts that the speaker does in fact have 'sense'—the intuitive sense of a poet who know how to use language to suit her own ends."[18]

Clifton's three earliest works were published by Random House, the same New York firm that released Maya Angelou's I *Know Why the Caged Bird Sings* in 1970 and that continues to publish Angelou's poetry and prose today. In 1980, with *Two-Headed Woman,* Clifton moved from the prestigious publisher, Random House, because she believed that a small press was more likely to keep a book of poetry in print. She first placed her books with the University of Massachusetts Press and later with BOA Editions.

MOTHERING AND WRITING

Good Times, although it was deeply concerned with the language and actions of people living in the inner city, was, from a political perspective, a late arrival in the organized struggle for racial equality. It was not published until 1969, six years after the March on Washington, at which more than 250,000 people gathered at the Lincoln Monument for speeches and declarations of freedom and Martin Luther King, Jr. delivered his famous "I Have a Dream" speech. During this time of political ferment Clifton remained mostly at home, writing poetry and attending to her young children. Not until *Good News about the Earth* (1972), her second volume, did Lucille Clifton write poetry directed toward the black power movement.

The Cliftons' neighbor, writer Eugenia Collier, said that during the civil rights movement she was personally drawn to writers more outspoken than Lucille. "Lucille was not overly militant," Eugenia said. "She had a quiet voice that focused on basic needs." Then in retrospect Eugenia added, "Maybe I didn't value her because of my own weakness."[19] In her own defense Lucille has claimed, "I was pregnant then and writing, perhaps producing more activists."[20]

Throughout her various moves—from Buffalo to Baltimore, to Santa Cruz, to Memphis, and back—Lucille Clifton's pursuit of her dual calling as a poet and a parent was uninterrupted. She seems to have experienced little guilt in trying to combine motherhood with earning a livelihood. In *The Feminine Mystique*, published in 1963 when Clifton was twenty-seven, Betty Friedan discussed the "career woman's guilt syndrome," a problem experienced, she claimed, by suburban housewives and other women from the middle class. Although Friedan gave a fleeting glance at the life of the black leader Sojourner Truth, her thesis had little if anything to do with the political and domestic oppression of black women.[21]

Black activists such as Angela Davis argued that black women were exploited both racially and sexually and that during the cult of motherhood that emerged in America in the nineteenth century, black women were still "slaves" and "chattel" in the eyes of the white man.[22] Refusing to accept the radical feminist view that men were the enemy, Lucille told Shirley M. Jordan, "I have been more messed up because of race than because of gender."[23]

Despite her claim that she was "just a housewife with four babies in diapers and no washing machine," Clifton is a descendant of the slave system that she traces to her great-great grandmother Caroline. Her first two books were written in the late 1960s and early 1970s during a period of political upheaval when black feminists were revisiting the issue of slavery from the slave mother's perspective. Among their sources were the narratives of Harriet Jacobs, Amanda Smith, Sojourner Truth, and other black women whose stories of the plantation past were coming to light in a time of black liberation.[24] Having recorded the journey of her Dahomey ancestor, Caroline Donald Sale, from freedom to slavery to freedom, Lucille Clifton, born Sayles, was consciously committed to writing about her slave heritage so that it could never be forgotten. Given her longing to remember her legacy, Clifton's burden was greater than that of most women writers: to record the black struggle and the women's struggle while writing poetry, doing housework, teaching, and caring for her six children. "My children have never known me not to be writing, not to be someone who writes poetry," she told Susan Somers-Willett in 1998.[25]

Lucille maintained her roles of writer and mother during the entire period when her children were growing up, offering them stability and a sense of security. Alexia Clifton said, "Being the youngest of the six, there were just siblings and parents all around and I felt taken care of and secure. I always remember that Mommy was a writer. She wrote books and that was who she was. Daddy was a traveler."[26]

Lucille from time to time wrote poems to her children, including "4 daughters" and "grown daughter" (*Next* 30, 31). Each of these poems contains unspecified references to a daughter: to a "she" or a "someone." The references in the poems are quite homely and domestic, with images of a sieve, a rind, and an onion peel. The poems were published in 1987, three years after Fred's death and shortly after the family, in a strong show of solidarity, had moved with their mother to Santa Cruz.

Lucille was beginning to receive public acclaim. In our interview of March 5, 2004, Clifton told me that one of her first publications was in a collection edited by Ira Zeff.[27] She remarked, "A number of people have a poem to King in that book. Yevtushenko, the Russian poet. And me. I was very tickled."[28] Lucille was also the first poet in the United States to read on the *Today* show, hosted by Hugh Downs; she read something from *Good Times*.[29] She appeared with Bryant Gumbel in the late '90s to discuss the *Huckleberry Finn* controversy stemming from Twain's repeated use of the word "nigger."[30] Clifton, who took a liberal stand in defending Twain's language, remembers that someone from Virginia had accused her of being a sellout.

In addition to *Good Times* and to her first children's book, *Some of the Days of Everett Anderson,* both published in 1969, Clifton tried her hand at short fiction, writing three stories, "The Magic Mama," "Christmas Is Something Else," and "The End of Love Is Death, The End of Death Is Love."[31] Each of these stories is a reworking of the poet's relationship with her mother.[32] Lucille also admitted to a reporter from the *Baltimore Sun* that she had written a script for the television show *Sanford and Son* that was rejected because it "lacked spark."[33] Yet it was neither in television script writing nor in short fiction that Lucille Clifton was to make her reputation. Instead it was in the areas of lyric poetry and children's books, genres that, although ostensibly separate, are often intertwined in style, character, and sentiment.

WRITING BOOKS FOR CHILDREN

For several years, from 1969 to 1971, Clifton was a literary assistant for the U.S. Office of Education in Washington, D.C., where the main focus of her job was dealing with children's books. In 1967 she and the poet Maxine Kumin had worked with the National Endowment for the Arts on the Poets in the Schools program. Meanwhile, Clifton had searched children's books used in three mid-Atlantic states as part of an investigation she was doing for CAREL (Central Atlantic Regional Educational Laboratory)[34] looking for characters that looked like her own children; it was during this time that she started writing books for children, an endeavor that has continued for three decades.

In her search, Lucille had not found many positive models for black children. The Baltimore Feminist Project, a local group of researchers informally sponsored by Rebecca Carroll of the Baltimore Board of Education and by Barbara Mikulski of the City Council, had arrived at similar conclusions, discovering that children who were black and female were grossly underrepresented in basal readers being used in the Baltimore school system. The Baltimore group studied books published between 1964 and 1975, roughly the same period during which Clifton had first questioned and then had begun responding creatively to the lack of stories for black children. Each of the five basal readers analyzed by the Baltimore Feminist Project had similar shortcomings: they presented black children in fantasy, rather than in reality; they gave inaccurate interpretations of minority group achievements; and they showed a bias toward white values.[35] In a "Postscript" discussing the updated Scott, Foresman *Open Highways* series, one of the researchers observed that, although there had been several important changes in connection with racial and sexual stereotyping, including more stories about African-American and Hispanic-American male children, the number of female characters had in fact declined.

In the 1950s and 1960s, the concerns of the Baltimore Feminist Project were being shared by activists in the civil rights and black power movements, and there was a surge of writing directed toward black children. Lucille Clifton, along with June Jordan and Rosa Guy, began writing books for children during this era. All of them are better known for their poetry and fiction than for their children's books.[36] Other African-American contemporaries combined the dual disciplines of adult literature and children's fiction. Maya Angelou and Toni Morrison, to name the two best-known authors, have been successful in both ventures, but have received far greater recognition for their contributions to adult literature. Unlike Lucille Clifton, neither Toni Morrison nor Maya Angelou turned writing children's books into a second career.[37]

Yet, having six young black children of her own provided a powerful impetus for Clifton's decision to write books that offered positive images of African-Americans and avoided racial stereotyping. She wanted her own children to be able to relate to the stories they read and to have "mirrors and windows. Mirrors in which they can see themselves, windows in which they can see the world."[38] Her own children, who were never formally taught black history in a school environment, learned it at home. They "got it at home. I know that black is beautiful; they know it too."[39] They were grounded in their heritage, sure of who they were.[40]

When one of the editors at Random House asked Clifton if she had ever written stories or poems for her children or their friends, her response was immediate and positive. Since her first publication in this genre, Lucille has written approximately twenty children's books. Many of them, *Everett Anderson's Christmas Coming* (1971) for example, have been reissued years after their original publication with new illustrations. Audrey T. McCluskey has rightly insisted that Clifton's "children's books are her most prolific literary product" and that any critic of her writing must deal with them.[41]

Most of her books for children follow the emotional development of one black male child, Everett Anderson, as he grows up in a large apartment complex. The Everett Anderson books, although they avoid racial bias, privilege the black male central character in the series. The conflicts generated by these stories are real rather than fantastic, as Everett Anderson adjusts to an absent father and a working mother. The losses evoked in the story are focused on human beings instead of, as is more typical in American children's books, on dogs, or kittens, or baby deer. Finally, and this is where Lucille Clifton's artistry is the most apparent, her Everett Anderson storylines have a development that is logical, even mathematical, as in the twelve months of *Everett Anderson's Year* or the five stages of *Everett Anderson's Goodbye*. Other books have a similar sequential development; for example, nine months of his mother's pregnancy or five stages of mourning.

The first book in the series, *Some of the Days of Everett Anderson*, received a good deal of critical attention when it was released. *The New York Times* found the verse to be "sprightly and without self-consciousness," and *Library Journal* admired Clifton's ability to reflect on her own black pride "without coyness or militancy."[42] *Some of the Days of Everett Anderson* was chosen as one of the *School Library Journal*'s Best Books of 1970. It is dedicated to Lucille's six children, whom she addresses by their nicknames: Sid, Rica, Chan, Gilly, Baggy, and Neen.

The book concerns one week in the life of Everett, a small black child; seven days bring him seven experiences. The setting for the nine poems that comprise the books, as for all of the Everett Anderson stories, is Apartment 14A in a large building in the inner city. Clifton is very aware that small children, like readers of her mature poetry, respond favorably to refrains, repetitions, and recurrences. The poems are written in childish rhymes that are occasionally overbearingly simple, as in he's six and "full of tricks." *Some of the Days of Everett Anderson* establishes certain themes found in all the Everett Anderson books; for example, Everett, although brave, is afraid of the dark and afraid of sirens. He depends on his mother and misses his Daddy, whose absence is "a black empty space."

One poem is dedicated to each day, except for Friday and Sunday, which are described in two overlapping poems, because it is payday and his mother is home for the weekend. The Sunday poem has a lovely poignancy. It comtrasts the vast proximity of the stars to the reality of living in the relative confinement of an apartment. "The stars are so near / to 14A / that after playing outside / all day / Everett Anderson likes to pretend / that stars are where / apartments end."

Everett Anderson's Year (1974) is a rhymed series of twelve poems, the equivalent of twelve months in the young boy's life. The saddest month is May, when Everett remembers a ride to the country with his father. July brings the wish to bake a Fourth of July cake, but there is no money. In September the boy questions the need to go back to school, because he already knows where Africa is. The month of December, which marks the close of Everett Anderson's year, has no rhyme. His Mama, who has held his life together since his father's absence, tells Everett about love and about endings.

In *Everett Anderson's Friend* (1976) Clifton moves outward from her character's almost exclusively black male world, as it opens up to include Hispanic relationships and the potential for a female friend. "Someone new has come to stay / in 13A, in 13A," the verse announces. Everett is at first disappointed when he learns that the new resident is a girl. He manages to avoid her, hanging out with the boys in 14B until one day he loses his key, an entry into his formerly secure world. His new friend, Maria, invites him into 13A; her mother, who speaks Spanish, makes tacos for him. The resolution to the story is "Lose a key, win a friend." As Dianne Johnson has pointed out, *Everett Anderson's Friend* is "an early barrier-breaking of sexism. Equally important is the subsequent barrier-breaking of ethnicity and cultural identity."[43]

In *Everett Anderson's 1-2-3* (1977) Clifton continues the mathematical structure in a series of thirteen short poems that explore his hostility toward his mother's friend, Mr. Perry, a bus driver who comes to live with them in 14A. Everett Anderson wants to be "2" with his Mama, not a "3" that includes Mr. Perry. The longest poem is a man-to-man discussion between Everett Anderson and Mr. Perry in which his rival acknowledges that he can never take the place of the boy's father. The set of poems is resolved in a triplet: "Mr. Perry and Everett too / know the number you need / is the number for you."

Everett Anderson appears a year later in the most imaginative volume, *Everett Anderson's Nine Month Long* (1978). His mother is now Mrs. Tom Perry, and she is pregnant. There are nine poems, reflecting both the nine months of his Mama's pregnancy and Everett Anderson's awareness of his mother's physical change: "Something is growing in 14A / Something resting inside a place / warm and soft." The rhymes and stanza structure are more complex than in the earlier books of the series, with the longest poem being a discussion between Everett Anderson and his stepfather about the forthcoming infant. The ninth poem, the end of the cycle, indicates the birth of Baby Evelyn Perry and of a new book.

Lucille Clifton has shown a particular fondness for *Everett Anderson's Goodbye*, published in 1983, a year before the death of her husband. "It's been very comforting. I've given it to adults many times. It deals with the five stages of grief. It has poems about each stage. It ends with 'whatever happens when people die / love doesn't stop, and / neither will I.'" Lucille admitted, "I didn't know how to end it, but the ending is hopeful."[44]

The five divisions of the book coincide with five stages of mourning. In his first confrontation with his father's death, Everett Anderson denies it, claiming that Daddy is everywhere. The second stage reveals his anger—at his mother, at Santa Claus, at Mr. Perry. In the third stage Everett tries bargaining with fate; he is willing to do anything if his father could be alive. The fourth stage shows the child sitting and staring, overwhelmed by his grief. The last section, acceptance, is also the longest, presumably because it is the most difficult phase in the mourning process to achieve. This brave and comforting book won the American Library Association's Coretta Scott King Award in 1984.

As of this writing, Clifton's most recent book in the series is *One of the Problems of Everett Anderson*. It was written in 2001 with pictures by the well-known illustrator Ann Grifalconi, the artist for *Everett Anderson's Year*, *Everett Anderson's Friend*, and numerous other books. *One of the Problems of Everett Anderson* concerns a boy who is worried when he discovers that his younger friend Greg is bruised. Everett, when he hears Greg crying at school, asks him why. "I can't tell you," Greg answers. "And he had the saddest, saddest face, / like he was lost in the loneliest place."

Everett Anderson is confused—not sure of what has happened, not wanting to tell the teacher, and not wanting to worry Greg's parents. Everett has a sister who plays a minimal role in the story. The boys, in this case both African-Americans, instead go to Everett's mother, who holds both boys by the hands and gives them the courage to try what is "new." As in many of the Everett Anderson stories and of Clifton's poems, it is the strong, comforting mother who offers solace.

Although the conclusion to *One of the Problems of Everett Anderson* is open to interpretation, the reader gets enough clues to guess that Greg is being bullied by other children and that Greg's problem might soon be Everett's problem as well if he is unable to discover what's wrong with his friend. The final illustration shows Everett and Greg, arm in arm, off to play baseball. They have numbers on their uniforms, a 6 and a 5, presumably their ages. Over one of Everett's shoulders there is a baseball bat while in the other arm he cradles his friend. In the background, beyond a chain-link fence, are three other children. If a battle were to ensue, Everett and his bat are prepared.

One of the Problems of Everett Anderson is a mixture of poetry and prose. The large, block lettering makes Everett seem younger than his age. Nonetheless, he is mature enough to take on the protective function of being the big brother. Like all of Lucille's books for children, this latest one deals with "the pains and joys of childhood in order to help children accept both emotions as part of the unique experience of being who they are."[45]

Clifton wrote other popular children's books outside the Everett Anderson series. One is *The Boy Who Didn't Believe in Spring*. The entire story is a pun on the cliché, "Spring is just around the corner." The story, written in prose, characterizes two boys, one black and one white. The central character is an African-American child named King Shabazz, a rather deliberate combination of the names of America's two greatest contemporary black leaders, Martin Luther King and Malcolm X (El-Hajj Malik El-Shabazz). The other boy is an Italian-American named Tony Polito. The illustrator, Brinton Turkle, emphasizes the interracial tenor of the male relationship through his pictures of the classroom and of the street. According to the back flyleaf, the story helped Turkle "rediscover New York—sketching boys' jackets, tennis shoes, buses, traffic lights, street signs."

The plot line of *The Boy Who Didn't Believe in Spring* is simple; King and Tony jump over a forbidden street crossing in search of spring. The boys pass the Church of the Solid Rock and a familiar Chinese restaurant. The more corners they turn, the farther away they are from home. Their journey takes them to a vacant lot, where Tony spots some yellow flowers breaking through the hard earth. On the front seat of an abandoned car the boys discover a nest containing four blue eggs.

The story ends in the lot, in a new season, as a yellow flower breaks through the concrete; perhaps it anticipates Clifton's later poem "spring song," with its powerful image, "the green of jesus / is breaking the ground" (*Good Woman* 106). Interrupting their shared discoveries, Tony's older brother arrives to take the boys home, much as Everett protects his younger friend Greg in *One of the Problems of Everett Anderson*. In this slight narrative Lucille suggests the affirmation of brotherhood, the wonderful sense of exploration, and the faith that an older, more responsible male is there to keep the boys safe.

The Boy Who Didn't Believe in Spring, like so many of Clifton's children's books, is centered on boys or on older men, as is *All of Us Cross the Water*. This book is a story written in prose that begins, "I got this teacher name Miss Wills." In the course of the story the central character, Jim, explores his lineage as he searches for his African name. A wise old man named Tweezer tells Jim that his real name was stolen long ago from his Daddy's Daddy and that during slavery no one was free: "All of us crossed the water." When Jim returns to the classroom he stands "straight as a king" and gives his African name of Ujamaa. The last line, like the first, points to the ignorance of his teacher: "Shoot, she don't even know what we talking about."

Amifika (1977) is another prose work, one that begins with a very happy mother instead of with a gloomy teacher. Amifika hears his Mama saying joyfully to his cousin, "Oh Katy, Katy, got a letter from Albert and he be home tomorrow." For Amifika the joy becomes a threat when he hears that some items will have to be thrown out to make room for Albert's return from the army. Fearing it will be he himself that has to be thrown out, the child hides under the sink, then in his Mama's laundry basket, then in a closet, and finally behind a tree, where he falls asleep. When Amifika wakes up he is in his own room, protected in the warm arms of his father.

Yet another story that centers on men is *My Friend Jacob*, about the relationship between Sam and his mentally disadvantaged older white friend, Jacob. Jacob teaches Sam to throw a basketball; Sam teaches Jacob to knock politely at the door. Their relationship is a reciprocal exchange between strength and intellect: "Jacob helps me to carry, and I help Jacob to remember."

As Hilary Holladay has observed, Clifton's books for African-American children often resemble a "balancing act" between male and female points of view.[46] One likely explanation for Clifton's early emphasis on male characters may be related to an understanding prominent in secondary and in higher education during the 1970s—that African-American men were far more devastated by racism than were black women and that young men were in particular need of black male role models. In his experience with educating black males, Freeman Habrowski discussed the difficulties confronting minority students at the University of Maryland Baltimore County, where he is the president. He contends that Lucille Clifton wrote the stories about Everett Anderson and other boys because she wanted our society to understand the issues and challenges black male children were facing in America. "She wanted to give families books they could use to give those boys opportunities to deal with what they faced every day."[47]

Clifton's first volume of poetry, *Good Times*, parallels this emphasis on male characters. Although it begins with poems about her mother and father, there are a noticeable number of poems devoted to males. Her poem "miss rosie" is a significant exception. By the time that the poems from *Good Times* (1969) through *Two-Headed Woman* (1980) were collected into a single volume, *Good Woman*, Lucille's exploration of gender issues was more intense.

Several of Clifton's books for children do have a female character in a significant role. In *Three Wishes*, for example, the central relationship is between a girl, Zenobia, and her friend, a boy named Victor. Zenobia finds a lucky penny, which entitles her to three wishes. As in the old folktale, she wastes them all until the story ends as it began, in friendship. This story was Lucille's contribution to the Emmy- and Grammy-winning children's book, *Free to Be ... You and Me*, edited by Marlo Thomas and dedicated to challenging sexual and racial stereotyping in children's music, poetry, and short fiction.[48]

Don't You Remember? (1973) is the story of Desire Mary Tate, a four-year-old girl who "remembered everything." Although the story begins in fairy-tale prose—"Once upon a time there was a four year-old person who remembered everything"—it immediately shifts to the portrayal of the realistic daily uncertainties of a black child. Desire Mary misses her mother, who works at a bakery. She envies her Daddy, who works at a plant, and her older brothers, who drink coffee. For her birthday she dreams of a black cake with her name in pink letters. So preoccupied is the passive child with her wishes that she actually forgets to remember her birthday until her family wakes her from bed and her dreams are fulfilled.

Three of Clifton's books about girls are aimed at a slightly older readership. One of these, *The Times They Used to Be* (1974), uses an unrhymed form with no right-hand margins, giving the appearance of being a poem but structurally resembling a paragraph format that makes it sound "adult." *The Times They Used to Be* evokes the good old days with its image of a family listening to *Amos and Andy* and *Hit Parade* on the radio and peeking through a window to see a television set, just as Elaine, Lucille, and Sammy Clifton used to do in the early days of television.[49] The narrative revolves around the friendship of two girls, one dark and the other lighter-skinned, one twelve and the other thirteen, who deal with such issues as a father in jail and an uncle who dies in a car crash. Some of Lucille's poetic motifs—war, death, funerals, ghosts, the female body, and religion—are woven into this somewhat somber story, which ends with the older girl, Tassie, getting her first menstrual period. The blood "got bigger / and looked like a hand spread out" (39). Tassie's grandmother and her Mama console her, assuring her that nothing's wrong.

Another story, *Sonora Beautiful*, (1981), is an E. P. Dutton "Skinny Book" of only twenty-two pages, written entirely in prose. It has a white female central character, Sonora, a young woman who is ashamed of her big ears, of her unusual name, and of the fact that her father is a poet. She finally realizes that both she and her parents, despite their irregularities, are beautiful.[50] Unfortunately, *Sonora Beautiful* is indeed a "skinny" text and its conclusion is obvious, suggesting that Clifton had missed the opportunity to develop her one white female character.[51]

The children's book that presents Lucille's fullest depiction of a female character is *The Lucky Stone* (1979), a novel for young teens. Divided into four sections or chapters, the prose narrative ranges from slavery times to the present, and each chapter describes a specific cultural and historical event. The story is told by Tee, the great-grandchild of Mrs. Elzie F. Pickens, an 80-year-old who likes to sit on her porch telling stories to her attentive offspring. The narrative is split into two components: stories about Tee's great-grandmother and stories about their strange neighbors, Mandy and Vashti. These tales are held together by a lucky stone that is passed from one family of women to the next until it finally comes into the possession of the narrator. The stone is the emblem of narrative itself: as Tee holds the stone in her hand she proclaims that, while the story became lucky for her, there is more to come, "and someday I might tell you about that too."[52]

The black-and-white illustrations by Dale Payson are rendered in marvelous detail, from the more intimate sketches of Tee and her great-grandmother in chapter 1 to the outdoor church scenes that crowd the text of chapter 2. As the narrative ranges from slavery times to the present, so the chapters themselves reveal Clifton's intense interest in the history of her people. She told an interviewer from *Jambalaya* that her books for children are "much more consciously thought out" than her poetry.[53]

Chapter 1 of *The Lucky Stone* pertains to slavery in the South and to Miss Mandy, a little girl who escaped into a cave when she feared being beaten by a boss for spilling a sack of cotton. During her year or so in the cave she sends signals to her fellow slaves by throwing to them the lucky stone, which is "black as night" with the letter "A" carved on it, for Amanda. The passersby leave her food and water as she, like the other slaves, waits out the time for freedom.

Chapter 2 involves another lucky event. After emancipation the former slaves are gathered around a platform to hear an itinerant minister and be saved. Mandy's daughter Vashti is waiting for her induction into the church when the strings of her pouch break, heaving the lucky stone away from the platform. In that split second, as she leaps to retrieve the pouch, lightning strikes the platform and Vashti is saved, physically if not spiritually.

Meanwhile the reader learns that Vashti has passed the lucky stone to Eliza's Mama in exchange for a glass of water. The narrative line also passes, with chapter 3 focusing on how Tee's great-grandmother threw the lucky stone at a circus dog who chased her through the fairgrounds until he was lassoed by the "finest fast runnin hero in the bottoms of Virginia" (42). The romantic rescuer, Amos Pickens, soon marries Elzie. In the fourth and final chapter Elzie F.

Pickens is in her eightieth year when she contracts pneumonia. Tee breaks the hospital's "No Visitors" barrier to see her beloved great-grandmother, who tells her that the lucky stone is on the bureau wrapped in a handkerchief.

At the end of the book, when the reader has come to accept the inevitable death of Tee's great-grandmother, the old woman is somehow healed. On the same positive note, Tee receives a Valentine card, the first in her life, from a secret admirer. She has the lucky stone, a symbol of her ancestor's survival, but she also has a Valentine, the conventional expression for love in American society. The inevitable cycles of death, love, and regeneration, so prevalent in Clifton's poems, are present, but made more palatable to a juvenile readership.

The lucky stone or its substitute (bones, fetishes, talismans, rocks, mounts, altars, and medicine pouches) is a familiar symbol both in Clifton's poetry and in the folk stories of many cultures. An African-American folktale traces the murder of a young girl, the daughter of a king, to her singing bones.[54] One Native American myth, "The Storytelling Stone," describes the manner in which tribal history came to the Iroquois when a young hunter exchanges the birds he has gathered for the stories that come from a flat stone deep in the forest. Soon other Indians follow, one after one, until the community is told that the storytelling is finished and that they should remember what they have been taught and teach it all to new generations.[55]

Lucille seems to have two personal talismans: the extra fingers amputated at her birth and "the Dahomey women gathering in my bones" (*Generations* 228). Both hold a prominent place in her poetry. Aware of the stone as talisman, friends and students have sent Lucille "lucky stones" from everywhere in the world.[56]

Of her numerous contributions to children's literature, one of her earliest, *The Black BC's*, is her most politically provocative. In it, the accustomed pattern of the "A is for Apple" text of standard preschool readers is given significant racial and historical meaning in an attempt to teach contemporary black history and its roots in slavery; for example, "A is for Africa" and "O is for Organize." *The Black BC's* is a book of contrasts. The simple poetry that introduces each letter is written against an informative, often impassioned prose commentary, and the black-and-white illustrations by Jamaican painter Don Miller are sometimes shocking portrayals of white-on-black brutality. Of the twenty-six letters, the S word, slavery, is portrayed most graphically, both visually and verbally.

The book begins as expected with the letter "A," a letter that is absent from the title, perhaps to indicate the absence of Africa from standard American history texts. "A is for Africa / land of the sun / the king of continents / the ancient one." A picture of an elephant separates the short poem from a prose description of the continent, its rivers, and its linguistic diversity. On the facing page is the first of many marvelous illustrations: a ragged map of Africa containing six portraits: five men and one woman.

The letter B is for "Books / where readers find / treasures for the heart / and mind." For this letter Lucille provides a brief history of African-American literature and lists some of the writers in the B category important to her development, among them James Baldwin and Gwendolyn Brooks.

The Black BC's lists several contributions made by black female poets, musicians, and activists, as in the letter "T." "T is for Truth / Sojourner the brave / and Harriet Tubman / the Moses of slaves." One of the alphabet poems is "N is for Natural / or real or true / the you of yourself / the self of you." The large illustration depicts a woman with an Afro, the kind of hair style Clifton and other Pan-Africans had adopted in the 1970s, perhaps to identify with sister Angela Davis, while the verse speaks to the kind of personal integrity Lucille has advocated throughout her career. A smaller illustration shows a young man grooming his hair in front of a mirror (literally, like her children, seeing himself mirrored in Lucille's book). Below it appears a quote from Malcolm X about avoiding self-hate.

However, most of the textual descriptions and the accompanying illustrations tend to emphasize men, which is natural because many of Lucille's alphabetical choices are capsule biographies of black male leaders: for example, Frederick Douglas, Martin Luther King, and Malcolm X. "X is for Malcolm / martyred when / he saw the brotherhood / of men." Like the tribute to Malcolm X, the entry on "Slavery" indicates stereotyping by gender: "brotherhood," "men," "man." "S is for Slavery / who can own a man / men own themselves / no one else can." The brevity of the verse form forces Lucille into using the generic word "man" instead of using the more politically acceptable forms of "he/she" or "people." Don Miller's black-on-white paintings reinforce the maleness of the text. They show black men being shackled by the Portuguese, their twisted limbs extending in a curved pattern from the left page to the right. All of the victims depicted are male. Although in the text Clifton refers to "human slavery," there is no indication of the terrible fate suffered by the women in an American slave population as they were bought and sold as pieces of property, separated from their husbands and their children.[57]

Identical abstract nouns are used for the letter Y: "Y is for youth / if any man / or men can save us / the young folk can" (44). In this verse she breaks the maleness with the use of the word "folk," indicating both male and female. In the illustration boys and girls of different races extend hands across two pages in an ironical reversal of the slavery picture.

Many of Clifton's books for children, and especially *The Black BC's*, cross the line between poetry and narrative, race and gender, America and Africa. As in *Generations* in which she connects to her lineage through her great-great-grandmother Caroline, so in her alphabet book she affirms the connections between the Mother Continent and the children of the Diaspora. When Caroline crossed the water she stayed, won her freedom, and passed on the line to Lucille, her six children, and their children to be—much as Lucille Clifton has passed her vision of children to all of her readers.

Clifton's contributions to children's literature are momentous, not only in their structure but in their mirroring effect. There is probably no other writer of stature of any race who has surpassed her work in this genre. Yet despite her voluminous work in children's literature, she prefers poetry. She once said, "I like doing children's books but my heart is in poetry. I'm a person of poetry, I think."[58] Given the test of time, many would ultimately agree with her.

THREE

Teaching, Politics, and So On

At the time of the March on Washington in 1963 and the civil rights advances of the 1960s, Lucille and Fred Clifton were living in Buffalo, where she was writing poetry and taking care of their six children. During the early 1970s, after the move to Baltimore, she continued to write both poetry and children's books that examined black issues, although no one could have called her an activist.

Fred, a dedicated black nationalist, had many friends on the political left who visited them in both Buffalo and Baltimore. One of them was Maulana Karenga, the man who introduced Kwanzaa, the Pan-African harvest ritual, to the United States in 1966. The introduction of the festival, which is celebrated from December 26 through January 1, coincided in America with the black power movement and has become a communal means for African-Americans to celebrate their African heritage.[1] When Channing was four, Karenga visited the Clifton house. To Lucille, who does not celebrate Kwanzaa, he looked like a black Santa Claus but he wore a caftan. She was astounded when Channing came bouncing into the house and said, "I can't wait for Santa Claus!"[2]

By the early 1970s many African-American intellectuals were involved in the Black Arts Movement. Clifton dedicated *Good News about the Earth*, originally published in 1972, to the "dead / of Jackson and / Orangeburg / and so on and / so on and on." It commemorates Jackson, Mississippi, the site of Jackson State College, where two students, James Earle Green and Phillip Lafayette Gibbs, were killed by police in May 1970 as they protested the Vietnam War and racial oppression.[3] She also eulogizes the dead of Orangeburg, South Carolina, where "firemen blasted protesters with hoses set at a pressure to remove bark from trees and mortar from brick."[4] As is typical of Clifton's style, she uses no capitalization and no punctuation in this dedication to the dead of Jackson and Orangeburg and so on in the 1987 reprint of the volume in *Good Woman*. The absence of such pauses gives the impression of an endless series of victims—as indeed there were.

Although her poetry from the 1970s continues to reflect her maternal and spiritual sides, it at the same time stresses a political concern for the Jackson State and Orangeburg tragedies, for the Kent State massacre, and for Panther Party leaders Eldridge Cleaver and Bobby Seale. The opening poem in *Good News about the Earth*, "after kent state" deals with the 1970 white-on-white shootings at Kent State University in Ohio, when students who protested the war were fired upon by National Guardmen; four of them, two males and two females, were killed.[5] In a strong indictment of racism in America she writes: "white ways are / the ways of death / come into the / Black / and live." There is no punctuation in the poem. In the 1972 version of the poem only the word "Black" is capitalized and is given the prominence of forming one single line, while in the 1989 version it is not capitalized (*Good Woman* 57). The formal aspects of this poem indicate that Clifton has clearly taken a stand on race: white is death; Black is life. However, the poem does not exclude whites, whom she invites to shed the ways of death by entering into Blackness.

Other political poems in this, her second book, are addressed to the leaders of the Panther Party, founded in 1966 by Bobby Seale and Huey Newton and revitalized by H. Rap Brown and Stokely Carmichael in Oakland, California in 1968 when the two nationalist groups they represented, the Student Nonviolent Coordinating Committee (SNCC) and the Congress of Racial Equality (CORE), merged.[6] In "apology (to the panthers)" she praises her brothers for their wisdom and "grieves(s) my whiteful ways." This alludes both to her being raised during the days when black women used bleaching cream to whiten their skin and, more significantly, to her absence from involvement in the civil rights conflict (*Good Woman* 62). The word "apology" has two meanings here: it is an expression of regret, but in its literary form it is a "formal or written defense of some idea, religion, philosophy, etc.," from the Latin form *apologia*.[7] Here the poet's "whiteful ways" seem to indicate her formal pursuit of recognition for her poetry at the expense of political participation in the black power movement.

The title of the volume, *Good News about the Earth*, serves as the concluding line of an eloquent untitled poem that links the Indian Trail of Tears with the African Middle Passage. She draws parallels between the Seminoles, who were forced against their will to resettle in the Oklahoma Territory, and Nigerians and Ghanaians, who were chained to the slave blocks in the American South. Clifton identified with American Indians, particularly with the Sioux warrior Crazy Horse, who was one of her great heroes. In a dynamic application of colors to depict racial difference, she claims that the good news about the earth is that white men will be buried under "red dust and black clay" (*Good Woman* 68).

HEROES

At the core of the volume is a poem sequence called *heroes*. The collection opens with "africa," in which "her bones / remember" the home of her people (*Good Woman* 73). After several other poems she introduces a structured sequence that addresses the leaders of the black power movement. The first three of the poems invoke their subjects by their names—malcolm, eldridge, and bobby seale—whereas the fourth, an untitled poem for "angela," is more veiled in content.

"malcolm" (80) is one of her most moving political poems. The dominant word is black, which is used three times in seven lines and twice to begin a line. The stark images of the poem—closed doors, shaved heads, rustling leaves, ambushed prophets—culminate with the lines, "and from their holes black eagles flew / screaming through the streets." In this final tribute to Malcolm X the natural world is reversed as eagles, airborne desert birds that are more common to Native American than to African-American symbolism, emerge from holes in the streets of New York to "scream" his death.

The second poem in *heroes* is entitled "eldridge," whose last name "cleaver" appears in the third line. The thirteen lines are elongated so that they visually resemble a knife or cleaver. This structure is reminiscent of a technique used by Renaissance metaphysical poets, such as George Herbert, whose poems "The Altar" and "Easter Wings" were formatted on the page to resemble their subjects.[8] Eldridge Cleaver, a year older than Clifton, was arrested for drug dealing in 1957 and was sent to San Quentin and then to Folsom Prison, where he read prison literature. His book *Soul on Ice* (1968) shocked his white readership for its denigration of women, especially of white women, whom he considered to be ogres. "Cleaver's attack on white women had a significant effect in discouraging the interracial sexuality common in the early 1960s."[9] Sherley Anne Williams, a noted black feminist, warned that black women should also be fully aware of the patriarchal, demeaning portrait of black women created by writers like Eldridge Cleaver, James Baldwin, and Richard Wright.[10] Cleaver's ideas about the "hyperpotent" black male hero, formulated while he was in prison, became the foundation for the black power movement.[11] Lucille's poem to Cleaver has no negative connotations; she praises the "man" who "will not / rust / break, or / be broken."

The third of her hero-poems is addressed "to bobby seale," whose full name, unlike in the earlier two eulogies, appears in the title. Based on a bitter pun about men, dogs, and impoundment, the poem advises "bobby seale" to "feel free / like my daddy / always said," a phrase that she uses frequently but with variations in her 1976 memoir, *Generations*. After co-founding the Black Panther Party in 1966 with Huey Newton, Seale was tried and sentenced for conspiracy in November 1969, probably because of his "inflammatory speeches," which the government used to "taint the other conspirators in the eyes of the jury."[12] The reference to her Daddy prepares the reader to expect a Daddy poem among her heroes.

The fourth poem of the series has no title. The word "angela," which appears four times in the text, refers to Angela Davis, who was arrested in California by the FBI in August 1970 for her involvement in an alleged conspiracy to free black activist George Jackson. Although the guns used in the conspiracy were registered in her name, Davis was acquitted.[13] The poem stresses Davis's "whiteness." Unlike many of the members of the black liberation struggle, Davis was a recognized member of the academic community, a tenured philosophy professor in the University of California system. Identifying with Davis, Clifton vows that if her sister is forgotten, "let our hair fall / straight on our backs / like death" (*Good Woman* 83). This reference to straight hair "like death" is a comment on Davis's trademark, a natural "Afro," a hairstyle that Clifton herself had chosen during the Pan-African movement of the early 1970s.[14]

In a strange shift of naming, the vaguely addressed poem to angela is followed by one entitled "richard penniman." Not a recognized leader in the civil rights movement, "richard penniman" was none other than the musician, "little richard," as he is so named in the sixth line of the poem. Like Bill Haley and the Comets, Little Richard was one of Lucille's cultural heroes. His performances of "Tutti Fruiti" and "Long Tall Sally" hit the charts in the mid-fifties. Penniman, who was born in December 1932, sang gospel as a teenager and left his hometown of Macon, Georgia, only to return in 1952 when his father was murdered and the family needed him for financial support. Little Richard reached his peak of popularity in 1956, when the Cliftons were in their early twenties.[15]

In her tribute she gives us Little Richard's full name, even though he was known primarily by his stage name, much as the downtrodden colored slave man was known as "robert" (*Good Woman* 20). Clifton's poem to Little Richard gives us snippets of Penniman's biography. Born in poverty, he took care of his twelve brothers and sisters when his parents died; he wears an apron over his trousers, indicating his nurturing qualities. When a white man calls him "faggot," one of Penniman's brothers replies: "you bet your faggot ass / he is / you bet your dying ass" ("richard penniman," *Good Woman* 84). Clifton's chastisement of the white man in this poem is one of her strongest statements about the combined themes of race and sexual preference in her early works.

This tribute to Penniman is followed by her well-known elegy, "daddy / 12/02–5/69." Its theme, like that of so many of Clifton's poems, is about memory and time: "nothing remembers, / everything remembers." In this poem of three stanzas she condenses the facts of Samuel Sayles's life, remembering when his leg was amputated, how he lived, and when he died. Immediately following is a "poem for my sisters" in which she shares their father's memory and stresses that his life and heroism have made theirs possible.

The *heroes* sequence reaches a crescendo in her poem for Fred, "the kind of man he is" (*Good Woman* 87). The poet identifies the racial characteristics of her husband, whom she describes as a "dark / presence with his friends, / and with his enemies / always." Critics note the erotic quality of the poem, especially the lines, "he fills / his wife with children." His wife seems to be suggesting that in "his comings and his goings," his arrivals and departures from political and spiritual missions, he has actually deposited each of his six children in his wife's uterus.

Of the many poems in *Good News about the Earth,* the *heroes* sequence demonstrates that although Lucille Clifton maintained her accustomed roles as mother, wife, and teacher during the black power movement, she at the same time used her poetic energy for political purposes. She had in *heroes* created a sequence that could simultaneously explore the contributions of Malcolm X, Bobby Seale, Angela Davis, Little Richard, Samuel Sayles, and Fred Clifton, much as in the *Black BC's* she had connected her cultural heroes—Harriet Tubman, Sojourner Truth, and Gwendolyn Brooks—through their places in the alphabet. The *heroes* section of *Good News about the Earth* presents a seamless approach to black history in which the guitarist mingles with the revolutionary and the living mingle with the dead.

During the early 1970s the black leadership of the Student Nonviolent Coordinating Committee (SNCC) decided that white people were no longer allowed to participate in its activities. Clifton connected this decision to Stokely Carmichael's strong opinions discouraging white involvement in the movement for black liberation.[16] Yet, about this time, the Cliftons decided to move to a white neighborhood, in which they were the only black family. They relocated to Dickeyville, a mill town in West Baltimore. The first year they were there, Lucille Clifton was invited to give the Fourth of July speech in the picnic grove. Somebody told her, "You're moving here and you are having a good time. When the first Jews moved here it was really rough."[17] Although she sensed some hostility from one of the Southern white women in the neighborhood, her children did not.

Clifton knows many black activists and is familiar with their personal histories, their wives, and their children. She is convinced that these public figures are not at all like they have been portrayed by the popular press. In particular, she is a close friend of Amina Baraka, Amiri's second wife; they enjoy getting together to talk about their children and their grandchildren.[18] One of Amiri Baraka's daughters by his first marriage, Hetty Jones, worked as an assistant to film director Spike Lee. Her mother, Hetty Cohen, is Jewish. Clifton remembers that on one occasion, when Hetty Jones and Spike Lee were downgrading white people, Amina said, "Well listen, remember when he is talking about white people he's talking about your mother."[19]

The entire Clifton family knew Amiri Baraka—or LeRoi Jones as he was known at Howard University when he and Lucille were classmates. A critic once commented that she was influenced by LeRoi Jones. She finds this assertion ridiculous because "LeRoi was a friend from home who wasn't even being Baraka at the time. If we influenced anybody it was each other. Nobody is thinking about literary influences when you're 17 or 18."[20] Amiri Baraka and Fred Clifton shared a friendship that dated back to their collaboration in organizing the Black Political Convention in Gary, Indiana. Alexia Clifton, the Cliftons' youngest daughter, remembers many of her father's political friends, especially Amiri Baraka, who was frequently at their house and who reminds her of her Dad. "I think he's a great guy," she said. "He's really misunderstood a lot."[21]

Clifton and her friends from St. Mary's College, Kathy and Michael Glaser, were in the audience when, Baraka, the poet laureate of New Jersey, read his poem, "Somebody Blew Up America," at the Dodge Poetry Festival in Waterloo, New Jersey, in October 2002. The poem created a stir because of its angry rhetoric in the wake of the terrorist attacks of September 11, 2001. However, Clifton said that nobody walked out or left after all the brouhaha, adding, "After hearing the attacks against Baraka, Michael didn't feel anything. He just wondered where Baraka got his ideas but he thought, 'Okay.'"[22]

CLIFTON AS TEACHER

Like Amiri Baraka, but radically different in tone and posture, Lucille Clifton is an educator, a person who takes the time to explain racial differences and to make people question their assumptions. Her goal is to tell the truth, even if some people might be offended. "As long as I tell the truth, I don't see why my mission is to assure people that they are comfortable. I used to worry. I used to think, 'I'm so harmless.' I always wanted to be like June Jordan. But I'm thought of in a different way by black folks. I guess I'm in a place all by myself."[23] A more militant poet than Lucille Clifton, June Jordan was born in the same year, 1936. She is the author of at least twenty books of poetry, including *Things I Do in the Dark* and *Naming Our Destiny: New and Selected Poems*. Although Clifton has been compared to many poets, from Emily Dickinson to June Jordan, she ultimately rejects such comparisons; she believes, as she writes in "won't you celebrate with me," that being "born in babylon / both nonwhite and woman" has left her without a historical model (*The Book of Light* 25).

Although politics occupies a part of Clifton's life, she is more passionate about her teaching; this role is one that that she embraces both in the classroom and in much of her poetry. As Mark Bernard White has argued, Clifton teaches with "subtle virtuosity" and with "indirection," using the poetic voice as one of several rhetorical ways to lead her reader to "significant self-perception."[24]

She loves her students, who bring out her powerful maternal instincts. Clifton's dedication to them is evidenced by the way she helps students explore questions affecting their own lives. For example, one of her students, a South Korean who had been adopted in America when he was an infant, had never identified with anything South Korean. He enrolled in Clifton's writing class under an anglicized name, which she found amusing. The student had heard about the slaughter of South Koreans by the Japanese when Korea was annexed by Japan in 1910; the Koreans were forced to learn the Japanese language and become Japanese citizens. During World War II, the Japanese brought in Koreans to work in the construction, mining, and shipbuilding industries. After the war ended the Japanese government branded Koreans as foreigners and forced them "to register as alien residents"[25] In assigning her student to write about Korea, he gained new insight into his heritage. Her student reported on the war and on how some of the Japanese would comfort the Korean women and children, taking them into their homes.

Clifton is not a typical faculty person who's interested in answers; what she wants her students to do is think of the questions. For instance, in teaching creative writing to children, she asked them to make a list of stereotypes. She told critic Charles Rowell that only the white students were unaware of stereotypes about themselves until children of other ethnic groups started to inform them.[26]

Teaching has often inspired her poetry. She wrote two series that revolve around her teaching, one about Memphis, where she spent a semester teaching as a visiting professor at Memphis State University, now the University of Memphis, and one about Santa Cruz, where she held a position from 1985 to 1989 in the years after her husband's death.

She told me that her term at Memphis made her nervous. In 1994 black students called the Memphis English department "Death Valley" because they had to take a required English class during their first semester. A failure in the course ended the student's tenure at Memphis State. The policy was similar to the literacy requirement of the 1960s in which black people were denied the right to vote if they did not meet certain standards established by whites. As a black educator, Clifton was made distraught by the severity of the Memphis English department.

A Term in Memphis is loosely structured on her 1994 journey from North to South, which is a reversal of the movement from South to North during the vast black migrations of the early twentieth century. The first poem, "shadows," is based on a prophecy, a message from the old ones that she will one day "come to a place / called Memphis." There she will receive signs from the earth, the fire, and the other elements, but most particularly from water—the water of the Mississippi River and the water of the ancient Nile. Until 2250 BCE the city of Memphis in Egypt, which sat on the banks of the Nile, was believed to be the largest city in the world. After the seventh century it was abandoned and became "an imposing set of ruins."[27] The poet, as she lies dreaming, hears the rush of the mighty, ancient river, and she sees the shadow of "another dusky woman," presumably her great-great-grandmother Caroline, who will be "dreaming a small boat / through centuries of water / into the white new world" ("shadows," *The Terrible Stories* 33).

A poem more overtly public in its content begins with a newspaper clipping: "Beckwith found guilty of shooting Medgar Evers in the back, killing him in 1963/-newspaper 2/94." What initially strikes the reader is the disparity between the two dates, 1963 and 1994. The murderer, Byron De La Beckwith, went unpunished for more than thirty years after civil rights worker Medgar Evers lay dead of a bullet wound. For three decades Evers's widow, Myrlie Evers-Williams, fought to bring his murderers to justice. De La Beckwith, age forty-two at the time Evers was murdered, was an opponent of integration and a founder of Mississippi's White Citizens' Council. Although he owned the gun that killed Evers, he was acquitted of the crime. Mrs. Evers went to live in California but later returned to Mississippi, finding new evidence against Beckwith. "On February 5, 1994, after deliberating for some seven hours, a jury of eight African-Americans and four whites convicted 73-year-old De La Beckwith of Medgar Evers's murder, sentencing him to life in prison."[28]

Although the Evers assassination itself is filled with potential drama, Clifton chooses to present the narrative from the point of view of the frail old man who was found guilty in 1994, two years before the publication of *The Terrible Stories*. In the poem, Clifton emphasizes the passage of time: "the son of medgar / will soon be / older than medgar" (*The Terrible Stories* 39). The poet's objectivity in reporting the trial of Byron De La Beckwith should recall her detached coverage of the Lorena Bobbitt case and of the Lawrence Powell case, both discussed in a later chapter.

Other poems in *A Term in Memphis* are concerned with the history of the slave trade and with the poet's own inadvertent participation in the buying and selling of flesh. When she enters the South she is wearing her mother's fur coat, with its blood still on her shoulders, "heavy and dark and alive" ("entering the south," 36). The dead coat is a reference to the thick coat of the fox who visits her apartment in the first sequence of *The Terrible Stories*, *A Dream of Foxes* (13–18). The dominant image of the Memphis sequence, though, is water, either of the river or of the ocean. The theme of the Middle Passage is painfully evoked in the poem "slaveships" (35), told from the point of view of the slaves who lie stinking and sweating in the belly of ships named "Jesus" and "Angel" as they cross the ocean from West Africa to the American South.

The Mississippi River is specifically named in "old man river" (38) and in "the mississippi river empties into the gulf" (37). The latter poem is a testament to the endurance of the murky river as it recycles through the centuries, whereas "old man river" is based on the contrast between the elegance of the white ladies and the "muddy" nature of the water and the "negras." The poem concludes with the lines *"don't say nothin' / must know somethin."* The highlighted couplet that ends the poem recalls the timbre of Paul Robeson's rich voice as he sang the famous solo for the London performance of *Showboat*.[29]

Although the last poem, "blake," seems a stranger to the sequence, its distance and language are enticements that lure Clifton from the horrors of the South to the "grace" of the North, where she sits at home "dreaming of blake, searching the branches / for just one poem" (44).

The sequence, *california lessons* (*Next* 81–86), consists of five poems in which Clifton remembers having been a professor at the University of California at Santa Cruz. These numbered poems, organized under a section entitled *SINGING*, range in subject matter, covering geography, history, botany, semantics, and metaphysics. Concise in their phrasing, they seem to parody the courses taught in the standard university curriculum. "1 geography," the longest poem in the series, is constructed on the contrasts between "here" and "over there," between California and Asia. As the enlightened gautama watches the water "astounded as siddharta," California sits on the edge of a darkening world. Siddharta Guatama was a "South Asian spiritual leader traditionally stated to have lived between approximately 563 BCE and 483 BCE." He became "the Buddha following a spiritual quest in which he learned that humankind could not avoid disease and death. Siddharta Guatama believed in moderation; he chose the path of Enlightenment." The poem begins by stressing distance: "over there is asia."[30]

Thus the poet sets up a recognizable contrast between Eastern and Western philosophy; Clifton, whose given name means "light," shared her husband's respect for Eastern religion and was suspicious of the "darkening" of insight represented by California. We witness this sort of geographical contrast in earlier poems, such as in the seemingly simple poem to her great-great-grandmother, "ca'line's prayer," where the "drought" of Virginia is compared to the glorious "rivers" of Dahomey.

From *Good Times* to *Next*, Clifton is using the language of her poetry as a form of global instruction. The place name *wydah* remains obscure until the reader consults a reference guide to West Africa, only to learn that *wydah* [Whydah] is at the western border of Dahomey in southern Benin and a major port in the slave trade.[31] "ca'line's prayer" ends, appropriately, with a prayer: "Ye Ma Jah" (*Good Woman* 33), which is related to the Rastafarian dialect that spread from Africa to Jamaica during the eighteenth century.[32] Clifton said that some of her poems from *An Ordinary Woman* and *Two-Headed Woman* are "written in a kind of Rastafarian dialect."[33] None of these references to West African, Southeast Asian, or Jamaican culture come easily to a chauvinistic American readership bred on familiar place names and mainstream poets.

The poem "2 history" is even more elaborate in its use of names as a teaching tool. In a question that echoes Keats's address to the "immortal bird" in "Ode to a Nightingale," Clifton asks, "what bird remembers the songs / the miwok sang?"[34] Just as in *Generations*, her intention in "2 history" is to foster the act of remembrance, in this instance not of her Dahomey ancestors but of California Indian tribes whose names she had learned while she was in residence there: the "mikwok," as well as the "pomo, shasta, esalen." The poet as teacher wants her reader to search out these names, to make these "peoples / not places" the frame of reference (*Next* 82). The Miwok are a group that once numbered 20,000 strong; the 1990 Census shows that only 3,500 people with Miwok ancestry still survive in California.[35] With so small a word she suggests the vastness and scope of a now almost forgotten people.

The other three tribes have suffered a similar fate. The Pomo had lived for centuries in the land north of San Francisco. They were a spiritual, sharing people who were virtually decimated by Spanish explorers and Russian traders.[36] The Shasta traditionally occupied the land on what is now the California-Oregon border. Like the Pomo, their numbers have dramatically decreased, from 3,000 in the eighteenth century to only 600 members in the 1990 Census. They died from poison, white vigilante attacks, feuds, and other natural and unnatural causes.[37] The final California tribe on the list is the "esalen" [Esselen], members of the Costanoan tribe considered extinct at the beginning of the last century. Through concerted political effort they were able to reinvigorate their culture and to stop a freeway from crossing over a sacred burial ground.[38]

Thus, as we observe in her Crazy Horse sequence, the poet has a tremendous respect for the Native American. She may also have some Indian ancestry from her maternal grandmother.[39] But although Lucille Sayles Clifton, an American woman of African descent, emphasizes above all her ability to trace her ancestors to their original homeland, she also encourages her students—black, white, Indian, or Asian—to use research as a tool for self-discovery. One of her primary techniques as a poet/teacher is to refer to a people such as the Pomo and expect her students to discover more on their own. She encourages them to use the Internet, the library, archives, and other sources to find the "few documented facts" available to them.

In the third poem of *california lessons*, a poem of three parts, Clifton tackles the subject of botany. The first stanza of "3 botany" is a citation from a botany lesson that addresses the pollination of flowers into figs. The third stanza is the shortest—"the fruit / is dark / and sweet." In between the two stanzas concerning a botany lesson is a reference to a lynching in Concord, Massachusetts, in which a "black man / was hung / from a fig tree" (*Next* 83). This richly associative poem is probably meant to recall Billie Holliday's recording of the song "Strange Fruit," about a lynching in the South. Holliday recorded the song in 1939, when Lucille was three years old.[40] When she was a student at Howard University Clifton was exposed to Billie Holliday's recordings through her professor, Owen Dodson. The poem, like the song, is about dark fruit, with the theme of botany signifying that under slavery dark people were raised and cross-pollinated to reproduce more slaves.

The setting of Concord has several associations as well. As the site of a battle during the American struggle for independence, Concord is a symbol of American freedom; now, in 1985, it is the site of race riots and a lynching. The Concord grape, like a fig, is a fruit used to satisfy the white man's taste. As in the first poem of the series, there is a sweeping shift from "here" to "over there," from the relative safety of Santa Cruz to the racial violence of the Boston suburbs. No matter where she is, the lynching stays in Clifton's memory. According to Trudier Harris, "to exorcize fear from racial memory is as formidable a task as attempting to obtain equality for black people in the United States."[41]

The fourth poem in the sequence, "4 semantics," is another overtly political poem, this time written in sympathy for the Japanese living on the West Coast who were put into internment camps during World War II because they were suspected of being enemies of the federal government. The last line reminds the reader that during their captivity "no doctor came." The poem recalls the unforgiving paranoia that people in the West, especially California, displayed toward the Japanese, even though they had been American citizens for many years.

The final poem in the series, "5 metaphysics," wheels the reader back to the Buddhist philosophy introduced in the first poem. In three lines it asks the question, "what is karma?" and answers it: "there is a wheel / and it is turning." Karma is a Hindu belief meaning "the sum of a person's actions, regarded as creating that person's present and future states of existence."[42] Originating in Hindu thought, it was later adopted by the Buddhists. Gautama Buddha preached that one must strive to change the results of one's karma, rather than to be a victim of desire. "When Buddhists talk about karma, they are normally referring to karma/action that is 'tainted with ignorance'—karma that continues to ensure that the being remains in the everlasting cycle of samsura [what is known as good karma or bad karma]."[43] In Buddhism the wheel of Dharma is a symbol for the continued enlightenment of the universe.[44] Both *california lessons* and *A Term in Memphis* show Clifton's great desire to learn from her environment and to translate her experiences with multi-diverse groups into her poems.

Merely by reading her poems, Clifton also serves as a teacher and educator. In higher education in America, black women have been "isolated, underutilized, and often demoralized."[45] Her very presence as a black woman in an auditorium filled with a primarily white audience can have an electrifying effect. When white people listen to Lucille Clifton, they are confronted with a different model, one that defies their expectations as she skillfully manipulates language in reversing the stereotypes of race and gender.

The section *SINGING* also describes her experience reading poetry to mostly white audiences. As in *california lessons*, the poems are numbered. The section is introduced by an epigraph from her fellow poet, Galway Kinnell: "one singer falls but the next steps into the empty place and sings..." (title page, *SINGING*) Occupying the empty space left by the white male poet, Clifton compares herself to a juggler, a dark spinner who can do fancy tricks. The first word in the *white america* sequence is "i" ("in white america," *Next* 71): "i come to read them poems." The words "i" and "them" immediately set Clifton apart from her audience (*Next* 71).

The sequence proceeds chronologically as her hostess escorts her through the "fourteen longhouses" that once held slaves ("2 the history"). In "3 the tour," the guide leads her through a finishing school for white women. Clifton writes, "smiling, she pats my darky hand," ironically using the racist term "darky" when in reality she is the honored guest ("3 the tour," 73). The fourth poem, which repeats the phrase "in this hall," points to the irony of her recitation in this hall that black women, and black women only, had scrubbed and scrubbed.

Two more poems complete the sequence. In "5 the reading" she doesn't look into the white faces but still manages to love the people in the audience. The final poem takes her to the end of the day with her reading completed. She feels like a "black cat / in the belfry / hanging / and/ ringing" ("6 it is late," *Next*, 76). The reference to the "black cat" in this somewhat innocent conclusion become more ominous with the word "hanging"—as in the hanging of the black man from the fig tree in "3 botany," a poem that later appears in *Next* (83) as part of the *SINGING* section.

Clifton does not intend to make life more comfortable for those who listen to or read her poems. Still, her international recognition as a teacher and poet has won her several university posts and an endowed chair in creative writing at St. Mary's College in Maryland. "My students inspire me," she told an interviewer for the National Council of Teachers of English. "They keep me young, keep me wanting to know what's going on in the world."[46] Nor is her teaching limited to the conventional classroom setting; she frequently conducts readings combined with writing workshops. Baltimore writer Eugenia Collier once participated in a workshop that Clifton conducted at Cave Canum in New York City.[47] "There was an emotion in that house I have seldom seen," Eugenia said.

Nevertheless, she has been ambivalent about her teaching career. In the 1990s she worked for a brief time as a visiting professor at the University of Memphis, a few miles from the Mississippi border, three decades after the start of the civil rights movement. Many of her poems reveal her aversion for Southern racism, poems that include the murder of Medgar Evers, the assassination of Schwerner, Cheney, and Goodman, and the enslavement of her great-great-grandmother. Her poetry from the Memphis period is somber, as have been her racially empowered poems in *The Terrible Stories* (1996) and *Blessing the Boats* (2000).

For Clifton, in contrast, teaching at St. Mary's has been a rewarding experience, one in which the poet learns from her students and is close to them; they call her by her first name. At the end of every class, her students join hands in a circle, just one of Lucille's methods for breaking down traditional barriers. She told Hilary Holladay that on one occasion, a white student from Arizona was standing next to a black one in the circle. The white student announced, "I'm from Arizona. This is the first time I have ever touched a black person." The two embraced. Lucille said to herself, "Oh, ok, that's why I teach. Now I understand why."[48]

One young man, Chris de Sousa, wanted to know more about the life of Mathias de Sousa, whose last name was the same as his. "Was there really such a man? That was his project," recalled Lucille.[49] People familiar with Maryland history would know that Mathias de Sousa was the first freed person of African descent living in the state. An indentured servant, he had to work for the Jesuits until his release in 1638. Later Mathias became captain of a trading ship and a trader in English goods. In 1641 he was an elected representative to the Maryland Assembly.[50] Clifton hoped that Chris de Sousa would find an ancestral connection through his project.

One day she told her students at St. Mary's College the story of a ship called *The Pearl*. On the night of April 15, 1848, seventy-seven slaves in the Washington, D.C., area stole silently to the waiting vessel in hopes of being taken to New Jersey, a free state. The ship was chartered from Daniel Drayton, a white man sympathetic to the cause. Mary Kay Ricks has identified the black leaders as Paul Jennings, Daniel Bell, and Samuel Edmonson; each of them either came from a prominent slave-owning family or was married to a freed black.[51] Because of the bad weather they were grounded in St. Mary's City and captured. What Clifton found so ironic was that her students were not angered by the fact of slavery; rather, they were incensed because the captured slaves had to walk from St. Mary's to Washington, D.C. In another version of the story the slaves did not walk to Washington but instead were dragged back on the boat in chains. Many of the most rebellious were then sold on the slave blocks of New Orleans.[52]

In either case it is, as Clifton has argued to her students, the horror of enslavement itself and not the means of transporting them that should arouse their passion. Additionally, the discrepancies regarding *The Pearl* incident point to the lack of reliable evidence concerning African-American history. Most of the information about *The Pearl* is from a book written in 1930 by John Paynter.[53] Like the history of Native Americans, the history of African-Americans has been primarily recorded by white historians who are unlikely to represent the feelings of the people about whom they are writing.

Clifton remembers a student who did research on the Tulsa riots in Oklahoma. She was particularly interested in the project because one of the men implicated in the Tulsa riots, a newspaper editor, A. J. Smitherton, had reportedly escaped with his family and five children, but authorities did not know what became of him. Although Internet searches suggest he was married in 1922 in Texas, the Cliftons, along with Ishmael Reed, had worked for him when he went to Buffalo. In Tulsa his paper had been called the *North Star*; in Buffalo it was the *Empire Star*.[54]

Clifton's commitment to black history is as apparent as her commitment to poetry and to teaching; they are virtually inseparable. It saddens her that so many young Americans, black and white, are ignorant of the civil rights movement. She believes that many students are so self-absorbed that it's hard to convince them that events surrounding black liberation are something they really ought to know about. In her classroom, she uses videos and tries to teach them the difference between a documentary and a movie. It annoys her that some people learn their history from movies like Alan Parker's *Mississippi Burning*, starring Gene Hackman and Wilhem Dafoe, who play two FBI agents investigating the 1964 murder of three civil rights workers, one black and two white: Michael Schwerner, James Chaney, and Andrew Goodman. Reviewers of the film were emotional in their response to it, but none more so than Pauline Kael, who wrote in *The New Yorker* that Parker manipulated "the civil-rights movement to make a Charles Bronson movie, and from his blithe public statements, he seems unaware that this could be thought morally repugnant."[55] From a historical perspective *Mississippi Burning* and other movies like it are "repugnant" because they feature white Northerners at the center of the action with passive Southern blacks providing the background. "Parker uses blacks only as victims—noble 'stick' figures to be beaten, lynched or burned in orgiastic explosions of slickly packaged pyrotechnics."[56]

Because of her commitment to authentic versions of history, Clifton often spends time searching through historical archives with her friend Kathy Glaser. One morning they studied the holdings at the Historical Society in Huntertown, Maryland, looking for an Underground Railroad stop in southern Maryland. Based in the North, the Underground Railroad was a network that helped those who had escaped the slave states of the South. It "was a loose organization of abolitionists, anti-slavery societies, and vigilance committees."[57] Clifton is convinced that such a system was operative in the South as well as in the North. "The archives say no, there is no record. But one tends to hear other things about St. Mary's County and its manor houses."[58] Given the opportunity, she should be able to enhance her research by using an interactive map of St. Mary's County as it appeared in an 1865 atlas, with an electronic search location for the name of the place or the person under investigation.

Clifton wants to know when the African-American presence was first felt in this country. "How did the slaves get here? The only person historians know of is Mathias de Sousa."[59] Other historians, however, claim that the first African in the New World was Anthony ("Antonio a Negro") Johnson, who first arrived in Virginia in 1621. A worker on a tobacco plantation, he bought his way out of bondage in the 1640s.[60] Clearly, Clifton loves poking into the past as she uncovers the kinds of factual materials that find their way into her poetry. As she had said in her remarks about the Sioux warrior Crazy Horse, "I'm a learner. If I'm interested in something, I find out, I research things. I'm extremely nosy."

Lucille's wide range of interest and her intelligent objectivity concerning human rights are constant sources of stimulation to her students, who have the freedom to "poke" everywhere, from Oklahoma to Japan, from South Dakota to South Korea, from Maryland to Mississippi, from poetry to documentary, under her gentle guidance.

FOUR

Generations Coming and Going

Lucille Clifton's life has been sustained by a vision of her ancestors and of those to come after her, best expressed in a memoir, *Generations*, written in 1976. *Generations* is dedicated to her father, Samuel Louis Sayles, Sr., "who is somewhere, / being a man."[1] Its publication coincided with the surge of interest among African-Americans in searching for their historical roots in Africa, an act of recovery generated in part by the publication of Alex Haley's *Roots* in the same year and by the celebrated television mini-series that followed it.[2] *Roots* had initially been published in 1974 as a *Reader's Digest* excerpt that Clifton may possibly have seen. Alex Haley's story and Clifton's story are similar. Two West Africans of noble descent are taken from their villages, enslaved, and brought against their will to the United States, where they are sold. They and their progeny live out their lives through several generations. It is interesting that both authors conclude their family line with the funeral of their father.

It is no accident that, as the black power movement gained in strength, many African-Americans became interested in tracing their origins. Books were published that offered guidelines for researching one's ancestors and tracing them to a specific tribe and geographical location in Africa. Maya Angelou, who lived in Ghana from 1963 to 1966, was caught up, like her American contemporaries, in the hairstyles, dress, language, and music of West Africa. As the central character in her own autobiography, she became "intoxicated" with her African ties and was pleased when an African woman identified her as a Bambara on the basis of her "height, hair, and skin color."[3] This interest in tracing African origins continues today. For example, in June 2005 Oprah Winfrey told *People* magazine that by doing a DNA search she had been able to trace her ancestry to the Zulu tribe of South Africa.[4]

Unlike Maya Angelou or Oprah Winfrey or Alex Haley, Lucille Clifton was well aware of her roots since childhood, when her "Daddy" used to tell her stories about great-great-grandmother Caroline, a Dahomey woman "born free in Africa" in 1823 and forced into slavery. Dahomey was a kingdom located in Benin, a part of Nigeria. "Dahomey reached the height of its power and prestige during the heyday of the Atlantic slave trade in the eighteenth and nineteenth centuries."[5] It was during this so-called heyday that Caroline was sent to America as a slave. Although she came from a culture that did not read or write, she told her great-grandson Samuel stories about her memories of West Africa and of her life in Virginia. As Suzanne Feldmann remarks in her introduction to *African Myths and Tales*, African stories "come to us from a world in which the word has not yet been divorced from the act of personal communication. A book can be read everywhere, at any time, by any literate person. It is addressed to everyone and to no one in particular. By contrast, the oral tale draws its vitality from the context of its telling."[6] The genesis for Clifton's memoir is the African spoken tradition, which in *Generations* she converts from the oral into the written, connecting her family through memories of Caroline. The memoir derives its power from the words of her ancestors, especially Caroline. It is through her agency that Caroline's descendants maintain a sense of order and a viable center; it is through Clifton's ability to write that the narrative is preserved.

In the intricate movement of her ancestors from West Africa to Virginia to Buffalo, Clifton accounts for her heritage through the individual voices of her relatives. This is in contrast to the first-person narrative that is more common among African-American autobiographies, such as in Frederick Douglass's classic, *Narrative of the Life of Frederick Douglass, an American Slave, Written by Himself* or, more recently, in Maya Angelou's *I Know Why the Caged Bird Sings*.[7] Clifton's choice is profound. It emphasizes her belief that only through the collective stories of her peoples from one generation to the next can she, a black woman and mother living in the present, exist at all. Through splicing the various stories in an innovative double-layering of citations and memories and by shifting from voice to voice, from father to mother to Mammy Caroline to Lucille, the text achieves a density that belies its short length. The multiple spoken voices reinforce its oral quality, which is one of the central features of the African-American slave narrative.

The slave narrative was almost always structured as a journey, originally from West Africa to America. "Through this method of speaking and writing, slaves recalled the harrowing journey from Africa to America and the atrocities of plantation life."[8] Great-great-grandmother Caroline, who had experienced such a journey, talked about it to her great-grandson, Samuel.

The earliest slave narrative to appear in print was probably Briton Hammon's 1760 story of how he endured under the slave system.[9] "Of the written narratives, many celebrated the achievements of literacy—of being able to read and write—as a major theme."[10] In contrast, Clifton's narrative begins as an oral history, for it was her "strong-willed father, an inveterate story-teller whose persona is so strong in this book, [who] provides her with the raw material for *Generations*."[11] Because her father could not write, "the very act of writing down Samuel's stories must have felt empowering and enobling."[12] In writing his story, it is Lucille Clifton who achieves literacy.

Generations tracks Clifton's journey northward in 1976, from Baltimore to Buffalo, to attend the funeral of Samuel Sayles. By this time Clifton was a recognized poet and writer of children's books. She makes the journey to her former home to join her sisters in mourning the passing of their father. In this contemporary slave narrative, Clifton emphasizes the female values of love and parenting, joining a company of black women autobiographers from Linda Brent to Maya Angelou to Nikki Giovanni.[13] Unlike male narrators, such as Frederick Douglass, women are more likely to play close attention to "women's issues such as rape, child care, and the stability of the family."[14]

The major verb in the narrative is "to say." Although her father could not write, he had the gift of "saying" or narration: "He had been a great story teller" (242). Verbs of telling or narration set the tone and create the point of view: "She said," "Daddy told me once," and "Daddy used to tell me." Clifton draws her lineage with subtlety, usually from the perspective of her father: "'Mammy Ca'line raised me,' Daddy would say" (230).

Both the first and the second sections of "caroline and son" open with the ambiguous referent, "She said." The first refers to a white woman telephoning Clifton with information about the Sayle family. The second refers to Clifton's sister Punkin [Elaine] calling from Buffalo to tell her that their father is dead. The parallel grammatical structure, "She said," introduces the female voice that controls the text. It eventually becomes Clifton's voice, modulated by other narrators that include her father, Job, Walt Whitman, her grandmother, her great-grandmother, the "first Black woman legally hanged in the state of Virginia" (240), and her great-great-grandmother Caroline, called Ca'line in *Generations*.

Clifton's story is not simply her own. It is filtered through the memories of those who came before her and especially through her father. "His life had been full of days and his days had been full of life," she writes of him with affection (242). This parallel phrasing, called *chiasmus*, recalls the rhetoric both of the black sermon and of the black slave narrative. Frederick Douglass, the former slave, became competent in the language of the master and in the master's rhetorical patterns, charting "how a man was made a slave," and as he put it in a chiasmus, "how a slave was made a man."[15]

As Caroline's crossing from West Africa is a replication of the slave narrative that had initiated Clifton's roots, so the death of her Daddy, Samuel Sayles, precipitates his daughter's journey from Baltimore back to Buffalo. Lucille,

Fred, and Lucille's brother Sam are in the car. "We all laughed," she writes. "Everything was funny" (231). The jovial attitude of the people riding to the funeral disguises the sense of apprehension that they must have felt as they traveled from Baltimore, an attitude that Clifton captures through her use of a slave metaphor: we "broke out of the city like out of chains" (231). Other metaphors in the memoir link environment and mood, as in "Smoke was hanging over Buffalo like judgment" (234).

Clifton's affectionate yet sardonic tone when describing her father is evident throughout the memoir, but especially in the description of Samuel's casket: "They were hiding his missing leg. The place where there was no leg was hidden. They were hiding his nothing" (238). The droning repetition of the words *missing* and *hidden* reveals Clifton's use of irony as the undertakers try to hide the reality of her father's absent limb, lost so long ago, when "his leg died. Just shriveled up and turned black and died." Samuel's doctors had to amputate the "black" leg before the poison spread. "Yeah, they got my leg but they didn't get me, he would boast" (*Generations* 255). In exploring the *missing* and *hidden* members of her father's body and of his family, Clifton brings them back to life; she "re-members" them. Memory functions throughout *Generations* to connect the past with the present and the future.

In this brief memoir the themes of family, heritage, slavery, and oppression emerge from Lucille Clifton's cultural experiences and are offset by themes of love, hope, and survival. In writing *Generations* she was assisted in her approach by her editor at Random House, Toni Morrison, her friend from Howard University days. Morrison advised her to speak her narrative into a tape recorder and then to write down some of the memories as she made the transition from oral to written composition.

Generations is divided into five sections or chapters: "caroline and son," "lucy," "gene," "samuel," and "thelma." These chapters are the basis of the Sayles genealogy, one that has the resonance of an Old Testament lineage. Great-great-grandmother Caroline and her husband Sam begat a son named Eugene, who begat a son named Samuel (Lucille's father), who married Lucille's mother (Thelma Moore). They begat a son, Samuel Sayles, and a daughter, Thelma Lucille Sayles, called Lucille. Thelma Lucille Sayles married Fred Clifton. They begat six children named Sidney, Frederica, Gillian, Alexia, Channing, and Graham.[16] All of these children were alive when Lucille Clifton's memoir was published in 1976. Although Clifton and her deceased father are the most conspicuous characters in the memoir, there is no chapter devoted to the author herself.

Critic Cheryl A. Wall has observed that in *Generations* "prose and pictures combine to create a singular text." Each section is introduced by a photograph that must be "read."[17] Shades and tones, the way in which a hand is placed on a shoulder, the time of year in which a snapshot was taken—these details create visual images that amplify Clifton's verbal descriptions and perpetuate the "ritual of remembrance."[18] *Generations* is held together by storytelling, by photographs, by the Bible, by the journey motif, and by a series of citations from Walt Whitman's *Song of Myself*. Walt Whitman (1819–1892) sings and celebrates his oneness with the cosmos in this most prophetic of American poems. Clifton is very fond of Whitman, who has written lines that she loves. At St. Mary's College she taught a creative writing class called *I Too Sing, America*, based on Whitman's "I hear America Singing" and Langston Hughes's "I Too Sing America." By choosing a white American male poet to introduce each section of the memoir, Clifton connects herself to mainstream poetry and culture. At the same time, in acknowledging Whitman's effect on black poets such as Hughes, she places her work within the African-American poetic traditions. The Crazy Horse sequence, discussed in the next chapter, is a further example of how she hears America singing. Through the rhythm and repetition in that sequence, she connects her poems to the chants of America's original peoples. Although she pursues each of these connections and contrasts in her works, *Generations* is most heavily weighed toward an understanding of the black family and of African-American heritage.

The title page contains the dedication to Samuel Louis Sayles, Sr. / daddy / (1902–1969). Below it is a quotation from Job 13:1 and 2: "Lo, mine eye hath seen all this, mine ear hath heard and understood it. What ye know, the same do I know also; I am not inferior unto you." Job is addressing the "worthless physicians" who had considered him to be less than them; perhaps this is an analogy to the racism and classism of America in the late 1960s. Although God seems indifferent to his pleas, Job keeps the faith throughout his trials, asserting his innocence yet claiming to be unworthy before the Lord.[19] The book of Job was one of Samuel's favorite Biblical texts; his eldest daughter Josie read to him from it as he was dying. Clifton seems to have chosen this particular quotation to assert her father's essential strength against any enemies who had considered him to be inferior. The citation from Job is followed by the words of great-great-grandmother Ca'line, the inspirational source of *Generations*: "Get what you want, you from Dahomey women."

CAROLINE AND SON

The first section, "caroline and son," opens with the exact repetition of the beginning of Whitman's *Song of Myself*: "I celebrate myself, and sing myself, / And what I assume you shall assume, / For every atom belonging to me as good belongs to you."[20] As if anticipating the DNA code, Clifton, by way of her literary ancestor Whitman, affirms that she shares the same atom that belonged to her great-great-grandmother, even though they might otherwise be very different. Samuel recalls Caroline as being a "dark, old skinny lady and she raised my Daddy [Eugene] and then raised me, least till I was eight years old when she died" (230). This verbal portrait does not resemble the mature poet or any recent photographs of her. It does, however, resemble Samuel's grandmother, Lucy, who was hanged for killing a white man.

Following the picture of Caroline and son and the quote from Whitman, the actual text begins with the words "She said" [no punctuation]. The "She" is a white woman who had called Clifton on the telephone in response to a notice the poet had placed in a Bedford, Virginia, newspaper inquiring about the name of her father, Samuel Sayles. The white woman, who is compiling a history of the Sale/Sayles family, doesn't remember a Samuel Sayles. Thus at the beginning of the memoir Clifton asks the question that is to continue to affect her poetry profoundly: "Who remembers the names of the slaves? Only the children of slaves" (227).

The basic impetus in *Generations* is to remember these slaves and to celebrate the "Dahomey women gathering in [her] bones" (228). In charting her ancestry Clifton provides the answer to her own real and theoretical questions: Where are the slaves? What are their names? In like fashion she later visits a graveyard and observes that the dead slaves lie silent and unmarked ("at the cemetery, walnut grove plantation, south carolina, 1989," *Quilting* 11–12). In *Generations* she addresses this same silence, this same historical anonymity; the memoir represents her efforts to give her ancestors a name and a place.

The remainder of the chapter focuses on the present, as Lucille, Fred, and Sammy make the journey from South to North, from Baltimore to Buffalo, for the family funeral. Their journey recalls in a smaller way the journey of great-great-grandmother Caroline on a slave ship that transported her from east to west; it also imitates the journey of Samuel Sayles as he moves from the land of the living to the place of the dead.

LUCY

Chapter 2, "lucy," begins with the Whitman citation: "I do not trouble my spirit to vindicate itself or to be understood; I see that the elementary laws never apologize." The severity of the quotation is appropriate to the section; its bitter tone sets the stage for Lucy's birth and death. As the narrator of past events, Samuel tells his daughter about the acquisition of the Dahomey girl Ca'line by old master John F. Sale. Because John's favorite slave desired the young woman, whom he had seen in an orchard, she became a gift from John's blind old owner, a lawyer. After they were married, Ca'line trained to be a midwife. They had seven or more children, one of whom was the girl they named Lucy, who grew to be a tall, skinny woman just like Clifton's great-great-grandmother was.

The Lucy chapter shifts from the present, with Samuel laid out in his casket, to the past, to her father's previous marriages and relationships, where he somehow always had a woman to cook and clean for him. But the focal point is Lucy. Samuel once said, "They tell me she was mean. Lucy was mean always, I heard Aunt Margaret Brown say to Mammy Ca'line one time. And Mammy just said no she wasn't mean, she was strong" (242).

The woman named Lucy had a sexual relationship with a white man named Harvey Nichols, who lived on a neighboring property with his wife and family. Harvey Nichols and Lucy Sale had a baby boy, Gene, Samuel's father, who was "born with a withered arm" (244). Lucy, blaming the father for her son's deformity, shot Harvey one night. She did not apologize for her crime, and she never tried to run away. Out of respect for Mammy Ca'line, Lucy was not lynched. There was a trial, and Lucy became the "first Black woman legally hanged in the state of Virginia" (240).

The scene with Ca'line witnessing her hanged child is one of the strongest pieces of writing in *Generations*. "And Lucy was hanged. The lady whose name they gave me like a gift had her neck pulled up by a rope and I can see Mammy Ca'line standing straight as a soldier." Ca'line stands in silence, "her mind closed around the picture like a frame" (245). Neither the mother nor her hanged daughter makes a sound. They realize, as Walt Whitman would years later, that "the elementary laws never apologize." Clifton never wanted to be called by the diminutive name of Lucy, perhaps because of the stigma associated with her great-grandmother.

GENE

The third chapter, "gene," shifts back and forth in time and tone; it moves from Clifton's getting ready for college to the amputation of her father's leg. The Whitman caption is precise: "What is a man anyhow? What am I? what are you?" The chapter begins with Samuel's definition of a man as someone who owns a house, has a son, and plants a tree. Lucille's sisters, Jo and Punkin, are married. Thelma Sayles is ill. None of the children share their storytelling and other amusements with Samuel: "We children were not close to Daddy in those days" (249).

Buried somewhere in the middle of the section is the death of Gene, Clifton's paternal grandfather and the father of Samuel Sayles. "My Daddy's name was Genie and he had a withered arm. He was born with it, oh but Lue, he was a handsome man" (251). Genie was the color of cinnamon with his father's light eyes. At Christmas he would load his arm with bricks and throw them at store windows while the police protected him out of respect for his mother, Ca'line. Samuel's Daddy died when the child was about six, and Samuel's mother "went to work in the tobacco plant and left us with Mammy Ca'line" (253). The concluding section records her mother's death and her father's health problems, including emphysema, a brain tumor, and a shriveled leg.

SAMUEL

As chapter 3 ends with Samuel's ailments, so chapter 4 begins with his death. The elegiac chapter opens with a quote from Walt Whiman's *Song of Myself*: "All goes onward and outward, nothing collapses, / And to die is different from what anyone supposed and luckier." The first two lines of the section show weather and grief in sympathy with each other: "The morning of my father's funeral was grey and wet. Everything cried" (259). Part 2 of chapter 4, "Samuel," is the most important one from a historical viewpoint. Through her written record the poet inscribes her father's oral account of his ancestry, listing the generations that descended from the union of Caroline Donald, "born free among the Dahomey people in 1822 and died free in Bedford, Virginia in 1910" and "Sam Louis Sale, born a slave in America in 1777 and died a slave in the same place in around 1860." Like her father before her, the poet can still recite the names of all of her ancestors from memory. It is through her father rather than through her mother, and through her father's view of history, not her mother's, that Lucille Clifton, born Thelma Lucille Sayles, is able to transmit her father's vision of his West African ancestry.

Stunned by the death of the patriarch, the mourners gather silently at the church, dressed in "stiff new hats and veils" (259). The family members then proceed to the cemetery, where Samuel is laid between his two former wives, Edna, mother of Josie, and Thelma, mother of Sammy and Lucille. His daughter recalls how she stands in tears, wanting to "*tell* him something" (261, emphasis mine). She holds the hand of her Aunt Lucille, who had come from New Jersey to Buffalo to honor her brother. The Samuel section ends in silence as Clifton hears not the sound of her father's voice but the bumping of his coffin: "My father bumped against the earth. Like a rock" (261).

THELMA

The fifth and final chapter, "thelma," is introduced by the longest of the quotes from *Song of Myself*. The four lines speak to the immortality of the spirit: "They are alive and well somewhere." The passage contains Whitman's famous words, "The smallest sprout shows there is really no death." Although it reinforces Clifton's links with her mother, the chapter is more about Lucille than it is about Thelma. It shows Clifton's approaching independence as she prepares to leave for Howard University. She writes lovingly about her maternal grandmother, Georgia Moore, who called the young woman "Genius" and who advised her to "keep her dress tail down" when she went off to college (267, 268).

In this last chapter, Clifton recalls that her parents had no closeness in their marriage: "After my brother was born, she never slept with my Daddy again" (272). Clifton and her sisters had tried to protect their mother from her husband's verbal abuse and fights. Once Punkin [Elaine] attacked her father with a broom, shouting, "If you hit Mama I'll kill you" (274). While having tests for the cause of her epilepsy, Thelma Sayles died in a hospital on Friday the 13th of February, 1959. It was raining. It seems obvious, from reading Clifton's later poetry, especially "the message from The Ones (received in the late 70s)," that she stored these early memories of her mother in her head and heart, where they were granted a special privilege and were considered sacred (*Mercy* 53–75). In her grief over Thelma's death, Clifton would have taken comfort in Whitman's line: "The smallest sprout shows there is really no death."

Cheryl Wall, in comparing Whitman and Clifton, writes that both authors "share aesthetic, political, and spiritual affinities. For both, the poetry of the Bible, colloquial speech, and popular music are key poetic referents."[21] Both believed strongly in spiritual communication. In matters of form, however, the two poets could not be more dissimilar. Clifton's lines, even in this prose work, are tight and crisp, whereas Whitman's *Song of Myself* sprawls at its edges as he documents "the sound of the belch'd words of my voice loos'd to the eddies of the wind" (I. 25) or witnesses "the blab of the pave, tires of carts, sluff of boot-soles, talk of the promenaders, / The heavy omnibus, the driver with his inter-rogating thumb, the clank of the shod horses on the granite floor," (II. 154–55), and so on, through a breathless list that runs from lines 154 to 166 without an end-stop. Clifton shares Whitman's compassion for the runaway slave (*Song of Myself*, II. 189–198) and his love for "the common air that bathes the globe" (I. 360). But in its seemingly limitless form, *Song of Myself* encompasses every detail of a vast continent, whereas *Generations* is on the surface a modest narrative about attending a father's funeral in Buffalo.

Generations ends emphatically, with Clifton's oft-quoted statement, "Things don't fall apart. Things hold" (275). "Things hold," she proclaims, inverting collapse into binding and separation into unity as she corrects two earlier writers, William Butler Yeats and Chinua Achebe, for their mistaken views.[22] Critic Jerry Ward claims that "*Generations* is a counterweight for Yeats's theory, because Mrs. Clifton wants to make a poetic argument for the possibility of having order, wholeness, affirmation, and a sense of place."[23] It is through Caroline that this "sense of place" gathers its full significance; she becomes, in Clifton's poetry and prose, an emblem for the shift in culture from West Africa to the American plantations of Virginia.

Caroline's endurance in America is a testament to Clifton and to her line-age: "Things hold." Clifton's insistence on cultural cohesion gathers full strength when seen in its historical context, at a time when people were dying in the Middle Passage and when European and American interests demoted black family members to so many pieces of property. The memoir ends posi-tively. She has a vision of her great-great-grandmother "standing in the green of Virginia, in the green of Africa" (276).

LATER TRAGEDIES

The death of Samuel Sayles suffuses the tone and subject matter of *Generations*. But since its publication in 1976 there have been other personal tragedies in Lucille's life—the death of her husband Fred from lung cancer on November 10, 1984, at the age of forty-nine and the deaths of two of her children, Frederica and Channing, in 2000 and 2004. In her mid-forties, when Clifton was still mourning the loss of her parents, she could never have anticipated these later tragedies, which would be so terrible and would occur so soon.

When Fred Clifton was diagnosed with lung cancer, people actually blamed him, claiming that he was doing it on purpose and that he wanted to die. This kind of remark greatly offended his wife, who knew him best. After all, it was she who married him.[24] In *Quilting* she has a poem, "4/25/89 late," that speaks to his early diagnosis and to the five years that have passed since his death. "Five" is a magic number, the number of years that the medical profession uses to estimate that a patient is likely to survive cancer. Clifton uses the number for ironic purposes; Fred has been dead five years, indicated typographically in the book by the five spaces between the date and the word "late." Five years ago, when he was assumed to be "well and safe," he was waiting to be "pronounced an almost ghost" (*Quilting* 63). The five years also mark the span of her widowhood.

When Fred was dying the family was living in a house with a garage that had been turned into a study. Fred slept in there while Lucille and two of their daughters took turns giving him his medicine. As he took his last breath several different flocks of birds, totaling perhaps several dozen, flew up to his window. They "just flocked there, just hovered there for about five minutes, then all flew away with his last breath."[25] Fred's last words to his wife were "Tell my story."[26]

She retells the story of Fred's death in a poem from *Quilting* (64): "as he was dying / a canticle of birds / hovered / watching through the glass." A canticle is a "song or chant, especially a nonmetrical hymn with words taken from a biblical text other than from the Book of Psalms."[27] Clifton's hymn, written without rhyme or meter, captures the nuanced differences between sound and silence, light and dark, bird and human. As the birds hover at the window, there is a "shattering of wing" marking the moment of Fred's departure. Some doubt the story, but she insists that it is absolutely true. A close friend of hers, poet Josephine Jacobson, a staunch Catholic, asked, "Don't you allow room in your life for miracles?"[28]

In addition to "as he was dying" and "4/25/89 late," there are numerous other moving poems that commemorate Fred Clifton. In *Next* she re-envisions his death and resurrection, his "rising and turning / through my skin" ("the death of fred clifton, 11/10/84, age 49"). The elegy is told from her dead husband's point of view. He is drawn into "the center of myself" and sees "with amazing clarity" not the "shapes of things / but oh, at last, the things / themselves" (*Next* 64). This poem is a reflection of the Buddhist philosophy that

Fred espoused during his studies of Eastern religions; the veil has been lifted from his earthly sight and he finally sees the "things themselves." It is at the same time a reiteration of the Pauline concept of death expressed in Corinthians I, chapter 13: "For now we see through a glass, darkly; but then face to face; now I know in part; but then shall I know even as also I am known."[29] This brilliant elegy is reprinted in *Blessing the Boats* (51).

Another poem from *Next*, "the message of fred clifton," also maintains the point of view of the deceased: "i rise." The risen spirit is "a nimbus of dark light." A nimbus has several meanings. It can be a "black rain cloud" but also a "bright cloud surrounding gods or goddesses appearing on earth."[30] Here the poet draws on a paradox that appears in many of her poems—that black is white and white is black. "the message of fred clifton" contains the lines that were to serve as the epigraph for her 2004 volume *Mercy*: "the only mercy is memory" (*Next* 66).

The poem "i'm going back to my true identity / fjc 11/84 [Fred J. Clifton 11/84]" refers to the month of Fred's death but not the specific date, which is unusual for this body of work. The lack of date suggests that the poem is set on the brink of death, when the man about to die seizes "a box of stars / for my living wife" (*Next* 65). He wants to give her the stars so that she will remember him as a man and not as a spirit.

One of the poems to Fred is both domestic and painful, filled with images of gaping wardrobes and abandoned clothing. Again it is told from Fred's perspective, as he observes "my wife" waking up to an open closet. Turning toward his side of the bed, she says, "'Darling / something has stolen your wonderful / shirts and ties'" (*Next* 66). It is not someone but "something" that has removed Fred's clothing and with it his former identity; the "something" is cancer.

Her memory of Fred is immediate, unrelieved by Asian philosophy or by Christian consolation. The cluster of memorial poems in *Next* seem to be a spontaneous overflowing of grief, rather than a planned sequence such as the series of poems to Crazy Horse that appears in the same volume. *Next* was published in 1987, three years after Fred's death and too soon to establish distance from it.

The Book of Light appeared in 1993, almost a decade after the death of Fred Clifton. The volume contains three special poems to Fred. One is an anniversary poem, "11/10 again," which is a philosophical playing with the concepts of light, radiance, and brilliance—all things Lucille. Extremely abstract, it was written at the peak of her spiritual phase and published in the volume that contained "brothers," her conversation between Lucifer and God. The only recognizable connection to her dead husband is in the title, which is the anniversary of his death (*The Book of Light* 19). In "again," a poem in seven parts, she refers to "a husband who would one day / rise and enter a holy house" (*The Book of Light* 64). In an untitled poem filled with phantoms, she writes about the long walk "through the widow's door" (*The Book of Light* 30).

Compared to the vivid Fred poems that appear in *Next*, the ones in *The Book of Light* are shrouded and ashen.

The Terrible Stories (1996) contains what might be considered Clifton's most spiritually complex poem to her husband, "evening and my dead once husband." Again one finds the familiar concept of Fred's "rising," but in this poem he is rising from the "spirit board." The spirit board refers to the Ouija board that is still a popular form of communication with the departed. Clifton had started to use the spirit board in the early 1980s to make contact with her dead mother. She told Akasha Hull that her communications with Thelma and other departed spirits led her from the "Ouija board, to automatic writing, to not particularly having to write because she could hear."[31] Automatic writing, which is a means of contacting other forms of intelligence by using one's own spiritual energy, takes place while one is holding a writing implement. The receiver of the communication can be in a trance or can be completely awake.[32]

The poignant poem, "evening and my dead once husband," duplicates the action of two persons touching a Ouija board. In the first twelve lines Clifton wonders why she is "fuss[ing] like a fishwife" about their "wayward sons"; she wants her "once dead husband" to answer her questions about loneliness, cancer, and the "wars against our people." Formally, the thirteen-line poem resembles a sonnet, with her questions occupying the body of the poem. Following a space that in a regular sonnet would be the thirteenth line, Fred, the source of spiritual energy, extends his hand on the Ouija board, and in the final line he spells out the eerie words: "it does not help to know" (*The Terrible Stories* 47).

During his lifetime Fred Clifton was a man with many answers, a philosopher who influenced a lot of people. When he was dying, people came from all over the world to sit with him. The house was virtually taken over by these people, which was difficult for his wife, as she is a very private person. Many of his friends felt that she had no special status with him because one of the things that yoga teaches is that nobody is special. Lucille, on the other hand, felt that her almost thirty years of marriage had made her special, as had their mutual efforts in rearing their children.

"By the end we knew he was going to die," his daughter Alexia said. "He was diagnosed with cancer in April of 1984. He went into radiation treatment. He was a real holistic vegetarian, a not-used-to-putting-anything-into-his-body kind of person. But what was he going to do? When you have lung cancer, you try not to have it. He started radiation, and it looked for a minute like he was getting better, but the cancer just started to spread. He went into the hospital in September of '84. By the time he came home we knew that he was going to die. So we weren't surprised."

Alexia continued, "He was eighty-something pounds. The doctor called one night and my Dad, amazing person that he is, had the presence of mind to, in this state, to ask my Mom, 'Tell him to give me a brain scan. It's not the medicine.' The doctor gave him one and called us one evening and said, 'I've stopped counting. It's just a matter of days.'" Lucille, Alexia, Gillie, Graham, and Rica were at his side. "We were around his bed, and then he just stopped breathing."[33]

The poet's grief at her husband's death is captured in her words: "In November of 1984 my beloved husband of almost 30 years died. I am making it because of my daughters, my sons, my woman friends. When I retreat into my room to just sit and stare or cry I can hear my mama speak through my four daughters. 'She don't have to act strong if she don't want to.' And they still love me."[34]

After Fred Clifton died, the family moved from Baltimore to California, where a teaching position at the University of California Santa Cruz was being held for the poet. Fred was cremated; his ashes were distributed in Santa Cruz. Although she could remember the time when she had thought that cremation was a terrible idea, she did not consider Fred's cremation a violation of her spiritual beliefs because she didn't believe the physical body is what we are.[35] All of the children, except for Channing who was in the Coast Guard, went to California and stayed with their mother at Santa Cruz. After six years, Alexia and her sister Gillian moved to Los Angeles.

The poet became angry when she spoke about Fred's leaving her, a hostility that grew in intensity after she too was diagnosed with cancer and he was gone, unable to nurse her as she had nursed him. She was mad at him because he was dead. She thought, "See there. I was with YOU!"[36] In "A Letter to Fred" she is explicit about her anger. It is a mournful passage written in prose, a fairly rare form for Clifton, which expresses her fury at surviving her husband's death:

> And anger. Especially anger at women with living mates. At survivors of cancer. At men older than 50. How dare they live, survive, grow old, and you did not. Who do they think they are? And who do I think I am to make such judgments? Ah, dear, I am the one who checked the box marked married for at least three years after my husband was dead. I am the one who still remembers the sick man more than the shy young boy. I am the lonely one who hums the old songs alone; I am the one who is left after so many are gone who remember. Fred, when the last one is gone, who will keep the past? Will the past exist? Did it ever?[37]

The anger expressed in this passage helps explain the epigraph to *Next*: "*See you later alligator.*" She is referring to a song recorded by Bill Haley and the Comets in the early years of their marriage: "See you later alligator / after a while crocodile."[38] The song is about a love quarrel that ends with the word "Goodbye." The ending helps to explain her anger, her feeling of being left behind. When filling out forms she still checked "married" after three years as a widow. The end of the three-year period of mourning coincided with the publication of *Next*.

Since Fred's death his widow has never been romantically involved with anyone else. Her poetry, her family, and her teaching have kept her well occupied. Still, she would have liked to have had a relationship, but in her opinion no one was interested in her. In one of her fox poems, published when she was sixty, she confesses to having strong sexual desires ("leaving fox," *The Terrible Stories* 16). At one point she went out with the president of St. Mary's College, the man who is Superman in one of her poem sequences. She was attracted to his unusually strong love poetry. In fact, he was a published poet, one of the young men Robert Frost invited to dinner at his house.[39]

In her poetry Clifton remembers this "Superman" and other friends from the past. After her brother Sam died, she continued questioning with renewed vigor the function of memory, wondering who besides her would remember her brother's death, her mother's suffering, or her husband's story. Much of her poetry is written to keep her husband and her ancestors alive, to tell their stories from an African-American perspective, and, projecting beyond the past, to tell the stories of her children and grandchildren.

One of the terrible tragedies of life is that our children grow out of their diapers, age, become adults, and sometimes die before we do. Since 2000 Clifton has lost two of her six children, Frederica and Channing. Frederica Clifton attended Harvard University and graduated from the California Institute of Arts in Valencia, California; later she worked as a graphic designer for Columbia Associations in Maryland. She died of brain cancer in August 2000 at her Columbia home. She was only thirty-nine. "She had a brain tumor while she was in art school," Clifton said. "Five years later, after the first brain tumor, when you're supposed to be free, hers recurred. It was more virulent and faster."[40] Her son Channing died of heart failure in January 2004.

She dedicates her 2004 volume *Mercy* to these two dead children, writing of their passing in a beautiful elegy, "april." Here she compares her lost children to fallen birds: "their birthday /is coming they are trying / to be forty / they will fail / they will fall / each from a different year / into the river. ..." ("april," *Mercy* 16). The many spatial gaps in "april," which vary from three to five to nine spaces in length, seem particularly appropriate in a poem meant to recall her grief at her children's lack of fullness. When read aloud, the gaps signal the long pauses of a mother in mourning. In another poem from *Mercy* she shares her grief for the lost two, comparing herself to a wolf-mother who carries her pain in her heart ("children," 19). Although Clifton feels some regret at her "manipulation" of the deaths of Channing and Rici, she told Hilary Holladay that her being a poet leaves her with no choice but to write about them.[41] She has not joined any parents' support group after these crises, believing that whatever happens, it's between her and God.[42]

Alexia Clifton, the youngest child, talked about the premature deaths of her sister and her brother: "The sadness and grief that I feel, and that we all feel as siblings, is the death of another sibling, which is something I had never imagined. I know it can't compare with what a parent must feel in losing two children in two and a half years. It's incomprehensible to me. I know what it must have done to her."[43]

Of the four surviving children Clifton's oldest daughter, Sid, works in Hollywood. She is a production person and produces films for Film Roman. Marlo Thomas, the producer of *Free to Be... You and Me*, had helped Sid get a college scholarship, but she did not use it, believing that if her mother did alright not graduating from college, she would too. And she has done well. "Sid's husband is a television writer who writes for a show about a smart-ass dog, *Family Guy*." Clifton's students are very impressed by that. They don't care that she's read at the White House, but *Family Guy* is different.[44]

One of the strongest themes in *Generations* is that the family lives on through their progeny. Lucille Clifton is very close to her children and to her grandchildren. Her granddaughter Bailey is a living example of a passionate belief in continuity. Bailey was born ten months after Frederica died. She was quite a surprise, because Sidney was forty-two when she gave birth. But the family knew somebody should have a baby to make up for Rica's death. Clifton likes to think there's a piece of Frederica in Bailey, whose full name is Bailey Frederica Clifton Goin Monnell.

In her storyteller's mode, Clifton told me an anecdote about a trip to the market with Bailey and her father. "He and Bailey were going through the aisles, and in California liquor is sold in the supermarkets. 'Oh, look, Papa,' she cried. 'There's Mama's juice!'"[45] Needless to say, Lucille loves this granddaughter. "She is so sweet. She is beautiful and tremendously articulate. At St. Mary's she's a legend. Bailey called her grandmother on the anniversary of Rica's death and said, 'Grandma Lucille? Remember, my name is Bailey Frederica Clifton Goin. Don't forget. Okay, bye!'"[46] One of the poems in the sequence *September Song* is dedicated to Bailey (*Mercy* 48).

At the 2004 "Tribute to Lucille Clifton" celebration that closely followed the publication of *Mercy*, she happily announced that another grandchild was on its way, a promise that has since been fulfilled. In 1976 Clifton had ended *Generations* with a list of her six children. That list now needs to be revised and expanded to include her grandchildren: Bailey Frederica Clifton Goin Monnell, Alexandria Monnell, Anpeyo Clifton Brown, and Dakotah Edward Brown..." And so the line goes on. And thus the generations continue, the comings and goings, much like the tide that carries one in and out, "water waving forever" as you "sail through this and that" (*Blessing the Boats* 82).

FIVE

Keeping the Story Alive

Many critics of Lucille Clifton's poetry have emphasized its intricate structures and her literary influences. James A. Miller has suggested "comparisons, contrasts, and connections" among Clifton and at least twelve American poets, from Emily Dickinson to Sterling A. Brown.[1] In his detailed analysis of the theme of light in Clifton's poems, Mark Bernard White discusses her use of tense, her grammatical structures, and her rhetoric, while in a particularly elaborate reading of Clifton's technique, Jeannine Thyreen-Mizignou claims that Clifton's patterns recall "African-American spirituals, such as repetition, refrain, call and response, characteristic adornment and dramatizing, suggestions of dancing and communal life, and various forms of traditional [N]egro expression, such as verbal nouns, asymmetry, and nouns used as verbs."[2] Such comparisons and interpretations have at times irritated the poet, even when she is often compared to Langston Hughes, a poet she greatly admires. Her poetry, she feels, is her own creation.

Stylistically, her poems, many of them untitled, are simple. In terms of form, Clifton has consistently preferred short stanzas of three or four lines, held together by a repeated word or phrase. This sense of unity and connection, implicit in individual poems, is augmented by the poems' organization into a series. She uses this format in her first book, *Good Times*, through the double voices of tyrone and willie b, and grander yet basically similar frameworks recur in her later volumes. Alicia Ostriker summarizes her technique: "The poems are short, unrhymed, the lines typically between four and two beats.

The sentences are usually declarative and direct, the punctuation light, the diction a smooth mix of standard English with varying styles and degrees of black vernacular."[3]

Unduly elaborate interpretations tend to minimize the role the poet plays in "receiving" the poem from wherever it originates. Clifton prefers to express her ideas of poetic conception in biological rather than in formalistic terms. The poet remains "open"; the poems "come." In a conversation with Sonia Sanchez she said, "I had been writing poetry for thirty years before I was published, but that's not the part that matters. What matters [is that] the poem wants to come and I'm here to receive it, try to be faithful to it and remain open to the possibility—and it shows up."[4]

This black poet has been faithfully receiving poems since childhood. No matter when they are conceived, her poems tend to focus on several dominant themes, among them race, gender, and spirituality, the latter being an aspect of her relationship with her sanctified mother.[5] Several of her volumes repeat selected poems, giving the reader a sense of familiarity and comfort, much like meeting an old acquaintance or recalling a memory dimmed by the passing years.

RACE

Of the themes given voice in her poetry, the most persistent is race, with the concept of race sometimes softened or sharpened by the intervention of a female *persona*. The *persona* is often portrayed by her great-great-grandmother Caroline, who was born in West Africa and who was perpetuated in the narratives that Samuel Sayles passed on to his daughter. Clifton's profound interest in history, which derives from Caroline and from her father, continues in her exploration of the American plantation, of Saint Mary's City, of the American West, and of contemporary global issues.

Her early poem "robert" reveals her desire to name her victimized subject. In "at the cemetery, walnut grove plantation, south carolina, 1989" (*Quilting* 11–12) she visits a historic site, where she notices that the buried slaves lie nameless and silent, their graves unmarked. She chants, "tell me your names." The silence of the forgotten slaves contrasts with the official, publicly proclaimed name of the plantation the poet is visiting. "Significantly, the silence seems to emanate from the poet's bones; what she doesn't know about the slaves amounts to things she doesn't know about herself and her own ancestry."[6]

Immediately following the poem about the Walnut Grove visit appears the recollection of another visit, "slave cabin, sotterly plantation, maryland, 1989" (*Quilting* 13). Here the slave is named "aunt nanny," a familiar slave name in the South and yet one so abstract that it is not a name at all but merely a substitution for "mammy." At the end of the poem aunt nanny hums to herself, "humming / her own sweet name"; only the slave nanny is privileged to know her own name. According to Hilary Holladay, "This small, private music, the most ephemeral of art forms, symbolizes the woman's core self. The wordlessness of humming is important here, for 'aunt nanny' is a nameless, essentially wordless entity. Her humming enables her to define herself on her own terms."[7]

Humming can also be a form of defiance, a wordless expression of unwilling submission. In Maya Angelou's 1970 autobiography, *I Know Why the Caged Bird Sings*, for example, three "powhitetrash" girls stand in front of Annie Henderson's store to taunt her. One of the girls exposes her private parts, while Momma Henderson, powerless to respond because she is black, hums a spiritual. One critic reads Annie Henderson's humming as a victory in self-control.[8] Humming is in certain cases a subversive form of music, the emission of sound without vocalization.

Clifton's most frightening poem about race is "jasper texas 1998" (*Blessing the Boats* 20), written to commemorate the death of forty-nine-year-old James Byrd, Jr., who on June 7, 1998, was beaten, chained by his ankles to the bumper of a pickup truck, and dragged along a country road, becoming "dismembered in the process."[9] An autopsy showed that "Byrd was alive and attempting to hold up his head as he was being dragged."[10] Byrd's daughter, Francis Renee Mullins, in a testimony on proposed Texas hate legislation, stated that after being beaten and chained and dragged her father was still alive: "The point in which you actually die after enduring a tremendous amount of pain and broken bones is when your head and arm are ripped from your body like a piece of paper is torn."[11]

The violence of Byrd's death caused the Reverend Jesse Jackson to sermonize that it could change America's bigotry into tolerance. He urged the crowd to join hands in turning "a crucifixion into a resurrection."[12] Other mourners were less conciliatory. A group of black-clad militants led by Khallid Muhammad condemned the white murderers and called Jesse Jackson "a puppet of the White House."[13] In a court hearing following the murder Lawrence Russell Brewster, one of the three men on trial for capital murder, confessed that Byrd's throat had been cut before he was dragged through the countryside and his mutilated body was deposited at the doors of a black church or cemetery.[14] There is little doubt that Byrd's murder was a hate crime.

The poem, which is informally dedicated to "j. byrd," is about separation—of body from head, of self from other, of death from life. The spaces or separations in the title emphasize the theme of separation and reinforce the horror of Byrd's decapitation. The reader, who has come to assume that the "speaking i" in Clifton's poetry is the poet, is shocked to hear her living, human voice transferred to the speaking head of James Byrd: "i am a man's head hunched by the road." The head is the chosen one, "chosen to speak by the members / of my body." The personal pronoun makes it clear that the detached head, with its oral capacity for articulation, is representing the other voiceless, scattered limbs just as, to use Francis Mullins's metaphor, "a piece of paper is torn." Decapitation is the ultimate castration.

In her handling of the talking head Clifton relies on two dominant traditions from her black heritage: the mythos of the talking head in African and African-American folk tales and the extensive literature in America concerning the atrocities of lynching. Among the Igbo of Nigeria there is a story about talking bones that, once retrieved, are able to reveal their victim's murderer. Additionally, the image of a talking skull can be found among the neighboring Nupe peoples.[15] In Byrd's case he cannot name his assassins. His head lies listless and bleeding in the dust while the mourners sing "we shall overcome" in distant undertones that recall the sounds of aunt nanny's hum in "slave cabin, sotterly plantation, maryland, 1989." From that Shadow Land that Lucille is so capable of creating, Byrd's head says, "if i were alive I could not bear it."

In his commentary on the West African folktale "Talking Bones," Richard M. Dorson makes an observation that has great bearing on Clifton's elegy to James Byrd, Jr. During the days of the plantations, dead slaves, assumed to be animals, were usually not buried, but were simply thrown into the woods to rot. One day John, the slave name in many of these stories, finds a talking skeleton in the forest and runs to tell Old Master. But when the reported speaking skeleton refuses to talk, the people beat John to death. Only after John is dead do the bones talk, saying, "Tongue brought us here, and tongue brought you here."[16] In other words, to trust your words to the white man is to die.

Although other black poets before Clifton had written about the horrors of lynching in their works—Claude McKay, Jean Toomer, Sterling A. Brown, and Richard Wright among others—the poem that almost completely captures the first-person point of view in "jasper texas 1998" is Wright's "Between the World and Me," published in 1935. It begins: "And one morning while in the woods I stumbled suddenly / upon the thing." The "thing" is a pile of dry bones surrounded by objects that indicate a lynching has occurred; these objects include cigarette butts, "a pair of trousers stiff with blood," and a "whore's lipstick." As the first-person observer stands in horror, he experiences not just that one lynching but all lynchings: being hung by the neck, being castrated, being tarred and feathered, being burned with gasoline. The poem begins as it ends, in a repetition of the lynching that the ashen bones have endured: "Now I am dry bones, and my face a stony skull staring in yellow surprise at the sun."[17] Wright's ending ellipsis, which further extends the idea of recurrence and repetition, serves as a warning to other black men who have heard his words made flesh. Trudier Harris informs us, "The speaker has not only experienced a baptism of fire; he has had his epiphany and moved from the lack of artistic expression to the creation of art."[18]

The poem "jasper texas 1998" offers no solace through art; there is no softening, no epiphany, no drawing back. The poet urges neither pacifism nor racial harmony in her elegy to a man who died, like Fred Clifton, at the age of forty-nine. There is no answer to Byrd's question, "why and why and why / should I call a white man brother?" As Alicia Ostriker observed, "Part of what separates white from black America, I suspect, is that if whites actually tried to imagine being black, we'd go mad with pain and rage."[19] When "jasper texas 1998" was first published in the literary journal *Ploughshares* it was awarded the Pushcart Prize XXV. Yet some readers expressed hostility toward the prize-winning poem because Clifton seemed to be blaming whites for Byrd's treatment while withholding her usual forgiveness. She said, "I don't want to be accessible to everyone. I'm really very private. As long as I tell the truth I don't see why my mission is to assure people that they are comfortable. I always wanted to be more outspoken. I guess I'm in a place all by myself."[20]

Just as she refuses to be compared to black poet Langston Hughes, Clifton sees herself as separated from the African-American literary tradition. She has been compared to June Jordan, a contemporary poet who helped foster the black cultural revival of the 1970s and whose poetry is, according to one anthologist, "antiracist, feminist, and avowedly political."[21] Comparing herself to Jordan, Clifton fears that her own poetry is elsewhere, in some harmless place where it doesn't disturb the reader. Yet nowhere in Jordan's works does one find a poem so unflinchingly outspoken and dreadfully clear as this elegy to the headless black Texan.

Like Byrd during his execution, the poet was unable, in writing her elegy, to call the white man her brother. Nor could she disguise the circumstances of Byrd's death and make his murder pretty. Her greatest fear is that even though it happened in 1998, just a few years ago, people will have already forgotten it. Ironically, although people may have forgotten the newspaper or television accounts of the execution of James Byrd or the deaths of the four little girls in the Birmingham church, these atrocities live on in the words of poets. That's where poetry is superior to journalism. As long as it's taught, the horror cannot be diminished. The story is told, is taught again and again and again. "jasper texas 1998" is now part of American literary history and will reach its audience for generations.

NATIVE AMERICANS

Clifton's concern for the victim spills over to other victimized people, as evidenced in her poems about Indians in "the killing of the trees"; in her sequence, *The Dream of Foxes*; and in her series of four poems commemorating the Sioux warrior Crazy Horse. There is a distinctive Native American sensibility in her poetry. She is a chanting poet, an African-American who, like the American Indian, tends to think in cycles. Like many Indians, she responds to nature and seeks a balance in the natural order. "For some reason Indian people, people who are Native American, have just been left out. And for some reason in books and poetry their spirituality—you know they are famous for that—these are humans just like the rest of us. I'm very into it and everybody's history, not just mine."[22]

In "the killing of the trees" (*Quilting* 39) she laments the lack of such balance, comparing the great fallen chiefs of the past to trees falling in the forest. She calls on the ancestors to keep their names in their tribal memories: "remember his name was Spotted Tail / or Hump or Red Cloud or Geronimo / or none of these or all of these" ("the killing of the trees," 39–40). Her chanting in "the killing of the trees" is identical to her chant in "at the cemetery, walnut grove plantation, south carolina, 1989" (*Quilting* 11–12): "tell me your names." It is one of her goals to keep the names of the past in her memory or to imagine them when the names have vanished from historical records.

In "the killing of the trees" Clifton refers to Pahuska, a name that seems to designate two distinct historic figures. One is an Osage Indian chief known as White Hair by the French. His village was on the Little Osage River in what is now the state of Kansas.[23] The other, a reference that seems more appropriate to Clifton's poem, is the long association between yellow hair and the hair of George Armstrong Custer, who was defeated by the Sioux and the Cheyenne at the Battle of Little Bighorn on June 25, 1876.[24] In a famous account of that battle, the Sioux Indian Black Elk describes the joyful war dance following the defeat of Pahuska and his Seventh Cavalry: "Long Hair, where he lies nobody knows / Crying, they seek him. / He lies over there."[25] Later in his autobiography Black Elk claims that the white men or Wasichus have won after all, forcing the Indians to accept an inferior way of life and to exchange their circular teepees for the white man's prison. The autobiography ends: "And I, to whom such a vision was given in my youth,—you see me now a pitiful old man who has done nothing, for the nation's hoop is broken and scattered. There is no center any longer, and the sacred tree is dead."[26]

Clifton seems to be using the Custer analogy in "the killing of the trees." Custer, the slayer of the Sioux, is reincarnated in "the killing of the trees" as a "pale man seated / high in the bulldozer nest." This construction worker destroys the forest just as the settlers of the nineteenth century destroyed the lives and habitat of the Sioux, the Cheyenne, and the Crow. Clifton told Naomi Thiers that she wrote "the killing of the trees" soon after she moved from California to St. Mary's City and observed workers cutting down trees to make way for tract homes.[27] As Black Elk ends his autobiography with the vision of a broken circle and a dead tree, so Clifton ends this clearly autobiographical poem witnessing the construction of new houses in southern Maryland. She watches the "pale man" bulldozing against the "old oak." Using Black Elk's metaphor of the circle, she extends her vision to include circling ponies and weeping children and trees that "huddle in a camp weeping / outside my window and I can see it all / with that one good eye." Her use of the word "camp" has possible Indian connotations.[28] The circle is broken and the tree is dead.

The sequence *A Dream of Foxes*, published in *The Terrible Stories* in 1996, is also related to Native American beliefs. Clifton has told many interviewers about her magical encounter with a fox who visited an apartment where she had been living. Even after she moved, the fox would return and sit by her door. The six fox poems (*The Terrible Stories* 13–18) range from guilt over the fox's being potentially endangered to an identification with the fox's sexual loneliness: "so many fuckless days and nights, / only the solitary fox / watching my window light / barks her compassion" (16). The compassionate, intelligent fox is similar to the totem or helping animal of Native American culture, an ambassador that aligns itself with a human protector and won't let go. It is a magical animal that, like the coyote, can alter shapes, not only its own but also the shapes of others. Blackfeet poet James Welch sees the fox as a trickster animal capable of changing fish into stars.[29]

Experts on the Indian lore of foxes claim that "fox medicine involves adaptability, cunning, observation, integration, and swiftness of thought and action"; fox medicine "teaches the art of Oneness."[30] All of these qualities except for swiftness of action belong to Clifton. Although over the years her ability to move has been curtailed by medical problems, what remain without question are her swiftness of thought, her powers of observation, and her adaptability. Like the fox, Clifton "teaches the art of Oneness," which the Lakota Sioux call *Mitakuye Oyasin*, "all are related." The concept "includes every human being on this earth, every animal down to the tiniest insect, and every living plant."[31]

Her sequence on the death of Crazy Horse is closely allied to the fox series and to "the killing of the trees" in its sensitivity to the natural order and its insistence on the function of memory. The Crazy Horse series (*Next* 1987) consists of four poems: "the death of crazy horse," "crazy horse names his daughter," "crazy horse instructs the young men but in their grief they forget," and "the message of crazy horse." Each of the poems is told from the point of view of Crazy Horse, known to the Lakota Sioux by his Indian name, Tashunka Witco. His name, according to Clifton, is translated incorrectly. The correct translation should be "Young Man Whose Horses Dance under Him as If They Were Enchanted"[32]

Tashunka Witco was the warrior who led the Sioux and the Cheyenne tribes to victory against the Seventh Cavalry at the Battle of Little Bighorn in June of 1876; three months later, he surrendered to the cavalry and was assassinated.[33] In her interview with Susan Somers-Willett Clifton laments that history is always recorded "by the winners of the wars. Even losers will try—for instance, the history of Little Bighorn was told by the losers of the war and makes it sound as though they were winners."[34] In her tribute to Crazy Horse, he, and not Custer, is "the final war chief / never defeated in battle."

The four poems explore a number of concepts: life, death, immortality, ceremony, origins, obligation, and remembering. These concepts, so prominent in the rest of her books, include too many ideas for so short a sequence, unless, of course, Clifton is making a statement through her use of an encapsulated form. Like so much early and contemporary Indian poetry, the ideas are presented in a circular manner, without a specific chronology. The naming of his daughter "They Are Afraid of Her" in the second poem, for example, occurs after the warrior's death, not at her birth, when Crazy Horse was alive. Neither the titles nor the personal pronouns nor the name crazy horse is capitalized. As we have seen, this form of punctuation is common to many of Clifton's other poems.

The use of the lower-case pronoun, though, seems to be inconsistent in her poems about Indians. In "the killing of the trees" (*Quilting* 39–40) she capitalizes each of the Indian leaders whom she names. However, in "the death of crazy horse" she capitalizes the names Wakan Tanka, Lakota, Wounded Knee, and the specifically named women but not the name of crazy horse. The unemphasized narrative "i" signifies that the great warrior is already a spirit "released from shadow," released from the rituals of naming, marriage, and battle. In this sequence the hero, gone from the wounded earth, addresses his listeners from the afterlife.

The first and longest poem of the sequence is preceded by an epigraph or introduction that simultaneously serves as a lament for the hero's death: "the death of crazy horse / 9/5/1877 / age 35." By including the age and date of the death of her subject as a part of her title, Clifton recapitulates the structure of her elegies to her mother and to her husband, both published in the same year as her Crazy Horse elegies: "the death of thelma sayles / 2/13/59 / age 44" and "the death of fred clifton / 11/10/84 / age 49." By emphasizing the brevity of the lives of her loved ones and by repeating the identically formatted titles, she is graphically bringing "Young Man Whose Horses Dance under Him as If They Were Enchanted" into her ancestral chambers.

In "the death of crazy horse" Clifton presents the basic symbols of Sioux cosmology: the sacred nature of the Black Hills, the division of the world into four directions, the hero on a quest, the unbroken hoop or circle, the belief in an afterlife called the Shadow Land, the idea that all are related, and the presence of the Great Spirit Wakan Tanka. Clifton capitalizes the name Wakan Tanka as she capitalizes Wounded Knee, where the Lakota Sioux way of life ended in 1890 when more than 300 Indian women and children were massacred by the Seventh Cavalry.[35]

In the first poem Crazy Horse foresees the massacre at Wounded Knee in South Dakota, an actual event that did not occur until thirteen years after he was taken prisoner and slaughtered by the U.S. government. Clifton also foresees the end of Crazy Horse as a man and father because he had no sons and because his daughter, named "They Are Afraid of Her," died of tuberculosis before she could bear a child. She also admires the fact that Crazy Horse kept his distance from the settlers, never allowing himself to be photographed.[36]

In keeping with her imitation of Native American techniques, Clifton chants and repeats the key stanza in celebration of her hero/warrior: "i am the final war chief, / never defeated in battle. / Lakotah, remember my name." Lakotah, the name of his people, is a word meaning "considered friends" or "alliance of friends."[37] Its effect in this poem is to place Clifton's hero within the alliance of the natural order and to perpetuate the concept of memory, as she had in "at the cemetery, walnut grove plantation, south carolina, 1989" (*Quilting* 11–12).

In the second poem the chanting and repetition, the rhythm and beat of the song, are more pervasive. Clifton begins the chant with the line, "sing the names of the women sing," much as Homer begins *The Iliad* with "Sing, goddess, the anger of Peleus' son Achilleus."[38] She also echoes Walt Whitman's "Song of Myself," Langston Hughes's "The Negro Sings of Rivers," and other poems whose subject is song, without being directly influenced by them.

Her twelve-line poem, "crazy horse names his daughter," falls within the ancient tradition of the Indian naming ceremony, as in the Native American chant, "I SING FOR THE ANIMALS," cited by A. Grove Day.[39] With a care for history Clifton "names" the four women who played a role in Crazy Horse's life: Black Buffalo Woman, White Buffalo Woman, Black Shawl, and, in the full last line, his daughter, "They Are Afraid of Her."

The third poem, "crazy horse instructs the young men but in their grief they forget," is addressed to his "cousins," who still mourn his death and gather to witness "grandmother earth," who "rolls her shoulders in despair" (*Next* 49). The first, third, and fourth poems, spoken from the Shadow Land, emphasize the concept of memory. More than a century has passed since Crazy Horse was murdered; the earth is still in agony. Using images of restoration, resurrection, "reboning," and rising, Crazy Horse calls for a restoration of spirit so that his "heart" may "rise / and rebone itself." Clifton uses the same image of rising in her several poems to her husband from the same volume: "rising and turning / through my skin," (*Next* 64) and "i rise up from the dead before you" (*Next* 67).

The themes of rising and resurrection are repeated in the final poem, "the message of crazy horse." Although suggesting the resurrection of Christ, these themes seem more akin to the Native American pattern of departure and return. The hero is one who by definition must separate from the community, initiate a meaningful action, and then return to the land.[40] The departed spirit of Crazy Horse loops back to the beginning: "i would sit in the center of the world, / the Black Hills hooped around me." Crazy Horse pledges his love for Black Buffalo Woman, asking her to listen, for the world's hoop is breaking and "fire burns in the four directions." The last line of the sequence is "i have seen it. i am crazy horse" (50). This prophetic tone reflects the similar vision of disintegration in the conclusion of Black Elk's autobiography. It also foreshadows the frequent use of the metaphor of fire, which was employed to horrific effect in Clifton's later two poems about the bombing of MOVE, an African-American community in Philadelphia set on fire by the authorities (*The Book of Light* 35–37).

Since her Buffalo childhood Clifton has been fascinated by Native Americans: "It is a handsome link, New York State and the Iroquois, the Mohawk, the five-nation confederacy."[41] Crazy Horse is one of the three dead men whom she has most loved, along with David of Jerusalem and Fred Clifton. She has searched her background for traces of Indian ancestry and suspects that her Indian heritage may have derived from Thelma's mother, Georgia Moore. Her maternal grandmother looked like a Cherokee, although she's been dead for so many years that her ancestry would be difficult to verify.[42]

Images connect in her head. She is intrigued by the fact that the great love of Crazy Horse's life, although they were not married, was Black Buffalo Woman—black like the poet. One needs to remember, though, that in Sioux legend there is also White Buffalo Woman, bringer of the peace pipe. Clifton incorporates both figures, White Buffalo Woman and Black Buffalo Woman. Like them, she is peaceful but strong. Not a traditional Christian, she works through the past, giving voice to mythological, historical, and religious people of other cultures. She blends myth and reality, making the myth real and reality the myth—a clever twist of phrasing that "works" for her.[43]

Like Crazy Horse, Clifton is a person who has tried to bridge gaps in culture. She shares the Native American vision of oneness, of connection, the feeling that "all are related." She told Susan Somers-Willett, "I am interested in the connections between things and how we are connected as humans—how everything is connected and how words are as close as we can come to try to define these connections."[44] It is her knowledge of her origins, best articulated in her 1976 memoir *Generations*, that enables her to connect to other nations. Clifton knows her roots lie in West Africa; only after these roots have been established can a cultural dialogue and a coalition of the willing occur.

THE MOVE CATASTROPHE

In her poetry Clifton remembers the Philadelphia authorities' unconscionable action against the black organization, MOVE. MOVE was a community in West Philadelphia founded in 1978 by John Africa and Donald Glassey. MOVE members espoused a "back to nature" philosophy and adopted the surname "Africa." They lived in a large twin house at 33rd and Pearl streets. Some neighbors, bothered by the lack of sanitary conditions in the community, appealed to the Philadelphia Department of Licenses and Inspections, headed by Philadelphia's white mayor, Frank Rizzo, to intervene. MOVE refused to admit health inspectors. A battle ensued, one officer was killed, and eight of the MOVE members were charged with murder.

MOVE then relocated to a row house owned by Louise James, where members reportedly trained for physical combat by jogging on the rooftops. W. Wilson Goode, a black politician, was at the time running for mayor. Even after Goode's victory as the first black mayor of Philadelphia, the group could not be controlled. Neighbors again complained about noises on the ceilings and the smell of human waste. Under Goode's leadership, the police fired ammunition on the MOVE site. On May 13, 1985, the police dropped a bomb on a supposedly unoccupied building. A fire spread rapidly, and the authorities decided to let it burn out of control. As a result, "62 houses burned to the ground; only Ramona and Birdie Africa escaped. Six adults and five children in the MOVE house died."[45]

As did the deaths of James Byrd and of Crazy Horse, the MOVE disaster of 1985 prompted the poet's compassionate response in a two-poem treatment, too short to be called a sequence. The first poem, "move," is preceded by a prose account of the catastrophe that has the detachment of a newspaper article (*The Book of Light* 35–36). However, at the end of the prose commentary the detachment ends and several other perspectives emerge. Again the reader is struck by Clifton's ability to assume the voice of the other.[46]

The poem "move" begins with the word "they": "they had begun to whisper / among themselves" about the wild people living next to them. Then, the words "move" and "away" become prominent; they are set apart by large spaces and become the only words in ten of the lines. One neighbor "turned his smoky finger / toward africa," the name that, as we know, each member of the commune had assumed but that could also be interpreted as a signal of betrayal of the motherland. In the third stanza a helicopter appears, and in the fourth a mother stands with her child in the smoke and ashes. They are evidently the two survivors. The point of view shifts in the fifth and final stanza from the third-person voice to address the complacent reader. The poet warns that if fire is preferable to difference, then "move / away" (*The Book of Light* 34–35).

The second poem, dedicated to MOVE survivor Ramona Africa, unites a prophecy of the Old Testament with its fulfillment in the modern age. Entitled "samson predicts from gaza / the philadelphia fire," it is again about the "they": "they will come for you / they will bring fire." If Ramona does not "bring the temple down," Clifton warns, "they will" (*The Book of Light* 37). Unlike the Biblical Samson, Clifton's super-strong hero, Ramona Africa, is a woman.

These two poems are from a section in *The Book of Light* entitled *Lightening Bolt*, which has other ominous uses of fire symbolism. One of them, "cigarettes," is a fantasy about her father's catastrophic burning down the family with a careless ash (46). The other, "fury," is perhaps her most important poem to her mother Thelma. It begins with the familiar theme of memory, "remember this," and describes her mother standing at the furnace, giving up her poems, which burn "jewels into jewels" (45).

MEMORY AND GENDER

Yet despite the somber tone of "the killing of the trees," the Crazy Horse sequence, and the two poems about the Philadelphia fire, some poems are purely celebratory. She and musician Gwyneth Walker wrote music and text for three clapping songs presented by two exuberant teenagers and accompanied by a women's chorus; the effect would probably resemble the unforgettable hand-clapping between Celie and Nettie in the 1985 film version of *The*

Color Purple.[47] One of her best-loved poems begins in celebration: "won't you celebrate with me" (*The Book of Light* 25).

In 2004 Clifton completed a new volume, *Mercy*. She figured that if she had said something good she should just quote herself. So the epigraph of *Mercy* is "The only mercy is memory," taken from one of her poems to Fred Clifton. In "wind on the st. mary's river" the poet writes about the silver-haired elders who try to cross the waters in search of redemption. But when the wind fails, "they sigh and still and descend." Clifton calls them by name—"Jeremiah Fanny Lou Geronimo." The names disappear and "we" see only the "white caps on the water" (*Mercy* 37).[48] The three capitalized names called forth in this poem identify Clifton with the three major themes explored in this chapter, race, gender, and religion, as they lodge in her memory.

As in many of Clifton's poems, some background is necessary if the reader is to understand the associations. Jeremiah was a biblical prophet in the sixth century BCE who predicted Jerusalem's destruction by the Babylonians. He was considered a traitor for believing that Egypt would conquer Judah and that the Temple would fall.[49] "Fanny Lou," not identified in the poem by her surname, Hamer, was born in Mississippi in 1917, the granddaughter of slaves. Fanny Lou Hamer was jailed and beaten when she and other protesters registered to vote. She later became an officer of the Student Nonviolent Coordinating Committee (SNCC) and co-founded the Mississippi Freedom Democratic Party, a group that demanded representation at the all-white Democratic presidential convention in 1954.[50] The third figure, Geronimo, is eulogized in "the killing of the trees" (*Quilting* 39–40) along with Spotted Tail, Hump, and Red Cloud. He was a Bedonkohe Apache and the leader of the last tribe to surrender to the U.S. authorities. Although his enemies considered Geronimo to be a savage, his own people valued his aggressiveness and courage. He died a prisoner of war in Alabama, prohibited forever from returning to his native Southwest.[51]

Even though the spaces between their names tend to indicate separation rather than connection, Clifton connects these three heroes in "wind on the st. mary's river" for several reasons. Given her attention to the sounds of words, it is possible that she has chosen their names for their cadence in the line. More important, in defying the power structure, the three culturally separate dissidents embody the spiritual values of three distinct cultures: Hebrew, African-American, and Native American. She once told Naomi Thiers, "I think to trivialize history, including the stories and practices of other cultures, is a great mistake."[52] Through her teaching and her poetry Clifton helps keep alive the various histories of the past and of the present, as the poem "jasper texas 1998" keeps alive the memory of James Byrd, Jr. and the sequence on Crazy Horse remembers his name among the Lakotah. The theme of memory is the connective tissue among these heroes and so many others who are nurtured by Clifton's imagination.

Memories of race and gender are important and intertwined elements in her poetry and in her children's books. Although a reader would not need to know Clifton's race or gender, such information is relevant. "A person can, I hope, enjoy the poetry without knowing that I am black or female. But it adds to their understanding if they do know it—that is, that I am black and female. To me, that I am what I am is *all* of it; *all* of what I am is relevant."[53] Her woman-focused perspective, although understated in her children's books, is nonetheless evident in *Good Times*, especially in the poem "miss rosie." Not until her 1974 collection, *An Ordinary Woman*, however, does she begin to focus on women's bodies. According to Ajuan M. Mance, the entire collection serves "as metaphor for the position of the black female subject within the larger society."[54]

Two of her most famous poems, "homage to my hips" and "homage to my hair," first appeared side by side in *Two-Headed Woman*, a collection that was published by the University of Massachusetts Press and that subsequently became part of *Good Woman*. *Good Woman* was a watershed moment; it contained all of her poetry published before 1980, as well as the 1976 memoir, *Generations*. "homage to my hips" and "homage to my hair" are love poems. The "nappy hair" and the "mighty hips" are positive enticements, loving come-ons directed to the black male. Written when she was in her early forties, they were obviously meant for Fred Clifton, who was alive and well when they were published. Many of her later poems were to reflect the loss of her husband and of her body, one long dead and the other aging and diseased.

The poem "homage to my hair" addresses the "black man" in a tone that is sexy and flirtatious. Her natural hair is "tasty on your tongue as good greens," she writes, in an image that evokes the down-home elements of natural hair and black cooking. The poem ends with an affirmation of hair, nature, and aging stated in the poet's inimitable black vernacular: "the grayer she do get, good God, / the blacker she do be" (*Good Woman* 167). The capitalization of God in this poem elevates it from the secular to the profound.

"homage to my hips" and "homage to my hair" bear Clifton's special stamp. They are funny, erotic, personal, and self-confident. They are held together by the personal "i" and by images of space: "these hips have never been enslaved, / they go where they want to go." Like many of her metaphors, the idea of enslavement refers both to woman's bondage and to racial bondage. The poem ends dynamically, with the hips. Like her twelve fingers, they are connected to magic: "i have known them / to put a spell on a man and / spin him like a top!" (*Good Woman* 168). When read aloud the poem reaches a crescendo from the downward movement of the *n* consonants ("man," "spin") to the lifting of the voice with the word *top*. The concept of spinning the man "like a top" is an erotic replication of the sex act, with a major reversal: the woman on the bottom is the one in control.

RELIGION

Nonetheless, it is Clifton's religious poetry that offers the greatest challenge to the reader, not only for its depth but also for its opacity. Her enduring engagement with the undercurrents of Judeo-Christian mythology begins modestly with *some jesus*, a group of sixteen poems in her 1972 collection, *Good News About the Earth*; its title may refer to the "Good News" Bible, a "popular edition during the 1970s."[55] Many readers familiar with the titles of her poetry but not with their inner substance think of her as a religious poet. Indeed, as a child she regularly attended church. She claims that the church was a great influence, "perhaps not as much in its subject matter as in energy."[56] However, when asked if she hears the voice of God she answers, "No, it's just an awareness of more than the physical. I think a lot of people have that and don't quite know what to call it. They talk about hunches, intuitions; well, I have intuitions a lot."[57]

Although she was raised a Southern Baptist, Clifton has told almost all of her interviewers that she is not religious. "I would like to live in a church," she jokes. "But I just don't want to worship in one."[58] She is in search of no single denomination, being comfortable at synagogues, in cathedrals, and at prayer meetings. According to Michael S. Glaser, "The spirituality that many readers see as central to much of her poetry may well be what enables her to write about such difficult subjects with patience, understanding, and even forgiveness. And, while she claims no particular religion, the life of the spirit infuses each of Lucille Clifton's books of poetry."[59]

Behind her Judeo-Christian tradition lie a women's tradition and an African-American tradition. Like Zora Neale Hurston in *Moses, Man of the Mountain*, she is able to use black dialect and colloquial English to transform Moses and other characters from the Old Testament into contemporary subjects, placing their struggles within a historical setting that is equivalent to the captivity of blacks under the institution of slavery.[60] According to Akasha Hull, "Clifton succeeds at transforming the Bible from a patriarchal to an Afrocentric, feminist, sexual, and broadly mystical text."[61]

The early sequence *some jesus* begins at the beginning, in *Genesis,* with Adam and Eve. There are six more poems about Old Testament figures—Cain, Moses, Solomon, Job, Daniel, and Jonah—followed by eight poems that elaborate on matters from the New Testament: John, Mary, Joseph, the disciples, Lazarus, Palm Sunday, Good Friday, and Easter Sunday. The content is perfectly balanced, with eight devoted to the Hebrew tradition and eight to the Christian. In her reading of "john," Holladay remarks on the poem's "stylized black vernacular" but also argues that the poem relies on certain meters from Hebrew poetry to achieve an "obliquely mournful tone."[62] The poems in the series have little capitalization and almost no punctuation. The series culminates in one of Clifton's loveliest poems, "spring song," with its metaphor of Jesus breaking the ground and opening his house.

The poem "mary" (*Good Woman* 99) is an example of how Clifton blends erotic images with religious ones. Mary experiences the visitation of the Holy Spirit as a "kiss / as soft as cotton." Given the gift of prophecy, she foresees the garden and the tree, the Garden of Gethsemane and the cross. In its literal context, however, the tree that she sees "between my legs" is a reference to public hair, and the lover in the poem is not only the Divine Presence but also her earthly lover Joseph, who ends the "joseph" poem calling out "jesus jesus jesus" in language that may imply a sexual release (*Good Woman* 100).[63]

Clifton's most dazzling religious poems appear in *Quilting* (1991) in a ten-poem series called *tree of life*. In her appreciation of *tree of life* Alicia Ostriker writes, "As in the 'some jesus' poems, the poet speaks through plural voices which seem to inhabit her. Hers is the voice of the mystified angels describing Lucifer's creation and fall in the first three poems, then woman's sensuous voice in 'eve's version' and man's sensually and intellectually desperate one in 'adam thinking.'"[64]

All but two of the poems in the sequence have "Lucifer" in the title or refer to him in the text. Lucifer is the former Prince of Light returning to reestablish his lost kingdom and seek vengeance against God. The poems are concerned with how Lucifer "illuminates" Eve and Adam. The opening inscription is from Isaiah 14:12: "How art thou fallen from Heaven, / O Lucifer, son of the morning?" The poet's initial concern is with the fallen "bringer of light" and not with Eve and Adam, whose fall is not recorded in the sequence. One must keep in mind that Lucille, whose name means light, has a natural inclination to associate herself with "lucifer six-finger" ("whispered to lucifer," *Quilting* 73).

In *tree of life* she attempts the impossible: rewriting two of the most solemn male religious tomes in Western civilization, *Genesis* and John Milton's 1667 epic, *Paradise Lost,* but in her own style. She develops the conflict between Lucifer and God in a set of typically short poems that begin with the birth of Lucifer as he broke from God's little finger, an image that not only suggests Michelangelo's famous fresco of the birth of Adam on the Sistine Chapel ceiling but also her extra fingers, severed at birth. The series ends with the poem "lucifer speaks in his own voice," as he dreams of Eve (*Quilting* 80). "Unlike Milton's Satan, whose evil emerges as a powerful, infectious force, the Lucifer of *Quilting* is primarily the herald of human sexuality."[65] Many of the words in the poems are sexual: "phallus," "thrust," "sweet delight," and "honey-tongue." In the final poem Lucifer imagines a "soft caress / along my long belly" (*Quilting* 80). Yet despite its erotic nature, the language of *tree of life* is extremely formal, with Lucifer addressing God as "thy servant" (75).[66] Unlike the earlier sequence *some jesus*, there is no attempt to reproduce or even to hint at an African-American vernacular.

Lucifer is also the center of *brothers*, published in the 1993 volume, *The Book of Light*. This eight-poem sequence is a "conversation between an aged Lucifer and God, though only Lucifer is heard" (epilogue to *brothers* 69). Although Lucifer speaks, there is no evidence in the poem that God is paying attention to him. Only the reader listens as he or she overhears Lucifer's argument with God. The form of *brothers* recalls the dramatic monologues of the nineteenth century, in which a poem "reveals a 'soul in action' through the speech of one character. The character is speaking to an identifiable but silent listener at a dramatic moment in the speaker's life."[67] In Robert Browning's "The Bishop Orders his Tomb at Saint Praxed's Church," for example, a dying bishop gathers his family round him and expresses his desire for a tomb of "peach-blossom marble" so elegant that Brother Gandolf, his earthly rival, will look from his inferior tomb with envy.[68]

In the Lucille/Lucifer dramatic monologue two old men meet at the crossroads to remember their former roles in the creation and destruction of the Garden of Eden. Not knowing God's purpose, Lucifer confronts his maker with a series of questions for which God offers no answers. In the sixth poem of the series Clifton uses as her title a line written by Carolyn Forché: "the silence of *God* is *God*."[69]

Forché's gaunt pronouncement, "the silence of *God* is *God*," cited in the sixth poem, is repeated with a variation in the last poem of the sequence: "_____ is *God*." By deleting the beginning of Forché's quotation, Clifton literally obliterates the beginning of God. In evoking His silence, Lucille/Lucifer indirectly challenges the Creator, calling him "the perfect / imperfection" and claiming that God is "beyond even Your own [God's own] understanding" (*The Book of Light* 70). By the end of this enigmatic short volume, Lucifer bows down and retracts his challenge, claiming that "to ask You to explain / is to deny You" (*The Book of Light* 76).

With the exception of the epigraph, Lucifer, in his guise as snake, serpent, and the speaking i, goes uncapitalized, whereas all pronouns and nouns related to God are in capital letters, a characteristic that we have noticed elsewhere in Clifton's religious poetry. In *brothers,* as in *tree of life*, there is a noticeable absence of black grammatical structures. Words like "lexicographer" (70) and "ineffable" (72) give the *brothers* sequence an intellectual remoteness that comes as a disappointment in a volume that contains both "fury," the poem about Thelma Sayles's burning her poems (*The Book of Light* 45), and the racially charged poem, "the earth is a living thing," with its ethnic images of a black bear, a black hawk, a black fish, and a girl with "kinky hair" (*The Book of Light* 34). When Hilary Holladay suggests that the title "brothers" might indicate the "possibility that God and Lucifer are true soul brothers," she seems to overlook both the formality of Lucifer's speech patterns and his echoing of the Protestant hymnal, as in the poem "how great Thou art" (*The Book of Light* 70).[70] The epithet "soul brothers," with its roots in black music, jazz, and black culture, pertains to younger, hipper, funkier men than the two worn-out apocalyptic antagonists of *The Book of Light*.

Of her biblical characters Clifton seems most at home with King David, whom she introduces in the curious dedication to the earlier volume, *The Book of Light*: "for Kathy / you sister david." Kathy would be Kathy Glaser of St.

Mary's City, a white woman who is Clifton's close friend despite their racial differences. The poet told Shirley M. Jordan that Kathy "doesn't understand the kinds of things that I have gone through in my life, but she does understand that I have gone through some things. And that can be enough. That can be as much as she can do. I appreciate that."[71] The dedication may be to Kathy, but the signature is Lucille's: "you sister david." In this three-word phrase, black vernacular sets the standard, and assumptions about gender are erased. David is a sister and a woman; David is Lucille.

Poems about David make their major appearance in the 1996 volume *The Terrible Stories*, a book that ends with an eleven-poem sequence entitled *From the Book of David*. David of Jerusalem (c. 1004–970 BCE) was chosen king of Judah after the death of Saul. He made Jerusalem his capital.[72] Clifton takes her poetic texts from Samuel I and II, selecting and transforming those materials that appeal to her sensibility. "My take on David and on Biblical people— because I write about that a lot—my take on them is that they were human. Not myth, not mythological creatures, but human beings."[73]

Her poem "the dancer" is a meditation on the meaning of David's life and on his place in history. In this first poem in the series, Clifton fantasizes about David as an old man looking back on his thirty-four-year reign. At the same time he dreams of holding young women between his legs; "lately I have begun to bed / with virgins," he confesses, reminding the reader of an aged Lucifer but also of Clifton's father Samuel, who fathered a child soon after his wife Thelma died.

In related poems Clifton describes David's male ancestors and his warrior past, as well as his coming to power through use of his brute male strength. The poem "enemies" deals with David's conflicting emotions of love for and hatred of his sleeping adopted father, King Saul. Another poem, "oh absalom my son my son," is one of her many elegies. Absalom was the "wild haired son" who had rebelled against his father and who had been tragically put to death against David's wishes (*The Terrible Stories* 67). According to the biblical source Absalom had been fleeing David's army when his hair was caught in a tree. Joab, a deputy of David, "took three javelins and plunged them into Absalom's heart while Absalom was still alive in the oak tree."[74] The detail about the wild hair must have appealed to Clifton, who was trying to break down racial stereotypes by transforming Absalom into a young black male, much as she had done with "john" in *some jesus*, with its brilliant opening lines, "somebody coming in blackness / like a star" (*Good Woman* 98).

David's violent maleness is softened by the hero's love for his wife Michal and for his beloved Bathsheba, expressed through lyric song. Like the goddess Kali, discussed in the next chapter, the prophet David reveals himself as a two-headed man, a person of contrasts, "bloody skull in one hand, harp in the other?" ("what matter of man," from *The Book of David*, *The Terrible Stories* 69). Through the vehicle of David's famed harp, Clifton molds the poem "bathsheba" into an erotic male performance in which "all of the blood in my body / gorged / into my loin" (*The Terrible Stories* 65).

David's pulsating stiffness in "bathsheba" provides a vivid counterpart to Clifton's sensational poem "lorena," published in the same volume and reprinted in *Blessing the Boats* (126). The amusing but sorrowful poem for Lorena Bobbitt, the 1994 housewife who made headlines for cutting off her husband's penis, is told from Lorena's perspective; it takes place in the seconds immediately following the castration. The limp "it" that she holds in her hand is both the measure of man and the master of man, demanding obedience "like the angels." As Lorena opens the window, she thinks that it "could fly" (*The Terrible Stories* 55).

As in "jasper texas 1998" the poet seizes the dramatic moment rather than its aftermath; Lorena was later acquitted by a jury in Virginia on the grounds of temporary insanity. Nor does she offer a feminist polemic, although Melissa Weinberger and others have argued that a biased press focused on the castrated male, rather than on the frequently raped and mutilated female: "John Bobbitt is a lucky guy; doctors were able to reattach his penis. No one is going to be able to sew Lorena Bobbitt back together."[75]

Under Clifton's deft fingers, David is multifarious and surely intact. He is both artist and warrior, both shepherd and king. When she was asked what three people from history she would invite to a dinner party, David of Israel was one of them. Her many religious characters—David, Kali, Wakan Tanka, Mary, and Leda—belong as much to myth as they do to an accurately recorded history. Subjected to Lucille's vision, they are molded into human beings.

THE BOOK OF LIGHT, BLESSING THE BOATS, AND MERCY

Blessing the Boats includes nineteen new poems as well as poetry reprinted from earlier editions. As in the 1980 collection *Good Woman*, *Blessing the Boats* gets much of its strength through its careful selection of Clifton's best-loved poems. Thus the poet suggests that poetry is hard to come by and that her cherished visitations from the mother/muse are to be remembered for their importance not only to literature but also to her life. *Blessing the Boats* won the National Book Award both for the new poems and the old ones, which are re-membered in its pages. Clifton seems to be acknowledging this paradox when she writes in *Mercy*, "The only mercy is memory."

Race, gender, and religion remain recurrent and painful themes. In his review of the book Daniel Donaghy comments that the poems "confront the aspects of life we'd like to avoid—chaos, pain, death—in an effort to overcome them."[76] Of the new poems about race, one is "jasper texas 1998" (*Blessing the Boats* 20). Another is "the photograph: a lynching" (*Blessing the Boats* 19). Written in three stanzas, the poem asks a series of five questions. The first two stanzas ask about the "they," who stare at the black man hanging from a tree while at the same they are smiling toward the camera. The third stanza shifts to the "we" point of view and is split into two questions. Will "all of us" be part of an accurate history? Will all of us be required to stare at the photograph? Here, through the medium of black-and-white photography, two races are joined together, whereas in the poem about Jasper we hear only a dead black man speaking from the dust.

Gender in *Blessing the Boats* is represented by numerous poems. Her most powerful poem about gender is "female," which had also appeared in an earlier volume, *Next*, published in 1988. The poem begins with the line "there is an amazon in us," a reference to her Dahomey heritage (*Blessing the Boats* 40).

Mercy consists of nearly sixty poems, all of them new. The first section, "last words," contains individual elegies—to her Mama, to Charlie Parker, and to each of her children—as well as poems about her own hospitalization and surgery. "last words" sets the tone for the remaining sections, which are generally somber meditations.

One of the poems from the second section, "stories," is entitled "Powell." Here Clifton breaks precedent in capitalizing Powell's last name. She informs the reader in a prose insert at the end of the poem that "powell was one of the officers who beat rodney king." The 1991 attack on black Rodney King by four white Los Angeles police officers has been better remembered than the murder of James Byrd because the Rodney King episode was videotaped and televised repeatedly. As one prosecuting attorney put it, "The common wisdom about videos and about video evidence is that it's the infallible witness—a witness whose memory doesn't fade, whose perceptions don't influence the way in which the event is recorded."[77] The police brutality was witnessed again and again by the public and later in the trials. After all four officers were acquitted in the first trial, riots in South Central Los Angeles broke out almost immediately. A new trial was ordered, and in April of 1993 Lawrence Powell and fellow officer Stacey Koon were found guilty and sentenced to thirty months in jail. A short time later, King received damages of almost $4 million in a separate trial against the officers present at the time of his beating.

Like the poems to James Byrd and Lorena Bobbitt, the poem "Powell" is told from the first-person point of view by a historical figure whose significance is amplified through Clifton's poetic discourse. It begins with an epitaph: "i am your worst nightmare / —black man to white." The internal "i" is uncapitalized, and the dream of terror is told from Powell's perspective. He hears voices, black voices, "nations of darkness / speaking a language i cannot understand." Fearing for his wife, his son, and his "golden daughter," Powell searches his dreams for a weapon as he finds himself surrounded (*Mercy* 34). "Powell" is a strong example of Clifton's phenomenal literary ventriloquism. She in effect becomes a camcorder, replacing the media accounts of the beatings with an "infallible witness," an internalized exploration of white paranoia.

Mercy ends with a section titled "the message from the Ones / (received in the late '70s)." Clifton recalls, "Those were poems that came to me in the '70s,—there isn't another way to say it—that came to me in the '70s, and I did not call them; they came and I wrote them down. It was like taking dictations."[78] The poems in the concluding section are untitled except for the first one, which bears the opening message, "your mother sends you this." It is written in the manner of some of the earlier messages revealed to the poet through the medium of Thelma; for example, in "the death of thelma sayles" (*Next* 51). Clifton evidently stored these messages from her mother in her memory for more than twenty-five years. At the end of the first poem the perspective shifts to the plural voice: "we are not she" (*Mercy* 53), "we will bring" (54), "we come" (55), and "we will call you / one eye" (56).

In the poem on page 64, "god" is evoked, and in the poems that appear on pages 65 through 69 Lucille is given a glimpse of the afterlife, where there is no hunger and no color, where one is neither one's brother's nor one's sister's keeper. Some of these poems echo the religious sentiments of earlier volumes, especially the silent dialogue of *brothers*, the major difference being that the poet is now the attentive listener, as the spirits, whom she calls the Ones, articulate their unchallenged messages.

Toward the end of "the message from the Ones / (received in the late 70s)" the reader notices a startling change. The poems cease to be sources of instruction or remembrance and become instead prophecies of doom. The spirits warn the poet that her "world is in grave danger" (*Mercy* 70). They send her the message that the polluted air and the poisoned water must be breathed again and drunk again when "you" return to earth (*Mercy* 72). "the message from the Ones / (received in the late 70s)" will remind some readers of Yeats's "The Second Coming," with its stark image of the collapse of the Christian millennial cycle and the beginning of a new one: "And what rough beast, its hour come round at last, / slouches towards Bethlehem to be born?"[79] Clifton's "end of a world" poem is softer and more discreet in its vision than that of Yeats—not a "rough beast" but a "something there" on a star that is "even now / preparing" (*Mercy* 75). At the bottom of the page, in large type, appears the text: "end of message."

An overview of Clifton's poetry indicates her preference for cyclical structures, such as the kind one finds in "the message from the Ones / (received in the late 70s)." Similar structures are apparent in her series of books on Everett Anderson as they deal with his father's absence or his mother's pregnancy. In her poetry, the cycles include elegies (to her husband Fred, to her mother Thelma, to her father Samuel, and others); birthday poems that mark the passing years; poems in a series (the fox poems, the poems to King David, the Crazy Horse sequence, Lucifer's poems to God, a series on Leda, and a series on Superman); and cycles within the poems themselves, as in her poem "cancer" (*Mercy* 26).

Clifton's birthday poems, although they celebrate the aging process, are at the same time reminders of death, hers and her mother's. The first of these, "the thirty-eighth year," tells of the death of Thelma Sayles. Its major thrust, however, is the poet's disappointment at being in the "middle" of her own life without having her mother to comfort her. In a poem that recalls the anguish of her mother's death at age forty-four, she confesses that at thirty-eight she "had not expected to be / an ordinary woman" (*Good Woman* 158). She expresses similar feelings in "poem on my fortieth birthday to my mother who died young." Now approaching her forties, she remembers when her mother tripped and fell into death at forty-four. Although in her thirty-eighth year Clifton had submitted to being "ordinary," two years later she announces stoically, "i have decided to keep running" (*Good Woman* 176).

In "birthday 1999," one of the new works in *Blessing the Boats* (29), Clifton uses the symbol of a train to represent the speed of time passing. The observer hears the train approach and can "almost touch the cracked / seat labeled lucille." She sees a woman standing on the platform. The woman sees the "bright train eye" approaching and expresses the desire to have someone undress her, someone to "stroke her one more time"; the "someone" is presumably, as in her earlier birthday poems, her mother. Structurally, the poem consists of nineteen lines, the first seventeen of them written in the third person. After the seventeenth line there is a space, followed by a two-line unit known as a couplet (or in this case a "coupler"). The poem separates or detaches, becoming first person: "it is a dream i am having / more and more and more."

Other sequences include three poems to Leda and four to Superman, seemingly strange companions among Clifton's cast of characters. A figure from Greek mythology, Leda was a Spartan queen, the wife of Tyndareus. She was raped by Zeus who, disguised as a swan, impregnated her with a set of twins, one of whom was Helen, the beautiful woman blamed for causing the Trojan War.[80] From Homer's *Odyssey* to William Butler Yeats's "Leda and the Swan," the seduction of Leda has been told from the male point of view. In the reversal of roles that we had noticed in "homage to my hips" and "lorena," the poet replays the seduction from the female perspective. She told Naomi Thiers that "visitations by a god are always like, here comes a swan, here's a bull. I mean, please, that's tiresome! So the poem is a personal note from Leda on visitations."[81]

The Leda sequence appears in a section of *The Book of Light* called "splendor." The series is presented as "leda 1," "leda 2," and "leda 3" (59–61). "leda 1" is one of the few poems in which Clifton uses the word "fuck." The last line of "leda 1" is "fucking god fucking me."[82] Leda is leftover goods, fucked by the lover-god and trashed by her family, who took away her children. She complains that her "father / follows me around the well, / his thick lips slavering," a line that possibly identifies the father of Leda with the poet's father, Samuel Sayles, condemned in the poem "moonchild" (*Blessing the Boats* 15). In "leda 2" the narrator shifts from the first to third person, drawing a parallel between Leda's "visitation" and the princes coming from the east to visit Jesus in the manger. Two bestial images—the inn "strewn with feathers" and the "fur between her thighs"—link Leda's seduction to the swan and the Greek myth to the Christian one. "leda 3" is subtitled "a personal note (re: visitations)." Like the language of Lucifer in "lucifer speaks in his own voice" (*Quilting* 80), "leda 3" is a verbal cascade of "stars spinning into phalluses" and serpents with "tongues / thick and erect." At the end of the Leda sequence the narrator sermonizes: "You want what a man wants, / next time come as a man / or don't come." The word "come" is an unmistakable reference both to reincarnation and to ejaculation.

The Superman series is also from *The Book of Light*, although it is scattered throughout the volume rather than presented, like the Leda poems, by numbered order of title. Superman, a product of D.C. Comics, became the hero of a 1940 collection of cartoons, a 1948 television series, and four films starring Christopher Reeve.[83] When she was a child Clifton must have been exposed to this man of steel, either in comic books or in serials shown in movie houses. He is an example of the American monomyth, a super/man from a distant place who enters the community and performs heroic deeds for the good of humankind.[84]

In the first of these poems, "if i should," dedicated to Superman's alias, Clark Kent, the poet revisits her shabby childhood, wondering, if she walked into its web, "who will come flying / after me, leaping tall buildings? you?" (*The Book of Light* 41). Her ironic question is followed by a "further note to clark" that promises her own form of heroism when, like Niagara, she batters the cliff and hangs to its edge (*The Book of Light* 42). In "final note to clark" she laments that her hero is only human after all: "we are who we are / two faithful readers / not wonder woman and not superman" (*The Book of Light* 47). Then, not wanting to stop, she ends the sequence with the most serious of the poems, "note, passed to superman." It begins with the line "sweet jesus, superman" and contains another casual profanity, "lord, man of steel." The "note" ends in recognition of Clifton's difference: "there is no planet stranger / than the one i'm from" (*The Book of Light* 48). She has identified the Superman, her faithful fellow-reader in this series, as a former president of St. Mary's College.[85]

As in her poem to Elvis Presley in the same volume, there is a poignant memory in what has passed away as "we ride the subways from the picture show, sure about / death and elvis, but watching for marvin gaye." She states flatly in the poem, "we have so many gone" (*The Book of Light* 22). This poem is another elegy to two great musicians born within a few years of Clifton—Elvis Presley and Marvin Gaye.[86] These elegies lie side by side with her poems to her mother Thelma, to her husband Fred, to her sister Josie, and to her father, all of whom were "gone" by the time she published *The Book of Light* in 1993. In contrast, the poems to Leda and to Clark Kent show the poet's lighter side. Her delight in popular mythology and comic books is similar to her pleasure in biblical heroes of the stature of David, King of Jerusalem.

Clifton's *Mercy* collection contains still another sequence, a seven-poem series entitled *September Song*. It begins on the morning of Tuesday, September 11, 2001, and ends at sundown on Sunday, September 17, 2001. This infamous week in the history of America has been recorded in reporters' logs, on video, and in documentaries. The poet's reaction to September 11 is discussed in the final chapter.

SIX

Fallen Body, Rising Star

I n "my dream about falling" Clifton refers to a "fruitful woman / such as myself" falling from a tree. She had thought she would always be a blossom; now she is an apple. Neither the apple nor the blossom nor the tree from which she falls is "forever" (*Next* 39). The poem "my dream about falling" was written in the three-year interval following Fred's death, at a time when Clifton was both commemorating her husband's memory and experiencing visitations from her mother. In 1987, when *Next* was published, she was fifty-one years old. The fallen fruit seems to represent the menopausal phase of female experience, what poet Anne Sexton had named the "November of the body."[1] Clifton did not achieve a "natural menopause." After Alexia's birth, she developed fibroid tumors. In 1987, while in California, she had a hysterectomy.[2] The metaphor of the fallen apple recalls the motifs of aging and physical deterioration that she addresses in some of her earliest poetry surrounding her mother's death.

Next was a time to mourn the past and to celebrate new generations; Clifton's daughters were grown, and she was anticipating a grandchild. As in "wishes for sons" where she had cursed her "sons" with menstrual periods, so in her poem to her unborn grandchild she wishes her "fantastic hands / twelve spiky fingers / symbols of our tribe" ("if our grandchild be a girl," *Next* 34). In her desire to connect the child to her Dahomey ancestors, she proclaims that the fingers will do "magic." The poem contains the term "abracadabra," a word chanted by stage magicians but having a special African meaning for the poet because it was a mystical word used by "a Gnostic sect in Alexandria [Egypt] called the Basilidians"; the word was "probably based on *Abrasax*, the name of their supreme deity."[3] Lucille, as the grandmother and the attendant god-mother, wants her granddaughter to wear the "extravagant gloves" of the Dahomey women and to participate in their rituals. The word "abracadabra" connects the godmother with magic, the good Lucille Clifton with her sinister counterpart.

In her earliest poetry Clifton had expressed the belief that being born with six fingers on each hand made her magical or "witchlike," a phenomenon that she addresses at several moments in her career, including the poems "I was born with twelve fingers" and "speaking of loss," which ends with the lines "my extra fingers are cut away. / I am left with plain hands and / nothing to give you but poems" (*Good Woman* 174). In *The Book of Light* she has a dream in which her "greater self" accuses her with "her extra finger" (29). The multiple fingers become once again a symbol of her "tribe" as she holds her hands against the light, re-membering them as "whole / alive twelvefingered" ("hands," *The Book of Light* 36). The theme of the lost fingers is expressed most intensely in *Mercy*, in which she describes how "the snips of finger / fell from the sterile bowl / into my mind." Often when alone or attending a religious ceremony she will raise these hands in a gesture meant to affirm her ancestry.[4]

Clifton perceives her extra fingers to be a sign of difference and of strength. More often, though, it is her race or gender, rather than her hands, which sets her aside, creating both difference and detachment. This distance enables her to see the murder of James Byrd, Jr. in all of its horror (*Blessing the Boats* 20) and to relate to the contemporary parable of Lorena Bobbitt, the castrating wife who, after being abused, cut off her husband's penis (*The Terrible Stories* 55). Both of these poems, like other forms of body alteration, such as wrist slitting, sub-incision [the splitting of the penis], and circumcision, involve the violence of cutting.[5] Although Clifton's fingers were removed immediately after her birth, she seems to re-member this "cutting" as part of her personal and tribal history.

It is important to recognize that Clifton contains within herself a desire to retaliate against abuses of person, race, and gender. In her case the anger may be intensified by her ambivalent memories of her abusive father, whom she continued to love. For years she kept her feelings about him a secret, not even telling her sister Elaine about their father's sexual advances until years after he had died.[6]

KALI, MENOPAUSE, AND MENSTRUATION

As admirable as she might be, Clifton admits that she is no saint. She confessed to her friend Michael Glaser that she has a "dark side" that she is obligated to reveal to her students; she expresses the "dark side" of her nature primarily through the figure of the Hindu goddess Kali.[7] Most of the Kali poems are in a section of *An Ordinary Woman* entitled "I agree with the leaves," a phrase that suggests the tea leaves used in fortune-telling. Kali is the ominous side of Clifton, whose familiarity with the attributes of the goddess shows her awareness of Southeast Asian culture. Kali has traditionally been associated with death, castration, and menstruation. She personifies the "fear of castration generated by menstruation—Kali, the maternal cannibal who decapitated her enemies and drank their blood."[8] In her aggressive nature Kali is sister to the Greek goddess Medusa and the Hebrew heroine Judith. The Gorgon Medusa would decapitate any man brave enough to look at her, whereas Judith, after being raped by Holofernes, cuts off his head.

In her fearsome aspect Kali resembles the old witch in the Grimm's tales, with her terrible face and her associations with child cannibalism and with menopause. Kali is black, which for Clifton is a form of racial sisterhood; but in Hindu mythology the color black has another meaning; black is the color of death and decay. The Kali poems are notable for their dreadful quality and for Clifton's identification with the Queen of Darkness, much as in her poems to Lucifer she had identified with the Prince of Light. She looks at Kali as "a dangerously powerful but not exactly evil spirit occupying her own body and soul."[9] In one Hindu depiction Kali is shown drinking her own blood from her castrated head, "enacting her own menstruation, in a psychic shifting from severed head to bleeding vagina."[10]

Clifton makes a tribute, an offering, to Kali by almost always capitalizing her name.

In a sequence of related poems Clifton explores the presence of this retributive goddess within herself, introducing her in an untitled poem and calling her the "queen of fatality." This black female goddess is the "bitch / of blood sacrifice and death" (*Good Woman* 128). Kali "determines the destiny / of things"; she is the "woman of warfare," the "dread mother" who exists "within ourselves." The poem ends with the line, "Kali, who is black." The poet relates to this ominous woman from Hindu mythology through her blackness and her motherhood.

In "the coming of Kali" Clifton portrays a goddess reminiscent of the biblical David. Presented as a double-sided figure, Kali is terrible on one side and soft on the other; she is "persistent with her / black terrible self" (*Good Woman* 135). In "she insists on me" Lucille offers her younger, more beautiful sister to Kali as a blood sacrifice. Although Lucille does not name her sister, it is obviously Elaine (Lane). The goddess refuses the poet's feeble offer: "she says, no i want / you fat poet with / dead teeth" (*Good Woman* 136).

Reminiscent of *the brothers*, the Kali sequence is a confrontation between sisters. It concludes with a defiant poem, "calming Kali," in which the speaker tells the "awful woman" to "be quiet" and promises Kali to give her "my blood to feed on." Importantly, this final poem, "calming Kali," ends in an act of identification: "i know I am your sister" (*Good Woman* 140). According to

Alicia Ostriker, "Admitting the goddess of death as a portion of herself—of ourselves—is Clifton's most radical move in *An Ordinary Woman*."[11]

The specter of castration is personified in Clifton's poetry by the severed head of James Byrd, Jr. and by the sharp cutting tool of Lorena Bobbitt. The poet's references to blood and to sacrifice are in keeping with Kali's mythological attributes: she offers her blood for the black goddess to "feed on," a reference to cannibalism and sacrifice, to being willfully consumed by the other. Kali is "a woman God and terrible / with her skulls and breasts" ("the coming of Kali," *Good Woman* 135). The woman in "lorena" exhibits no blood. Still, her connections with Kali are clear. The magazine *Vanity Fair*, one of the many media outlets intrigued by Lorena Bobbitt's revenge, did a special article in its November 1994 issue that showed photographs of Bobbitt "wet and dripping in a bathing suit."[12] In the popular imagination Bobbitt, like Kali, embodies the castrating woman. Bobbitt's attack on her husband aroused fears, especially among men who abused their wives, that it could happen to them.[13]

"Wet and dripping" has another connotation for women. Some of the flood stories in Hebrew, Babylonian, and Greek mythology have been related to men's fear of the powers of women's blood, of their menstruation. Menstrual blood is both a universal symbol of disaster and an ordinary monthly reminder of fertility. In "she understands me" Clifton connects the image of Kali to menstrual blood: "it is all blood and breaking / blood and breaking." "she understands me" is one of her most elusive poems. A "thing" drops out of a cage, its bars wet. Images of "emptying" and wetness become repeated cycles in the poem, which ends with the lines, "she is always emptying and it is all / the same wound the same blood the same breaking." The breaking and returning wound indicates a connection between Kali's repeated, bleeding wound and the breaking blood of menstruation ("she understands me," *An Ordinary Woman* 137). In a related poem Clifton imagines that for women the world "seems a landscape of / red blood and things / that need healing" ("she is dreaming," *An Ordinary Woman* 138). The Kali poems, interspersed between two sections entitled "sisters" and "i agree with the leaves," were published in 1974, nine years after the birth of her last child, Alexia. Lucille was thirty-eight years old. Images of blood seem to erupt in her poetry of this period.

Flowers, fluid, the witch, and the moon are frequent images in Clifton's poetry.[14] Very often these symbols connote menstruation. Occasionally the Hindu goddess, Kali, disguised as the witch, represents menstruation for the poet. The witch is a menstrual analogue that seems to have gained credibility in the writings of women analysts such as Mary Chadwick, who argued that traits of irrationality, perversion, and cannibalism were recognizable symptoms of the menstruating and the menopausal woman.[15] One can find the menopausal hag featured in independent feminist publications, such as *Broomstick*. "The Change" is a 1986 story from *Broomstick* about a woman whose "change," a term usually meant to describe menopause, occurs at the full moon. The central character, Hilde, discovers that her arms and hands are furry and that she has become a werewolf.[16] In "hag riding" Clifton assumes the familiar posture of the witch or old hag when in 1996 she writes, "but when I wake to the heat of morning / galloping down the highway of my life / something hopeful rises in me" (*The Terrible Stories* 26).

Clifton at times refers to menstruation in a light-hearted way. For example, "wishes for sons" is the wonderfully satirical poem about male menstruation referred to in the introduction. In this poem a witch blames men everywhere for their failure to understand women and their bodies. She curses them all with the discomforts and inconveniences that beset women during their menstrual periods; she wishes that they will have to consult the same unsympathetic doctors that are available to women. "wishes for sons" was first published in the 1991 volume *Quilting*, a collection of poems written between 1987 and 1990 that was nominated for a Pulitzer Prize. It is also one of the poems chosen to be reprinted in *Blessing the Boats* (71). However, some readers find the poem cruel, outlandish, and inappropriate in its disrespectful treatment of menstruation.

"wishes for sons" is an amusing reversal of sexual roles. Yet its position in *Quilting* and in its reprinted form in *Blessing the Boats* places its farcical idea of a man menstruating near three solemn poems about this exclusively female function. "poem in praise of menstruation" is written in five stanzas, each of which has the word *river* in its first line. Clifton's "river," so prominent in *A Term in Memphis* (*The Terrible Stories* 1996), has been compared to Langston Hughes's muddy Mississippi in "The Negro Speaks of Rivers."[17] It may also recall the song "Cry Me a River," which Julie London recorded in 1955 when Lucille was nineteen and enjoyed popular music.[18] Clifton's crying river is a beautiful river of blood, one that returns "each month / to the same delta" ("poem in praise of menstruation," *Quilting* 36). *Webster's New World College Dictionary* defines a delta as a "deposit of sand and soil, usually triangular in shape, which forms at the mouth of some rivers." The word "delta" thus visually suggests the vagina, the triangular part of the body that is the mouth of the womb.[19] Unused menstrual "deposits" drain from this womb each month in the form of menstrual blood, which also contains "mucus, fragments of uterine mucous membrane, and scaling cell tissues from the vagina."[20] The repeated, cyclical structure that we had noted in the previous chapter as perhaps the most consistent expression of Clifton's technique also resembles the menstrual process—the periodic building up and sloughing off. Menstrual images also go forth in the tidal flow of her prize-winning poem, "blessing the boats:" "may the tide / that is entering / even now the lip of our understanding." (*Quilting* 83). The lip is the entrance to the mouth [of the womb], just as the delta is the entrance to the vagina.

A second poem about menstruation, this one written as she psychologically prepares herself for artificial menopause induced by her hysterectomy, is less hopeful. "poem to my uterus" is an elegy that mourns her forever-to-be-lost fertility. It is addressed to "you uterus / you have been patient / as a sock." This wonderfully comfortable image of a uterine "sock" has its counterpart in another poem, in which she compares her womb to a "brown bag" tightened like a "good lunch." After the bag burst in their "honeymoon rooms," she writes, we "wiped the mess and / dressed you in our name" (*Good Woman* 124). From this womb or sock or bag the six Clifton children emerged. Now, she complains, they want to "cut you out." In a shift of person, Clifton writes that her uterus is "my bloody print / my estrogen kitchen" (*Quilting* 58). The image of the "estrogen kitchen" is an accurate one, implying the build-up of nourishment in the uterus during each menstrual period that enables pregnancy to occur but that is bled out if it does not.

A companion poem, "to my last period," is somewhat lighter in tone, beginning with a similar direct address to her uterus: "well girl, goodbye, / after thirty-eight years" (*Quilting* 59). The poem is written in two stanzas of seven lines each, possibly to recall the fixed shape of the sonnet, but the poem's form is far from graceful. She addresses herself as "well girl," although she did not felt exceptionally "well" when she was menstruating. She feels like a grandmother gazing at a photograph of her former self; the "hussy" is gone and she now finds herself "beautiful." One gets the sense from "to my last period" that menstruation has always been problematic for the speaker, that it would arrive, "splendid in her red dress," bringing some sort of trouble.[21] It would be a mistake, though, to make a case that these poems were written in chronological order; when Clifton composes she prefers to spread out her works in progress on a table and see which poems "call" her, rather than to place them in a biological or psychological sequence.[22]

Lucille Clifton joins other women poets writing about menstruation and menopause between the 1930s and the beginning of the twenty-first century. Her poetic model from high school, Edna St. Vincent Millay, wrote a poem called "Menses," one of the earliest poems written about menstruation. Millay's poem, written from a male point of view, reveals man's fear of the "poison" that is menstrual blood.[23] One might also compare the "poem to my uterus" to Anne Sexton's "Menstruation at Forty." As she approaches menopause, Sexton regrets that she has never borne a son. Instead of representing fertility, her menstrual days are death days, symbolized by bleeding flowers and fallen rose petals.[24] Anne Sexton, Sylvia Plath, and Erica Jong address this intimate topic from a female perspective; their poems tend to anticipate menstruation, to celebrate it, and to lament its passing.

Relying on research conducted for *The Curse: A Cultural History of Menstruation*, Hillary Holladay compares in detail the menstrual images of Lucille Clifton and Sylvia Plath, citing numerous poems by each poet, including Plath's "Moonrise" and Clifton's "poem in praise of menstruation." In "Moonrise," for example, Plath uses colors to signify the menstrual cycle. She contrasts white, the color of death, with red, the symbol of fertility; she hopes that her "white stomach may ripen yet."[25] In "poem in praise of menstruation" Clifton's moon symbolizes a "woman's kinship with the natural world."[26]

Menstrual images include the vagina, the swelling waters, and the increasing menstrual flow. "The poem's conclusion further exalts menstruation by placing it in a religious and mythological context."[27] Holladay concludes that, although both poets are "bracingly honest," Clifton, because of her interest in feminist and African spirituality, finds a mystery in menstruation that Plath does not. Clifton's poems about menstruation are in stark contrast to the "irony and anguish" found in Plath's poems about the subject.[28]

For girls, the timing of menarche or their first menstruation varies greatly, depending on diet, health, and other factors. However, twelve is the average age for American girls to experience their first period.[29] It is quite clear from "moonchild" and from statements made to a number of interviewers that Clifton had been sexually abused by her father when she was approaching menarche—by the age of twelve and possibly earlier. In "moonchild" Lucille alludes to her incestuous relationship with her father, who cradles her in the moonlight. The poem's subject matter is strongly pubescent, with Lucille and Elaine giggling together about boys, bras, and French kissing, until Lucille reveals the fact that her father has been teaching her about sex. The word "moon," one of the most common symbols for the menstrual cycle, appears five times in the poem, often enough to emphasize its regularity and significance to Lucille and Elaine, two girls who are "ten years old" and on the brink of menarche (*Blessing the Boats* 15). But in Clifton's "moonchild" the conduct of Samuel Sayles is irregular, not regular; it is not a monthly reminder of fertility, but an unpredictable signal of invasion.

Lucille Clifton's most insightful observation of the menstrual process is found in the poem "blood," included in *Mercy*. "blood" builds upon the contrast between women's blood and men's blood, although both types share the same color. A young woman presses a scarf "against her bleeding body." Men "will march to games and wars / pursuing the bright red scarf / of courage." For thirty years a woman will continue "emptying / and filling"—as in menstruation, as in the flow of tides. Men are less regulated by tidal forces. They go to war to become heroes: "some will die." In contrast, a woman is an "ordinary girl" in an "ordinary room" (*Mercy* 28).

"blood" incorporates a number of menstrual symbols in its four stanzas. There is the scarf that the girl presses to her body as a kind of sanitary protection. There is the ebb and flow of the tides, the "emptying and filling" that represents the periodic filling and emptying of the endometrium, the lining of the uterus. There is the girl's closeness to her sister, the moon, which is frequently a symbol of death and menstruation. For Sylvia Plath and for William Butler Yeats the moon, like menstruation, moves through a series of predictable cycles. In *A Vision* Yeats constructed a philosophy of history on the movement of the moon, writing: "Twenty-and-eight the phases of the moon, / The full and the moon's dark and all the crescents."[30]

Clifton insists that these lunar movements are "ordinary"; they come to an "ordinary girl" in an "ordinary room." By repeating the word "ordinary" the poet confirms the commonplace aspect of menstruation, its dependable regularity. The word "ordinary," used so insistently in "blood," recalls the title of her watershed collection, *An Ordinary Woman*, published in 1974. Unfortunately, when the bleeding is not ordinary but irregular the excessive flow can indicate that a woman is ill and possibly has an ovarian tumor or a liver disease.[31]

Men, in contrast, are not regular. They retreat to the external world, measuring their worth in games or battle. They too bleed, but in a different way. The poet's gender-specific contrasts between male and female bleeding have been explored elsewhere—by poets, by theorists, and by psychoanalysts. The authors of *The Curse* have actually discovered the curious fact that some men want to bleed like women do. Many preliterate societies practice the rite of sub-incision, in which the penis is split to resemble a vagina. These and other rituals have enabled men to participate in the rhythmic cycles exclusive to women.[32]

In a book entitled *Male Fantasies* Klaus Theweleit examines the relationship between war and male blood, using the language of menstruation in sections entitled "The Red Flood," "Erasing the Stain," "All That Flows," and "Street of Blood." "Theweleit cites a passage from a German drama that connects soldiers' blood and the menstrual flow; continuing the analogy, he observes that battle, like menstruation, is 'regular' and 'violent.'"[33] In her poem "blood" Clifton suggests this male violence, stating that men at every moon are "pursuing the bright red scarf of courage." Here she alludes to Stephen Crane's *The Red Badge of Courage*, the novel about a young man who experiences the blood and gore of battle during the American Civil War. Images of blood constantly recur in Crane's novel. In the last chapter alone there are references to a "crimson oath," a "bloody soldier," "the red sickness of battle," the "place of blood and wrath," and other aspects of male bleeding.[34] Clifton might also be referring to the fact that "at every moon" warriors have traditionally hidden so that their presence cannot be discovered.

In a series of four *shapeshifter* poems that convey her fear of her father, the poet links Samuel Sayles to the moon through images of shapeshifters or werewolves, creatures who are legendarily affected by changes in the moon. The full moon has the power to change men into beasts, usually into some grotesque version of the wolf, in which their bodies are covered with hair and fur.[35] In her first *shapeshifter* poem Clifton writes about beasts who "wear strange hands / they walk through the houses / at night / their daughters / do not know them" (*Next* 77). The hands are the hands of the violating father, who had touched his daughter in secret places. No one—not the moon, not the mother, not the light who is Lucille—can protect this "prettylittlegirl" from his dreadful hands ("shapeshifter 2," *Next* 78). The third poem of the sequence depicts a little girl lying quietly in bed, still and silent, hoping that the beast will not appear and that "the full moon may not / find him here" (*Next* 79). The brutal reminiscence of her father concludes as the same little girl hides her head in a pillow, unable to tell the world her secret. The moon, so often an image of menstruation, becomes in the *shapeshifter* series an appalling male eye, the light by which her father can illuminate his daughters' darkened room.

In a poem dedicated to Edgar Silex, a poet, storyteller, friend, and colleague, Clifton questions the nature of their respective fathers: "whose father is that / guarding the bedroom door ... not yours not mine" ("a story," *Mercy* 29). The poem, "a story," is a brief retelling of life with her father, who hid outside his daughters' room, whose wife went mad, and whose son killed himself, which in "Hon's" case was with drugs and alcohol. Who is this father? What manner of man is he? The process of trying to find the answer to these questions marks the beginning of what Clifton calls "this storytelling life." Storytelling eventually becomes the key to her survival. Part elegy, part autobiography, "a story" ends like a fairy tale, but with all of humanity embraced in her wish for survival: "we survive / to live not happily perhaps but / ever after" ("a story," *Mercy* 29).

ILLNESS AND DEATH

In an earlier series of nine painful poems published in 1987, Clifton tells a different story, this one about the illness and death of Joanne C., a twenty-one-year-old friend from Grenada who died of leukemia. Leukemia, a form of cancer caused by a high concentration of white cells in the bloodstream, has its own associations with blood. The treatment for any type of leukemia in its advanced stages is chemotherapy.[36] *The Death of Joanne C* is an important sequence interspersed among the other major elegies, including the ones to Crazy Horse, to Fred Clifton, and to Thelma Sayles. Hilary Holladay describes the Joanne sequence as "among Clifton's bleakest."[37]

Unlike most of her sequences, an exception being her poems about Superman, the Joanne poems are not set aside in an individual grouping. As Greg Kuzma has noted, the sequence gains much of its potency from its casual arrangement, so that each Joanne poem in the volume, like each day in a terminally ill person's life, might be the last.[38]

The poem "chemotherapy" begins with the lines, "my hair is in pain. / my mouth is a cave of cries." The speaker sees a room filled with "white coats shaped like God" (*Next* 58). The word "chemical" appears three times in the poem's short nine lines. In another poem, there is also a "message" such as one finds in the elegiac verses to Fred and Thelma published in the same volume. In "the message to jo" the poet, in her role of empathetic ventriloquist, uses images of war and blood to signify Joanne's surrender to cancer: "my blood is a white flag, / waving. / surrender" (*Next* 62). In several of the poems a figure in white hovers by the bed, representing Joanne's nurse but also her mother, who insists that she live. In this series, red is the color of life and white the color of death. In "leukemia as dream/ritual" Joanne feels sympathy for the others in her room who are dying (*Next* 61). The poem "incantation," with its repeated word "cancer," anticipates Clifton's repetition of the word "cancer" in the poem by that title (*Mercy* 26). The shortest poem of the Joanne sequence established the name of the book, *Next*, and points to the inevitability of death: "the one in the next bed is dying. / mother we are all next, or next" (*Next* 60).

Clifton has had her own experiences with ill health and medical intervention, having had surgery at the Johns Hopkins Hospital in Baltimore numerous times: she underwent two operations on her left breast, a lumpectomy in 1994, and a mastectomy in 2001; the implant of her daughter's kidney in 1997; the removal of a cancerous abdominal tumor in the fall of 2000; and an operation to remove an overactive parathyroid gland in late 2001 or early 2002. The poet has faced mortality—her husband's, her parents', two of her children's, her friend Joanne's, her own—with unparalleled courage and pragmatism. Taking it on the chin, she remarked, "I have said that it is only me who would have two different cancers at the same time!"[39]

Her first breast cancer, a small but malignant tumor, was discovered in 1994, and it was treated with a lumpectomy. After the excision, she was not terribly afraid because the cancer was detected early. But it recurred in 2000, at about the same time she was diagnosed with renal cancer. In 2001 she had a mastectomy, in which the entire breast was removed.

Her poems about breast cancer are loosely clustered in a section from *Next* subtitled "From the Cadaver." A cadaver is a dead body or corpse being prepared for dissection, a reference not only to the fallen state of Lucille's body but also perhaps a note to the critics who will someday scrutinize the text. The first poem in "From the Cadaver" is about the Amazons, legendary Greek women warriors from the mythical kingdom of Cappadocia who were skilled with the bow and arrow. When a baby girl was born, the mother removed the infant's right breast to facilitate her use of weaponry. "From this custom, their name was derived: in Greek, 'amazon' means "having no breasts.""[40] In "amazons" Clifton fuses the Greek myth with a historical reference to her ancestors, the Dahomey Amazons, a brave and fearless female regiment of the eighteenth and nineteenth centuries so named because of their resemblance to the semi-mythical Amazons of Greece.[41] Although studies show that the breasts of the Dahomey women warriors were intact, the poet nonetheless finds the image of body mutilation an effective way to describe her lumpectomy.[42] Clifton parallels the valor of these fighters to her own, their victories over their adversaries to her personal one. Her ancestors, "each / with one nipple lifted," beckon to her as the poet answers the phone to hear this message: "cancer early detection no / mastectomy / not yet" ("amazons," *The Terrible Stories* 21). Despite its awesome content, "amazons" is a hopeful poem that ends with a celebratory "circle dance" among her sisters; one of these sisters is "audre," a reference to poet Audre Lorde, who died of breast cancer in 1992, four years before the publication of *The Terrible Stories*.[43]

When Clifton brings Audre Lorde back to life at the end of the poem, she includes her sister-poet as part of her vision of the "rookery of women" who were the amazons; "rookery" is another one of Lucille's richly ambivalent words. A rook is defined in *Webster's New Collegiate Dictionary* as crow; a rookery is a breeding ground for gregarious birds or animals like penguins and seals. In its rarer meaning still, it is a tenement house. Each of these meanings conveys the sense of being part of a black sisterhood like the Dahomey Amazons.

The second breast poem in "From the Cadaver" is a frightening but amusing dream where one breast whispers softly to the other as it fears removal for cancer ("lumpectomy eve," *The Terrible Stories* 22). Hilary Holladay notes that this poem is a "love poem for the speaker herself as well as an elegy for the lonely, love-starved, synecdochical breast."[44]

"lumpectomy eve" is followed by "consulting the book of changes: / radiation." The *I Ching* or *Book of Changes* is a Chinese tome so complex that the great philosopher Confucius was said not to have approached it until he was seventy. Like the Buddhist concept of the mandala, the *I Ching* is a sacred source that Clifton has used in some of her poems. People consult the *I Ching* to find wisdom during moments of momentous change.[45] Her momentous change is in this case the diagnosis of the cancer itself, followed by radiation therapy that alters her cellular structure.

Like her poem to the amazons, "consulting the book of changes: / radiation" begins with the maternal image of Clifton holding her breast: "each morning you will cup / your breast in your hand" (*The Terrible Stories* 23). The poem is written in the second person, a detached form she does not use very often. She seems to be looking down from above at the "you" in the poem who is riding in a bus to the "house of lightening" for radiation therapy. As she ["you"] rides through the city, she asks questions pertaining to light or lightning: "where is the light in one leaf / falling?" The question itself is in the form of a Chinese proverb, whereas the participle "falling" echoes the apple, no longer a blossom, falling from the tree. As in so many of her poems, the "you" wishes that she were "a child with kin," someone with a mother or with a loving man, perhaps her husband or her father. At the end of the poem she asks herself: "will i begin to cry?" The answer shifts back to the impersonal "you": "if you do, you will cry forever."

"1994" is a birthday poem; the poet leaves her fifty-eighth year with a scarred and damaged breast. The images in the poem have to do with cold. It is so cold that icicles are "hanging off / the one mad nipple." Other images include "a thumb of ice," "a cold and mortal body," weeping icicles," and a "shivering life." The "birthday" signals the end of the year; in reality Lucille was born on the 27th of June, in a warm season. In this extraordinary poem, the poet combines the fear of cancer with the fear of racism (*The Terrible Stories* 24); having breasts is as dangerous as wearing "dark skin."

Although these poems from *The Terrible Stories* were not necessarily written in order, their appearance in a cluster suggests the idea that cancer creates a connection among humans, as explored in the poem "scar." After the breast cancer, Lucille Clifton continued to live with her severed breast, what in a bizarre image she calls her "empty pocket flap" ("scar," *The Terrible Stories* 25). In like manner we must learn to live with the truth of our conditions. The poem "scar" embraces the collective "we": "we will learn / to live together." The primary meaning of these short, clipped lines is apparent: Lucille Clifton, a survivor, will learn to live with only one breast. But the greater implications form the foundation of her humanism: blacks must learn to live with whites; Israelis must learn to live with Palestinians; men must learn to live with women; Lucifer must learn to live with the God of Light.

Clifton has learned to live with breast cancer and her mastectomy. She relives that experience by reprinting poems written earlier. In *Blessing the Boats*, poems about her last menstruation and her breast surgery, reprinted from *Quilting* and *The Terrible Stories*, serve as reminders of the poet's Job-like torture.

There are new poems as well that concern both her mastectomy and her dialysis for kidney failure. In *Mercy* is found "in the mirror," a poem about her one breast that "leans against her chest wall." The poem is based on the pun of "t and e and a and r," which represents both a "crying" and a being "torn away" ("in the mirror," *Mercy* 27). The pun on the word "tear" recalls the needing and kneading pun of her poem "to thelma who worried because i couldn't cook" (*Good Woman* 175).

She mourns the "gash ghost of her sister," which refers to her other breast and also possibly to one of the spirits with whom Clifton may have been communicating. The title "in the mirror" suggests that Clifton is staring at a reflection of her misshapen body, although the text of the poem does not specify this point of view. In the poem "dying" (*Mercy* 13), Clifton observes "a woman / lying in a hospital hall" and realizes that she is that woman. She sees a moon rising from the woman's breast "and I saw that the moon was me / and I saw that the punctured bag / of a woman body was me." The first-person pronoun is capitalized in the middle of the poem but not elsewhere. "dying" has the kind of distance and objectivity that one notices in "birthday 1999" (*Blessing the Boats* 29), where "lucille" had used the symbol of a train to represent the passing years. The observer could "almost touch the cracked / seat labeled lucille." The "cracked seat" would be a reference to her physical state after undergoing the breast surgery.

Her most significant poem about cancer is bluntly entitled "cancer." Like her three separate bouts with the disease, the poem is written in three stanzas. It is based on a series of structural repetitions: the first time, the second time, the third time. In each of these stanzas Clifton learns that she has a new cancer. In vivid language and with an abundance of metaphors she describes what it is like to be told you have cancer. In the first stanza the waiting room is "twisting crimson," and the other patients are "dolls / watching from their dollhouse chairs." Stanza two is the briefest. You "hear a swoosh." You fall down a well. You try not to drown. By the time the poet and her readers get to the third stanza, there is a sense of exhaustion stemming not only from the announcements concerning the disease but also from the repeated form. It is "the third time and you are so tired / so tired." She resolves the situation by walking out of the hospital and into a movie theater, where you stand "staring at the screen with your living eyes."

What makes "cancer" so effective is its repetitious nature. As you hear the word again and again, it becomes almost unbearable to hear it another time. Some of the poem's strength is also achieved through contrasting images of life and death: "the angel uniforms the blood / machines" are busily trying to save your life. Comfort comes only from the dead images on the movie screen perceived with "your living eyes" (*Mercy* 26). "cancer," like the related poem, "consulting the book of changes: / radiation," is written in the second person, a form the poet uses to establish an emotional remoteness (*The Terrible Stories* 23). The impersonal "you" is also Clifton's way of drawing other cancer victims into sharing her awe-filled experience.

Clifton's kidney failure occurred in 1996. When she mentioned problems with urination to her doctor, he told her she should see a nephrologist, a physician who specialized in kidney disorders. But before she had time to consult the specialist, Clifton went to the bathroom one day, and according to her daughter Alexia, "It was really scary. This was an immediate problem. She then made an emergency doctor's appointment. The doctor told her, 'Your kidneys just simply aren't working.'"[46] Because of her malfunctioning kidneys, she had to go on dialysis for ten months. Alexia said, "Just watching that process, how draining it is, how difficult it is ... made a kidney transplant a better option than dialysis."[47] Although most patients generally are dialyzed through the arm, Lucille had to do it through the neck. After five hours on dialysis, a patient is always very cold. The confinement and the lack of energy are terrible. Fortunately, St. Mary's College had a good support system so that Clifton could continue to teach; she had dialysis three days a week and taught on the other two.[48]

In a new poem from *Blessing the Boats* entitled "dialysis," Clifton begins by describing her kidney condition with complete directness and without metaphor: "after the cancer, the kidneys / refused to continue." Not content to depict her own suffering, she turns to the blind man who drips blood on the tile and to the ninety-year-old woman who "cries for her mother." As if in a dream, metaphors then come to the distraught poet. She sees a house on fire. Then "something crawls out of the fire / cleansed and purified. / in my dream i call it light." As the reader knows, the light is "Lucille," grateful to be alive even though she has lost so much.

The kidney failure was unexpected; Clifton was shocked at the news and was upset further to learn she would need a kidney transplant. While she was suffering through these health troubles, her friends sent her letters that reflected their personalities and relationships. Amiri Baraka sent a note saying if she did not get well he was going to call the police. Sharon Olds sent her all kinds of little drawings of kidneys.[49]

Members of the family knew that they were all going to be tested to determine who would make the best match as a kidney donor, and they all agreed that whoever was the best match would undergo the procedure necessary to prolong their mother's life. The best-matched donor has not only the same blood type but also a certain antigen or antibody match. Because there were six children from whom to choose, doctors were looking for a three-antigen match, at least half of a certain type of tissue. Gillian and Alexia were tested first. Gillian was a three-antigen match. Alexia, however, was a four-antigen match, which was closer than thought possible between a parent and child and closer even than between siblings.[50]

When Clifton entered the operating room in July 1997, her fear for her daughter Alexia was far greater than her fear for herself. The only time Alexia saw her mother nervous was when they were wheeling Alexia down first to take out her kidney. Lucille cried out, "No, no. Wait. Wait. You can't take my baby in." The surgery was performed by laparoscopy, which is less invasive than an open nephrectomy. Alexia was in the hospital for three days and her mother for five days.[51]

"donor," Clifton's tribute to Alexia, is one of her most powerful poems. Like the *persona* in "the lost baby poem" (*Good Woman* 60), the pregnant mother tries those methods to abort her child that were available to a woman facing an unwanted pregnancy in the 1970s: coat hangers, pills, "the everything i gathered against your inconvenient bulge." Yet the fetus persists, "refusing my refusal." The mother now hopes that the donor's kidney will stay intact, refusing to be rejected, just as the unborn child had stubbornly refused to be aborted. The poem works through a series of connections and ambiguities. Alexia, addressed in the poem by her nickname "lex," is "buckled in" and "fastened to life." The words "buckled" and "fastened" signify not only the hospital gurney but also the umbilical cord that had connected them at the infant's birth, the healthy kidney fastened over the failed one, and a mother's close attention to her child's seat belt. Clifton balances a thwarted abortion with the shrewd irony that the nearly "lost" child has become the donor and therefore an "angel," a giver of life.

Clifton is very proud of her new kidney, which the surgeons placed on top of the one that had failed to function, as is the accustomed procedure. But the other kidney atrophied and became cancerous; the renal tumor weighed twenty pounds. Her doctor said there was a fifty-fifty chance that the renal cancer would recur. So every time Lucille gets a headache she thinks, "Oh god, here we go again. Some of the deaths are so dreadful. Why not me?"[52]

Lucille had a doubling of separate cancers; the renal cancer occurred in 2000, at about the same time that the breast cancer recurred. However, the breast cancer recurrence was not from a metastasis, which is the spread of an original cancer to another organ in the body, but a new cancer. Another recent surgery has been performed on Clifton's parathyroid, a miniscule set of glands located near the thyroid that can produce an excess of calcium level and may cause kidney stones.[53] When *Blessing the Boats* was nominated in 2000 for the National Book Award, Clifton, one of five prominent American poets competing for the honor, was tremendously excited. She had previously been nominated for the Pulitzer Prize in 1991 and for the National Book Award in 1996, but this time she had the faith that she might win. Two of her daughters, Alexia and Gillian, attended the ceremony in New York with her. Clifton approached the podium, her twenty-pound tumor disguised by an ample gown. "I knew about the tumor," she told one reporter, "but I didn't know how big it was."[54] She was advised to have surgery immediately, but she insisted that the operation be postponed until after the ceremony. She told the doctor, "I'm sorry, I'm a finalist for the National Book Award. I'm going. We can have the surgery on hold, but I am going to the National Book Award."[55] She went. And she won.

Today Lucille Clifton is approaching seventy, although she doesn't feel old. It irked her somewhat when, at the 92nd Street Y *10th Muse* program, she was introduced as a "senior poet." She thought to herself, "I'm not a senior. I feel like a young poet. I feel like somebody who's got a lot to do."[56] She also has two new granddaughters on whom to lavish her affection.

In her poetry Clifton charts her fears about illness, conveying her awareness that cancer, like Kali or kidney failure, is a possibility within each of us. In an eloquent tribute to his colleague, Edgar Silex connects his story with Clifton's, his suffering with hers. Using the metaphor of a soaring eagle, Silex claims that it is life that has made them poets, pain that has made them whole.[57] As Lucille once told Michael Glaser, another good friend from St. Mary's College, "I don't write because I have a mission to heal the world. My mission is to heal Lucille if I can, as much as I can."[58]

SEVEN

Her Lasting Gift

One of Clifton's most popular poems is "won't you celebrate with me," which appeared on the program for "A Tribute to Lucille Clifton," distributed at Hunter College in November 2004. "won't you celebrate with me" is an invitation from a woman "born in babylon / both nonwhite and woman" (*The Book of Light* 25). Although every element has conspired against her, she has survived.

Her family and community, her students, her readers, and the members of her profession celebrate Clifton's survival. She is a daughter, a mother, and a grandmother, a poet, and a writer of children's books. According to Freeman Habrowski, Clifton "is an intellectual giant capable of being down to earth," with an "ability to speak the truth with courage and simplicity."[1] She is a friend, a "whole human," as she insisted in a poetry reading and conversation with Sonia Sanchez. "I am a whole human. I don't think of that as a theme, first of all, but if it is, I'm a whole human. It is human to be angry, it is human to be glad, it is human to be afraid—all of that. I wish to express in all of my humanness. I wish to see myself wholly and to be seen wholly—I wish to see others wholly and to have them see me wholly."[2]

In an earlier celebration of Clifton's poetry in Bethesda, Maryland, during National Poetry Month in April 1999, Maryland laureate Michael Glaser described her enormous appeal:

Readers value Clifton's poetry for many reasons. Some see her as an African-American poet documenting the struggles of her people. Others see her as a feminist who speaks out for women's rights. Some see in her a woman who has been abused and who has the courage to write about it. Some regard her as a survivor of cancer. Others find comfort and insight in her poems about being a mother or a widow. Many readers treasure her poetry for its crystal clarity of language, and most value her work for its spirituality and its struggle to salvage what grace we can.[3]

Of Clifton's many gifts, one surely is her spirituality. Her poem "the gift" is about a woman who, struck on the head, begins to sees things that other people do not. She can see "the sharp wing of things" and the splendid colors emanating from the bodies of her mother and her sisters; she is able to predict her mother's death. When the seeing woman is dead and in a coffin, her "sewn eyes" shine colors "of purple and crimson and gold." The poem is semi-autobiographical; it was this gift of seeing that enabled Clifton to make contact with her departed relatives, first through the Ouija board and later through automatic writing.

Clifton's family extends beyond her own bloodlines to the African-American community, where many of her contemporaries are highly regarded critically but relatively unsung writers. Explaining her personal debt to Clifton, Eugenia Collier said, "I always wanted to write. When Lucille and I were neighbors in Windsor Hills, my husband said, 'Lucille Clifton had six children. You have only two. Why can't you write?'"[4] Eugenia now has three children and seven grandchildren. She writes when she can. Understanding the problems of trying to succeed as a black woman writer, Clifton said with sadness, "Eugenia Collier never got what she deserves as a writer."[5]

Clifton has had an enormous influence on Eugenia Collier and on other poets and writers. She once advised young authors, "If something can start you, then something can stop you. Keep writing. Trust the poet in yourself. Trust the language. No poet ever gets exactly where they want to."[6] Additionally, she has maintained long-term friendships with Sharon Olds, Sonia Sanchez, Mary Oliver, Toni Morrison, Maxine Kumin, Gloria Oden, and many other women poets.[7]

Many of Lucille Clifton's distinguished poet-friends have been guest readers over the years at St. Mary's College. Two of them, Sonia Sanchez and Sharon Olds, are very different from one another. Sonia Sanchez is a revolutionary poet, a wiry black woman with roots in the Black Arts Movement of the sixties, whereas Sharon Olds is a tall, reserved white woman whose poetry can be even more disturbing than Lucille's; for example, the volume *The Gold Cell*, with its poems "Outside the Operating room of the Sex-Change Doctor" and "The Pope's Penis."[8]

It is hard to resist comparing Lucille Clifton to Maya Angelou, perhaps the most popular contemporary black poet. Each woman was sexually abused as a child. Each has transcended racial and economic barriers to become a major writer. Each has received honorary doctorates from American universities without having graduated from college. Each has taught creative writing and has held chairs at distinguished academic institutions. Each is an accomplished poet, autobiographer, and writer of books for children. However, Angelou, a far more prolific writer than Clifton, enjoys the stature of being a public figure and television personality; Clifton is more contemplative and private.

Lucille Clifton knows Maya Angelou, of course, and has been in her company on several occasions. Writers she knows more intimately are Mary Oliver and Gallway Kinnell, both of whom have participated in the St. Mary's College poetry series. Oliver, who was born in Cleveland, is a year younger than Lucille.[9] "Mary doesn't go anywhere but she came to us to read. She's a wonder. We've had Richard Wilbur and Amiri Baraka. That range of people. I like those guys."[10] Like her friends Sharon Olds and Sonia Sanchez, Amiri Baraka and Richard Wilbur are quite different, but she is friends with both. Baraka, an acknowledged black radical, was Clifton's friend from Howard University, LeRoi Jones; Wilbur is a poet friend she became close to through the lectures at St. Mary's College. She admires them both.

Another noted poet, Josephine Jacobsen, had been a long-time friend of Clifton's. Like Lucille, she had read at the Angel Tavern, a poetry bar in the Fells Point area of Baltimore, a neighborhood on the verge of being artsy. Both Jacobsen and Clifton had also been readers at the College English Association and other Baltimore area venues. Clifton thinks that if there were a dictionary word to describe "lady" it would be Josephine Jacobsen, who was a lady in the very good, positive, wonderful sense of that word. Jacobson, the author of many books of poetry, including *In the Crevice of Time*, died at the age of ninety-three of kidney failure. After Jacobsen's death, Lucille Clifton was one of three Maryland poets to celebrate her work in a televised memorial service, the other two being Michael Collier and Elizabeth Squires.[11]

Clifton also knows the poet Clarinda Harriss Lott, who with Dyane Fancey organized the poetry series for the Angel Tavern. Clarinda's poem, "Answering Crows," still screeches in one's ears during those gray hours of the morning.[12] Another frequenter of the Angel Tavern was poet and translator Anselm Hollo.[13] Clifton told me that, although she is fond of Hollo, he used to frighten her children, who were afraid of him because one evening in Baltimore, when a poet they admired was reading, Anselm hollered out, "Stop, stop, no more guitar." They were afraid he would yell at their mother.

Although she has traveled across the country to do poetry readings, at the time of this writing she has never visited Africa, the continent that has been so great a source of inspiration.[14] She was particularly inspired by Nelson Mandela, who helped organize the African National Congress in 1944, demanding full citizenship and free education for all people of South Africa. During the 1960s, in a period of political struggle that paralleled the American civil rights movement, he was accused of treason and sentenced to life imprisonment until he was released in 1990 after serving twenty-seven years of his sentence.[15]

One of Clifton's poems is dedicated to Nelson Mandela's wife Winnie, who, during the twenty-seven years of her husband's incarceration, had risen to political power. In the ominous poem, "winnie song" (*Next* 16), Clifton describes a "dark wind" blowing through South Africa, spreading a fire that has burned Winnie Mandela's house and that has been burning in Africa for a century. The repetition of the similar words, "Mendala, Mandala, Mandala," creates the sound of chanting. There are two "mendelas" and two "mandalas" in the poem's thirteen lines. The mandala in sacred geometry and art is symbolic of the Buddhist word "manda," which means essence. Its origin or center is a dot. The center reaches outward to an "outlying square," the symbol of the four-gated physical world. In Buddhist tradition the mandala contains the presence of the holy man, the Buddha. Often a ring of fire is found at its outermost circle.[16]

In "winnie song" Clifton uses images from Buddhist philosophy to focus her tribute to the Mandelas. The South African leader has been locked "in a cage" in the center of the universe, a representation of the sacred qualities of the Buddha. The chanted words "Mandela, Mandala" appear four times, which is a sacred number in Buddhist geometry. The fire surrounds Winnie's house at the outer ring of the mandala, creating the "homelands into home."[17]

Another poem to Nelson and Winnie Mandela, "February 11, 1990," celebrates Nelson's release from prison. By creating a title that is a date, Clifton includes Mandela among her other heroes like Fred Clifton and Crazy Horse, for whom she wrote poems with titles that are also dates. In a splendid, erotic image Clifton locks the long-separated couple, apart for twenty-seven years, in a sexual embrace: "walk out old chief, old husband, / enter again your own wife" (*Quilting* 10). Unhappily, their reunion was short-lived; the celebrated couple divorced in 1996 on the grounds of adultery.[18]

Clifton's poetry has reached an enormous audience beyond America and Africa. Her first book, *Good Times*, was translated into Norwegian and then into other languages. Among the Norwegians, the Germans, and other northern European people there is an interest in African-American and Native American literature; this interest is shared by Japanese readers and critics as well. The Japanese translations of Clifton's poetry are beautiful and colorful but difficult to decipher. Her name is usually the only thing the poet can understand.[19]

Clifton can surely find her name on the paperback cover of the National Book Award winner, *Blessing the Boats*. Designed by Geri McCormick, the multi-toned cover features a gold medallion announcing Lucille Clifton as the winner of the popular award. The moon-like medallion in the top right corner is poised above the painting, "Siren's Song," by the African-American artist Romare Bearden (1911–1988).[20] Bearden was known for his visual translations of Homer's *The Odyssey* into illustrations involving black subjects. On the cover of *Blessing the Boats* a black man is shown hanging from the mast of the ship, which in Homeric literature would depict Odysseus's request that he be tied to the mast so that he could hear the forbidden song of the sirens.

But there is an alternative interpretation to this classical story. If viewed as a commentary on slavery, the bound figure conveys the atrocities of the Middle Passage, when slaves were bound to the inner bellies of ships. The man bound to the wooden mast also suggests someone who has been lynched or crucified. Clifton had addressed the horrors of lynching and of the Middle Passage elsewhere in *Blessing the Boats*, in the fearsome poem "slaveships" (121) and in the poem to James Byrd, Jr., the decapitated man from Texas (20). But in the volume itself Clifton is somehow at peace as she blesses the boats and their innocent cargo.

The poem "blessing the boats" made its first appearance as the concluding poem of *Quilting* (1991). It is a tradition in a seafaring community that a priest or his representative blesses the departing boats, praying that God might protect the sailors as they begin their voyage. The poet serves as such a priest in "blessing the boats," blessing both the ships that leave the harbor and the memory of the slave ships that once entered it. Using the image of the entering and outgoing tides, she wishes that "you in your innocence / sail through this to that." Although Clifton can be painfully specific in poems like "slaveships," the quiet power of "blessing the boats" rests in its abstractions, in its "this" and its "that." The wide-ranging nature of the poem makes it possible for a myriad number of connections. The insurance company AIG, for example, admired "blessing the boats" enough to reproduce it in a charmingly illustrated series of poems entitled *Well-Versed*, which was attached to the June 13/20, 2005, issue of *The New Yorker*. The attachment included poems by Robert Frost, Edna St. Vincent Millay, David Filer, and several others.[21]

In the summer of 2005 Clifton was asked to contribute a poem to accompany an exhibition at the Maryland Institute College of Art (MICA) of an inspired collection of paintings celebrating Baltimore. Her untitled poem is in the left-hand margin next to the first painting, a cityscape by Bill Tamburrino. Because it is the only marginal note in the series, its slender fifteen lines are made to bear the weight of the city's cathedrals and cemeteries and monuments. The poem begins with a direct reference to the "line of this gallery"; the word "line" appears three more times in the poem. At the end of the poem Clifton returns to the initial "line": "beautiful awful city / we believe in that line." [22] Although in painting, a "line" refers to a connecting pattern that is part of a design other than shading, in poetry a line is the single unit in the organization of a stanza. Through her references to the "line," Clifton connects the visual arts and the art of poetry.

George Ciscle, guest curator of the MICA exhibit, hinges the first four paragraphs of his brief review of the exhibit on Clifton's fragile poem and on the way its "line" connects the paintings exhibited in the gallery. Despite his visual orientation, the curator attends to the voice of the poet to achieve an understanding of how the various paintings and the city of Baltimore are interrelated; the phrase "beautiful awful city" reflects a belief that the viewer "accept all of it—the beauty and the awfulness, the good and the bad are all part of the same line."[23]

In the final analysis, Lucille Clifton is an optimistic and forward-looking person who believes in lines, in continuity, in connections among people. She believes that even with her cancers, the worst has never happened. As she explained to Michael Glaser, "The *worst* has *never* happened to me. Because even in my imagination, even when it seems like something really, really bad has happened, I can imagine something worse than that. And it's not an either/or. What it means is that even in the face of this madness there still is, 'it *could have* been even beyond that,' but it wasn't."[24]

What she envisions as "the worst" could be a recurrence of her cancer, but it is more likely to be global annihilation and a world that ends in fire or in ice. Or is the "worst" a prophecy of her death, not now but at some time? Yet in her poetry she often scorns death and is quite open about her own mortality. She jokingly told Marilyn Kallet, "On my gravestone it's going to say, 'She almost did it'"[25] Those who know Clifton and her poetry would argue that she in fact is doing it and has done it. It is her courage in the wake of global madness that makes her gift to others so great.

Yet despite her bravery, she could never have imagined the deaths of two of her children.[26] The epigraph of *Mercy* is "the only mercy is memory," a line taken from the elegiac poem, "the message of fred clifton" (*Next* 66). By using this memory of Fred as epigraph, and by writing the title poem "mercy" in response to her father, Clifton creates a strange kind of family reunion. After Channing died on January 13, 2004, she asked her publisher to send back the manuscript so that she could include the elegies to her lost children.[27] *Mercy* begins by announcing the birth dates and death dates of Frederica and Channing. Her elegy to Frederica, "after one year," uses Native American images to intensify its effect. The poem is especially lovely in its mourning of her daughter's untimely entry into "Lake-Too-Soon." Rica's death parallels the storm that "would / alter the landscape of our lives" (*Mercy* 17). Her elegy to Channing is a three-line poem that suggests the abbreviated Japanese form, the haiku ("sonku," *Mercy* 18).[28]

As Clifton continues to write, her fame as a poet has grown. Eugenia Collier, addressing the issue of Clifton's legacy, said, "I haven't realized what it is yet. As she matures she will continue growing in wisdom. Her poems are meant to raise consciousness, to point out the basic strength and beauty of our culture." She continued, "The black community holds the key to whatever humanity there is in this country."[29]

There have been numerous tributes to Clifton in the past several years. Some of these have been regional, such as the celebration of National Poetry Month in Bethesda, Maryland, in April 1999; others have been national. The New York celebration in 2004, devoted exclusively to the achievements of Lucille Clifton, was sponsored by the Poetry Society of America, with other groups, including St. Mary's College of Maryland and Clifton's publisher, BOA

Editions, Ltd., offering further support. The distinguished participants included Sharon Olds, Galway Kinnell, Haki R. Madhubuti, Toni Morrison, Sonia Sanchez, Maxine Kumin, and eight other writers who read one or two selections from Clifton's work as well as one poem of their own.

Haki R. Madhubuti, the former Don Lee, is known for an early essay in praise of Clifton's poetry. "Her originality," he wrote, "is accomplished with everyday language and executed with musical percussion, pushed to the limits of poetic possibilities. Lucille Clifton is a lover of life, a poet who feels her people."[30] At the 2004 Hunter College tribute Madhubuti read a poem he had written in her honor. Toni Morrison, Clifton's former editor, read from the beginning of *Generations*. When willowy Sharon Olds read "homage to my hips" with a sassy swaying of her torso, the audience went wild. The final reader, Sonia Sanchez, read "donor" and one other poem. And then, in a lyrical soprano voice that resonated with rhythms simultaneously recalling the African chant, the slave song, and the spiritual, Sanchez announced her Sister Lucille.

The honored poet sat regally with two of her daughters in the front row and then rose and ascended the platform to thunderous applause and a standing ovation, elegant in a glittering evening gown. Clifton acknowledged her gratitude to her family and friends, to those who had assembled to pay tribute to her poetry and to her person. She announced that she was going to be a grandmother again; she mentioned her cancerous kidney, her thwarted abortion, and the ironic fact that her youngest child, whom she had tried to kill in the womb, was the one who saved her life.[31] When someone cautioned her about saying too much, she said, "I can say anything I want. These are my friends." Although her eyes turned to the people on stage, they seemed to encompass everyone in the theater who felt the gift of her warmth.

For her own reading she chose *September Song*, a seven-poem sequence from *Mercy* written in memory of the seven days from the morning of Tuesday, September 11, 2001, through Monday, September 17, at sundown. Like the fox cycle and the elegy to Crazy Horse, *September Song* is structured in a series of poems. Its subject matter, though, is excruciatingly immediate, a topic all too ominous to an audience sitting in upper Manhattan not that far from Ground Zero. She had presented an earlier version of the 9/11 cycle at a reading with Sonia Sanchez in New York City in 2002.[32]

The song, "September Song," written by Maxwell Anderson and Kurt Weill, was first recorded by Bing Crosby in 1946, when Lucille would have been ten.[33] In using it as the title of her sequence, Clifton suggests an anti-lyric, much as Marc Estrin did in a caustic 2004 review by that title that appeared in *Counterpunch*.[34] Both the poet and the reviewer use the title to pinpoint the events in the week after the bombings of the World Trade Center and the attack on the Pentagon. Teresa Ballard compares Clifton's empathy toward the incidents of 9/11 to the grief a mother would feel while attending a dying child. "She is going to patiently explain what we need to know."[35]

The first poem, "1 tuesday 9/11/01," begins with the words "thunder and lightning," the sort of natural storm Americans expect to hear about, but no one in the country seemed prepared for the city-storm of 9/11. Clifton's moral voice, heard throughout the series, is nowhere clearer than in this first look at the horror. God, who has always blessed America, is teaching us that "no one is exempt" from grief. As it began in thunder, so "tuesday 9/11/01" closes with the illusion of unity: "the world is one all fear / is one" (*Mercy* 43).

In the second poem Clifton records the reactions and retaliations following the bombings. "2 wednesday 9/12/01" is structured around a repeated refrain, "this is not the time": "this is not the time," the poet warns, to condemn the terrorist in his mosque, and "this is not the time" to fill the streets with the blood of Arab children. She wishes that all could be joined safely under a single flag and under the "single love / of the many tongued God" *Mercy* 44). The many-tongued God is a reference to the Pentecost, in which the Holy Spirit descended upon the apostles in fiery tongues to give them the gift of languages.[36] The image points to the enduring diversity of languages and cultures in the Middle East.

The third poem, "3 Thursday 9/13/01," is the shortest and the most violent. It depicts firemen climbing "like jacob's ladder / into the mouth of / history" (*Mercy* 45). In this context, Jacob's ladder refers to a ladder to heaven on which Jacob saw angels ascending and descending (*Genesis* 28.10–17). In the storm of 9/11 stairwells and elevator shafts replace the fireman's ladder. Although the Lord had promised not to forsake Jacob, many of the firemen perish in the wake of the bombings, consumed by fire and fallen buildings.

In "4 Friday 9/14/01" Clifton uses the collective pronoun "we" to draw a distinction between the two Americas: one of us is weeping for the first time, and "some of us" have never felt safe" and have "wept before." Here she refers to the social injustice experienced by blacks in this country and asks whether remembering the injustices of the past is a form of treason, alluding to the fact that many people from the political left who had criticized the government during the week of September 11 had been accused of betrayal and insubordination.

"5 saturday 9/15/01" is the fifth day, the day of the Sabbath when Jews celebrate their holy day of rest. In this puzzling poem she commemorates the death of a Jewish infidel who died for his faith. After his death the "world was filled with miracles," a possible reference to Jesus as rabbi. "5 saturday 9/15/01"concludes with the question that had haunted the earlier sequence, *Tree of Life*: "who can understand the gods" (*Mercy* 47).

In "6 sunday morning 9/16/01" the poet has reached a tentative inner peace. She looks at St. Mary's River while drinking her coffee. The river, so dominant a symbol in her poetry, "flows / as if nothing has happened" (*Mercy* 48). In this love poem for her granddaughter bailey (bailey fredrica clifton goin monnell), she ponders the infant's future in so violent a world. The poet is "consumed" with feelings of love and hate and sadness.

The week-long sequence, subtitled *Rosh Hashanah,* concludes at sundown on Monday, September 17. Traditionally Rosh Hashanah, the Jewish New Year, is a time for personal introspection and prayer, both on an individual and a national level. It is followed by Yom Kippur ten days later, when prayers are said at the Yizkor (remembrance) service for the victims of the Holocaust and for heroes who fought in the defense of Israel. "In the Prayers of 'Yizkor,' 'May He Remember,' we ask Hashem to 'remember' the souls of our loved ones who have passed away." Rosh Hashanah is also a time to create connections between the living and the dead.[37] It is the custom that Jews bury their dead as quickly as possible. Under these circumstances the corpses—whether Jew or Muslim or Irish Catholic—trapped under tons of rubble, cannot be found for burial. The irony is clear.

"7 monday sundown 9/17/01" is subtitled "Rosh Hashanah." It is written in eight lines of four couplets that are carefully designed to repeat both structure and content. The first two stanzas or couplets both begin with the biblical phrase, "i bear witness." This clause has been used to identify the victims of the Holocaust as well as the survivors of the American slave system. Clifton is applying both meanings in her repetition of the term.[38] The third stanza contains the repeated phrase "apples and honey," the traditional foods of Rosh Hashanah.[39] In the final couplet Clifton once again challenges the epic writer John Milton, who in *Paradise Lost* had charted the Fall of Man and the Expulsion from Paradise.[40] She had confronted Milton earlier, both in *brothers* (*The Book of Light*) and in *tree of life* (*Quilting*).

Her final response to that terrible week in America is a paradox: "what is not lost / is paradise" (*Mercy* 49). Although much has been taken away, much remains; we are graced with what is left. Strangely, Clifton leaves us with a Judeo-Christian resolution. Other than the single reference to Arab children in "2 wednesday 9/12/01," there is little sense of the cultural diversity for which she is known.

At the end of her reading Clifton received a second standing ovation, but she shared it with the other writers, those who had given so much during their lives to pass on the legacy of their gifts. The poets convened on the stage for greetings and picture-taking, glad to be with their honored colleague.

Many literary critics have celebrated Lucille Clifton's gift. Peggy Rosenthal, for example, is intrigued by Clifton's "minimalist mode." In her works "we see a poetry so pared down that its spaces take on substance, becoming a shaping presence as much as the words themselves."[41] Erica L. Still praises what is perhaps Clifton's greatest asset, her ability to tell the truth without any sort of embellishment: "Her truth is forthcoming, spare, economical, limited—it does not drape itself in too-large language, it does not protest too much, it does not presume to speak of that which it does not know."[42]

Edgar Silex, the young poet whose office was adjacent to hers, adds his eloquent tribute:

Whenever Lucille is around my soul flies, it soars above, on winds of possibility. This was a person who had been dirt poor like me. She knew suffering that comes partly from our shared American experience and partly because it was divined. I always felt that both of us had been born with the same kind of wings. Our wings had been cut, they had been wounded and every day someone somewhere was trying to clip them. And though they were always in tatters we had learned to preen and heal them with words. And somehow, some wind had caught them and we flew. And now, Lucille's poems form an eagle rounding in the sky above us.[43]

Clifton continues to spread her beautiful wings as she participates in one major ceremony after another. In October 2005 she did back-to-back performances in New York City. One was to pay tribute to America's poet laureates, even though she herself had never been granted this title; the other celebrated the achievements of poet W. S. Merwin. The Merwin tribute was held at the 92nd Street Y in New York, where Clifton had received the Discovery Award more than thirty-five years earlier. However, travel is more difficult for Clifton than it was in the past. "In the old days," she says, "I could hop from a plane to a train very easily."[44] She took such activity in stride.

Not content to be satisfied with her frequent readings and with serving as a voice for the Academy of American Poets, Clifton is currently working on a collection of poems tentatively titled *Colored Women*. Poems about women in history who have a special significance for her pan-African vision, they recall earlier ones to Winnie Mandela, to Harriet Tubman, and to Eve, the mother of us all. Among her subjects for the projected series are Mary Magdalene, Sally Hemings, Pocahontas, and Aunt Jemima, all of them reinterpreted in Clifton's keen search for historical truth.[45]

In Catholic theology Mary Magdelene was the woman who anointed Christ's feet, stood at the foot of the cross, and was "the first witness of his Resurrection."[46] Yet there is no hint, either in Catholic doctrine or in Dan Brown's heretical novel, *The Da Vinci Code*, that Magdalene was African.[47] In *some jesus*, her innovative treatment of heroes from the Old and New Testaments, Clifton had deliberately presented her biblical characters, including John the Evangelist and Lazurus, as people of African heritage through their use of "black English." One recalls her portrait of Daniel—"when a man walk manly / he don't stumble" (*Good Woman* 96)—and of John: "somebody coming in blackness/ like a star" (*Good Woman* 98). According to Akasha Hull, these and other religious figures are "demythologized, debunked, leveled through ordinary imagery and contextualizations."[48] Presumably Clifton will depict the much disputed friend of Jesus in the New Testament as an African. Many nontraditional scholars, in fact, have claimed Mary Magdalene to be the original Black Madonna.[49]

Sally Hemings, although she lived many centuries after Magdalene, is another historical figure shrouded in myth. Historical records are replete with references to President Thomas Jefferson, but were silent on his mistress, Sally

Hemings, until 1802, when a reporter for the Richmond *Recorder* claimed that the slave, owned by Thomas Jefferson, allegedly had an intimate relationship with Jefferson when he was in Paris with his daughter. Sally had at least six children whose birth dates were carefully recorded by Jefferson.[50]

As for Pocahontas, Clifton remembers a day when she was teaching at Santa Cruz and had attended an exhibition of Indian artifacts at the University of California at Los Angeles. Pueblo Laguna critic and historian Paula Gunn Allen, who spoke during the the exhibition opening, said that the bones of her ancestors were locked away behind the glass. Later Clifton heard a young man brag that he had seen the "real" Pocahontas; he was referring to a romanticized depiction of the Powhatan woman that he had seen in an art gallery.[51] Clifton intends to set the story straight as she rescues Pochahontas from the misconceptions of the past, as Paula Gunn Allen did in her 2003 biography, *Pocahontas: Medicine Woman, Spy, Entrepreneur, Diplomat*.[52] Clifton is, after all, like Pocahontas, a "Medicine Woman" whose poetry and spirituality have enabled her to bridge the gulf between the living and the dead.

The most unusual figure in Clifton's projected biographical series is Aunt Jemina, who was actually a real person. Nancy Green was born a slave in Kentucky in 1834. "A Black storyteller and one of the first (Black) corporate models in the United States,"[53] Nancy Green became the logo for the R. T. Davis Milling Company, which marketed Aunt Jemima Pancake Mix at the Chicago World's Fair in 1893. "Green was a hit, friendly, a good storyteller, and a good cook." As America's "Pancake Queen" she toured the country until she was killed in a car crash in 1923.[54] It would be tempting to stereotype Nancy Green, as it has been the custom to stereotype Pocahontas. But the truth—and Lucille believes, as did Fred, in telling the truth—is that both women were independent entrepreneurs and diplomats in their own right.

These character studies are still in the planning stage. During our telephone and email conversations of mid-October, 2005, I repeatedly asked Clifton for a recent poem. On October 27 I received the first draft of "new orleans." The poem was addressed to Mary Jane and signed in her own pen, "Lucille Clifton 2005."

new orleans

when the body floated by me
on the river it was a baby
body thin and brown
it was not my alexandra
5 months old
it was not even my city
or my river it was a dream
but i thought somewhere
there is a space in a grandmothers

sleep if she can sleep if she is still alive
and i wanted her to know that the
baby is found here in my heart and
i will never forget her i swear

Perhaps there is folly in an attempt to explicate a poem so anguished that
its dampness gathers in the bones. Like her elegy to James Byrd, Jr., "new
orleans" is written from within; it takes its content from the images of real
brown people whose floating bodies were caught by television cameras during
the days of August 29 through September 2 when Hurricane Katrina demolished the Gulf Coast. In "new orleans" the drowned child who "floated" on the
river is not "my alexandra" but someone else's grandchild, one of the countless unidentified black children who died during Katrina and its aftermath. As
is typical, Clifton treats the tragedy abstractly, as in a dream. But there is one
specific word that bears the weight of the surrounding space: "alexandra."
Alexandra is Bailey's sister, the infant daughter of Gillian Clifton-Monnell.
How close her name is to the name of Alexia, Clifton's youngest daughter and
the "angel" in "donor" who refused to be aborted.

The name of the child is literally deleted from the poem: "it was not my
alexandra." Nor is the poet identified as the infant's bereaved grandmother. Yet
the poet vows never to forget the infant—as she has never forgotten the West
Africans who rode in the bellies of slave ships or the firemen who climbed into
"the mouth of / history" (*Mercy* 45). Again we see Clifton's overwhelming
compassion, not just for her own generation but for babies and grandmothers
everywhere, victims who live forever in her heart and in her words.

Clifton celebrated her sixty-ninth birthday on June 27, 2005, still standing
firm by the beliefs that she has expressed throughout her career. One is that a
writer must speak the truth. Another is that poetry is a mixture of intellect and
intuition, with intuition being the stronger of the two.[55] A third is that many
people who write poetry have their priorities confused. "People wish to be
poets more than they wish to write poetry, and that's a mistake. One should
wish to celebrate more than one wishes to be celebrated."[56] Lucille Clifton,
though, is a poet who deserves to be celebrated. She is a wise woman, a
shaman whose words have won the respect of those who have read her work
or who have been fortunate enough to have met her.

Notes

INTRODUCTION

1. Kalamu ya Salaam, "Historical Background of the Black Arts Movement," *The Magic of Juju: An Appreciation of the Black Arts Movement*, http://www.black-collegian .com/african/bam1_200.shtml.

2. "Lucille Clifton," African American Publications, http://www.africanpubs.com/ Apps/bios/0366CliftonLucille.asp?pic; Chinua Achebe, *Things Fall Apart* (London: William Heinemann), 1958.

3. Hilary Holladay, "Song for Herself: Lucille Clifton's Poems about Womanhood," in *The Furious Flowering of African American Poetry*, ed. Joanne Gabbin (Charlottesville: University Press of Virginia, 1999), 282.

4. "*Brown v. Board of Education*: About the Case," http://brownvboard.org/summary.

5. Lucille Clifton, in discussion with the author, March 5, 2004.

6. The My Lai Massacre was a massacre by American soldiers of hundreds of Vietnamese civilians during the Vietnam War. The Trail of Tears (1838–1839) was the forced removal of 14,000 Indians, mainly Cherokees, from Georgia to Indian Territory, a journey on which approximately 4,000 Indians perished. The Salem Witch Hunts marked the persecution of people, mostly women, accused of consorting with the devil in the 1690s. Its history has been preserved most dramatically in Arthur Miller's 1952 play, *The Crucible*.

7. Susan B. A. Somers-Willett, "'A Music in Language': A Conversation with Lucille Clifton," *The American Voice* (Summer 1999): 92.

8. Lucille Clifton, cited by Jannette J. Witmyer, "Poetry in the Key of Life: Lucille Clifton," *Jubilee* (April 2001): 27.

9. Charles H. Rowell, "An Interview with Lucille Clifton," *Callaloo* 22 (Winter 1999): 57.

10. Somers-Willett, "A Music in Language," 76.

11. *Blessing the Boats* was one of the 835 titles submitted. These awards and honors are commonly listed in the articles and press releases about Clifton. Specific information on the National Book Awards is from American Booksellers Association, "Literary

Award Winners: National Book Awards," http://www.bookweb.org/news/awards/1289.html.

12. "Chesapeake Bay History," Chesapeake Bay Program, http://chesapeakebay.net/info/aframer.cfm.

13. Maggie O'Brien, cited in "Three-Time Pulitzer Prize Nominee, Lucille Clifton, Wins National Book Award," *Baltimore Times*, November 24–30, 2000. From the collection of Professor Margaret Reid.

14. Lucille Clifton, in discussion with the author, June 21, 2005.

15. Sonia Sanchez is the winner of an American Book Award and the author of many books of poetry, including *We a BaddDDDPeople*, *Wounded in the House of a Friend*, and *Shake Loose My Skin*. Joanne Gabbin, Professor of English at James Madison University, is known for her book on poet Sterling A. Brown and for her editing of a major anthology, *The Furious Flowering of African American Poetry*.

16. "Fire and Ice," originally published in 1920 in *Harpers Magazine*. See Edward Connery Lathem, ed., *The Poetry of Robert Frost* (Henry Holt and Company, 1979), 220.

17. Lucille Clifton, in discussion with the author, March 5, 2004.

18. Hilary Holladay, *Wild Blessings: The Poetry of Lucille Clifton* (Baton Rouge: Louisiana State University Press, 2004), 196.

19. Edgar Silex is the author of at least three volumes of poetry, including *Through All the Displacements* (Willimantic, CT: Curbstone Press, 1995) and *Acts of Love* (Willimantic, CT: Curbstone Press, 2004).

20. Galway Kinnell is the author of numerous volumes of poetry, including *What a Kingdom It Was* (Boston: Houghton Mifflin, 1960) and *Mortal Acts/Mortal Wounds* (Boston: Houghton Mifflin, 1980).

21. "Her Story: 1971–Present," 230–231. *Ms. Magazine,* http://www.msmagazine.com/about.asp.

22. Flo Kennedy, cited under "abortion" in Ambrose Bierce, *The Devil's Dictionary* (New York: Oxford University Press, 1999).

23. Jacob and Wilhelm Grimm, *"Sleeping Beauty,"* in *Grimm's Fairy Tales* (1812–15), illustrated by Trina Schart Hyman (Boston: Little, Brown, 1977).

24. Janice Delaney, Mary Jane Lupton, and Emily Toth, *The Curse: A Cultural History of Menstruation* (Urbana, IL: University of Illinois Press, 1993).

25. "Her Story: 1971–Present." 230–231.

26. Gwendolyn Brooks, "The Mother," in *Black Voices*, ed. Abraham Chapman, 461 (New York: Penguin Books, 1968).

27. Holladay, *Wild Blessings*, 70.

28. Anne Sexton, "The Abortion," in *No More Masks!: An Anthology of Twentieth Century Women Poets*, ed. Florence Howe, 192 (New York: HarperCollins, 1993). Like "The Sleeping Beauty," "Rumpelstilskin" is from the Grimm's collection.

29. The "abortionist" was the famous Dr. Robert Douglas Spencer, who performed the operation on women rich and poor during the 1950s, at a time when there were no safe clinics as there are today. Brett Harvey, *The Fifties* (New York: HarperCollins, 1993), 24.

30. Eugenia Collier, in discussion with the author, October 18, 2004. See Eugenia Collier, *Breeder and Other Stories* (Baltimore: Black Classic Press, 1994).

31. Clifton, cited by Naomi Thiers, "Lucille Clifton," *Belles Lettres* 9, no. 4 (Summer 1994): 88.

CHAPTER 1

1. "Epigraph," *Generations: a Memoir*, in *Good Woman: Poems and a Memoir 1969–1980* (New York: Random House, 1976).

2. "Depew, New York Detailed Profile," http://www.city-data.com/city/Depew-New-York.html.

3. Lucille Clifton, in discussion with the author, March 5, 2004.

4. Hillary Holladay, *Wild Blessings: The Poetry of Lucille Clifton* (Baton Rouge: Louisiana State University Press, 2004), 199.

5. Cheryl A. Wall, "Sifting Legacies in Lucille Clifton's *Generations*," *Contemporary Literature* 40, no. 4 (Winter 1999): 554.

6. Elaine Philip, in discussion with the author, July 6, 2005.

7. Ibid.

8. Eisa Davis, "Lucille Clifton and Sonia Sanchez: A Conversation," *Callaloo* 25, no. 4 (2002): 1058.

9. Clifton, cited by Michael S. Glaser, "I'd Like Not to Be a Stranger in the World: A Conversation/Interview with Lucille Clifton," *Antioch Review* 58, no. 3 (Summer, 2000): 318.

10. Reynolds Price, cited by Edward Whitley, "Lucille Clifton (1936–)," in *African American Autobiographers: A Sourcebook,* ed. Emanuel S. Nelson (Westport, CT: Greenwood, 2002), 71.

11. Holladay, *Wild Blessings,* 10.

12. Wall, "Sifting Legacies," 553, 567.

13. Linton Weeks, "Poetry's Persistent Listener," *Washington Post*, C1, November 18, 2000. From the collection of Professor Margaret Reid.

14. Lucille's accusation of her daddy as an "old lecher / old liar" should recall Sylvia Plath's poem "Daddy," with its venomous last line, "Daddy, daddy, you bastard, I'm through." See Sylvia Plath, "Daddy," in *The Norton Anthology of Literature by Women*, ed. Sandra Gilbert and Susan Gubar (W. W. Norton, 1985), 2208–2209.

15. Lucille Clifton, in discussion with the author, June 21, 2005.

16. Ibid.

17. Elaine Philip, in discussion with the author, July 6, 2005.

18. Maya Angelou, *I Know Why the Caged Bird Sings* (New York: Random House, 1969).

19. Clifton, cited by Glaser, "I'd Like Not to Be a Stranger," 320.

20. Susan B. A. Somers-Willett, "'A Music in Language': A Conversation with Lucille Clifton," *The American Voice* (Summer 1999): 74.

21. Elaine Philip, in discussion with the author, July 6, 2005.

22. "On Strength Gotten from Others," Lucille Clifton Biography and Bibliography, http://www.math.buffalo.edu/~sww/clifton/clifton-biobib.html. The term "sanctified" means "made or declared or believed to be holy; devoted to a deity or some religious ceremony or use;" as in "a consecrated church" (http://www.wordreference.com/definition/sanctified). Both Lucille's mother and her Grandmother Moore were sanctified.

23. Clifton, in Glaser, "I'd Like Not to Be a Stranger," 318.

24. Lucille Clifton, in discussion with the author, March 5, 2004.

25. Clifton, cited by Glaser, "I'd Like Not to Be a Stranger," 314.

26. Elaine Philip, in discussion with the author, July 6, 2005.

27. Ibid.

28. Fabian C. Worsham, "The Poetics of Matrilineage: Mothers and Daughters in the Poetry of African American Women, 1965–1985," in *Women of Color: Mother-Daughter Relationships in 20th Century Literature,* ed. Elizabeth Brown-Guillory (Austin: University of Texas Press, 1996), 177–231.

29. Holladay, *Wild Blessings,* 143–145.

30. Akasha Hull, "Channeling the Ancestral Muse: Lucille Clifton and Dolores Kendrick," in *Female Subjects in Black and White: Race, Psychoanalysis, Feminism,* ed. Elizabeth Abel, Barbara Christian, and Helen Moglen (Berkeley: University of California Press, 1997), 341.

31. Worsham, "The Poetics of Matrilineage," 331.

32. Elaine Philip, in discussion with the author, July 6, 2005.

33. Ibid.

34. Ibid.

35. Ibid.

36. Ibid. When Elaine was a young woman she won competition after competition for her singing. Being "bashful," she never pursued voice as a career. She now sings in her church choir.

37. Ibid.

38. Ibid.

39. Robert Frost, "Nothing Gold Can Stay," in *The Poetry of Robert Frost,* ed. Edward Connery Lathem (New York: Henry Holt, 1979).

40. Modern American Poetry, "About William Stafford," http://www.english.uiuc.edu/maps/poets/s_z/stafford/about.htm.

41. For a discussion of Lucille Clifton's use of automatic writing, see Hull, "Channeling the Ancestral Muse," 330–348. This aspect of Clifton's poetry is discussed in chapter 5.

42. Alicia Ostriker, "Kin and Kin: The Poetry of Lucille Clifton," *American Poetry Review* 22, no. 6 (November–December 1993): 5.

43. Lucille Clifton, in discussion with the author, June 21, 2005.

44. Holladay, *Wild Blessings,* 141.

45. Lucille Clifton, in discussion with the author, June 21, 2005.

46. Ibid.

47. *The Council Chronicle,* NCTE (September 2001).

48. Alonford James Robinson, Jr., "Howard University," *Encarta Africana* CD-ROM (Microsoft Corporation, 1999).

49. Lawrence Otis Graham, *Our Kind of People* (New York: HarperCollins, 1999), 68.

50. Ibid., 68.

51. Robinson, "Howard University."

52. See *The Oxford Companion to African American Literature,* ed. William L. Andrews, Frances Smith Foster, and Trudier Harris (New York: Oxford University Press, 1997), under "Brown, Sterling A.," 104–106; "Dodson, Owen," 222–223.

53. Eisa Davis, "Lucille Clifton and Sonia Sanchez: A Conversation," *Callaloo* 25, no. 4 (2002): 1064.

54. Frederic Kelly, "A Woman with Words," *Baltimore Sun Magazine,* 9, 11, January 27, 1974. From the collection of Professor Margaret Reid.

55. Horace G. Dawson, "The Legacy of Patricia Roberts Harris at Howard University," http://www.huarchivesnet.howard.edu/0005huarnet/harris.

56. Lucille Clifton, in discussion with the author, March 5, 2004.

57. Lucille Clifton, in discussion with the author, June 21, 2005.

58. Reed later wrote several experimental novels such as *Mumbo Jumbo* (New York: Scribner, 1996). See *The Reed Reader* (New York: Basic Books, 2000).

59. Obituary, "Fred Clifton, 49, Activist Wed Poet Laureate," *Baltimore Sun*, October 1984. From the collection of Professor Margaret Reid.

60. Elaine Philip, in discussion with the author, July 6, 2005.

61. Editor's insert from Lucille's out-of-print "Letter to Fred," written five years after his death, published in *Essence* (November 1989) as "A Letter to Fred." From the collection of Professor Margaret Reid.

62. Somers-Willett, "A Music in Language," 81.

63. Lucille Clifton, in discussion with the author, June 21, 2005.

64. Jannette J. Witmyer, "Poetry in the Key of Life: Lucille Clifton," *Jubilee* (April 2001: 26). From the collection of Professor Margaret Reid.

65. Hull, "Channeling the Ancestral Muse," 340. After Fred's death, Lucille began to receive messages from him.

66. Lucille Clifton, "A Letter to Fred."

67. Freeman Habrowski, in discussion with the author, November 17, 2004. Habrowski was an early leader in the civil rights movement. See "The Role of Youth in the Civil Rights Movement: Reflections on Birmingham," in *African Americans and Civil Rights: A Reappraisal* (Washington, DC: Associated Publishers, 1996).

68. Eugenia Collier, in discussion with the author, October 18, 2004.

69. Lucille Clifton, in discussion with the author, June 21, 2005.

70. Jonathan Kozol, *Free Schools* (Boston: Houghton Mifflin, 1972).

71. Alexia Clifton, in discussion with the author, July 26, 2004.

72. Davis, "Lucille Clifton and Sonia Sanchez," 1069.

73. "Fred Clifton, 49, Activist Wed Poet Laureate."

74. Martin Dyer, in discussion with the author, December 23, 2004.

75. Lucille Clifton, "A Letter to Fred."

76. Martin Dyer, in discussion with the author, December 23, 2004.

CHAPTER 2

1. Marilyn Kallet, "Doing What You Will Do: An Interview with Lucille Clifton," in *Sleeping with One Eye Open: Women Writers and the Art of Survival*, ed. Marilyn Kallet and Judith O. Cofer (Athens: University of Georgia Press, 1999), 84.

2. Florence Howe, ed., *No More Masks!: An Anthology of Twentieth Century Women Poets* (New York: HarperCollins, 1993), 469.

3. Susan B. A. Somers-Willett, "'A Music in Language': A Conversation with Lucille Clifton," in *The American Voice* (Louisville: Kentucky Foundation for Women, 1999), 79.

4. Lucille Clifton, in discussion with the author, March 5, 2004.

5. Chad Walsh, "Review of *Good Times*," *Book World* (March 8, 1970): 7.

6. Bryan McLucas argues that there is nothing "sub-standard" about AAVE [African American Vernacular English] and claims that the "biggest problem that AAVE speakers face is prejudice." Bryan McLucas, "African American Vernacular English," http://arches.uga.edu/~bryan/AAVE/main.html.

7. For an analysis of this technique as it relates to e. e. cummings and to the new black poetry, see Hilary Holladay, *Wild Blessings: The Poetry of Lucille Clifton* (Baton Rouge: Louisiana State University Press, 2004), 19–20.

8. Dick Gregory, *Nigger* (New York: E. P. Dutton, 1964).

9. William Blake, *Songs of Innocence*, 1789, in *The Poetry and Prose of William Blake*, ed. David V. Erdman and Harold Bloom (Garden City, NY: Doubleday Anchor, 1970).

10. In *Good Times* (1969) Clifton capitalizes the names of Jackie Robinson and Muhammad Ali. When *Good Times* was reprinted in the collection *Good Woman*, their names are in lower case; "Miss Rose" (1969) becomes "miss rosie," for example. Similar discrepancies exist in the 1972 volume *Good News about the Earth*. I am generally citing the more familiar 1987 text in both instances.

11. "Buffalo Soldiers," http://buffalosoldiers.net.

12. Gwendolyn Brooks, "We Real Cool," in *The Norton Anthology of African American Literature*, ed. Henry Louis Gates, Jr. and Nellie Y. McKay (New York: W. W. Norton & Company, Inc., 1997), 1591.

13. See *The Concise Columbia Encyclopedia*, ed. Judith S. Levey and Agnes Greenhall (New York: Columbia University Press, 1983), for brief summaries of both wars.

14. Elaine Philip, in discussion with the author, July 6, 2005.

15. Charles H. Rowell, "An Interview with Lucille Clifton," *Callaloo* 22, no. 1 (Winter 1999): 62.

16. Maya Angelou, *Even the Stars Look Lonesome* (New York: Random House, 1997).

17. Alicia Ostriker, "Kin and Kin: The Poetry of Lucille Clifton," *American Poetry Review* 22, no. 6 (November–December 1993): 4.

18. Holladay, *Wild Blessings*, 18–19.

19. Eugenia Collier, in discussion with the author, October 18, 2004.

20. Lucille Clifton, in discussion with the author, March 5, 2004.

21. Betty Friedan, *The Feminine Mystique* (New York: W. W. Norton, 2001), 353, 98.

22. Angela Davis, *Women, Race, and Class* (New York: Random House, 1981), 6, 7.

23. Shirley M. Jordan, "Lucille Clifton," in *Broken Silences* (New Brunswick, NJ: Rutgers University Press, 1993), 48.

24. Eileen Stetson, "Studying Slavery: Some Literary and Pedagogical Considerations on the Female Slave," in *All the Women Are White, All the Men Are Black, But Some of Us Are Brave*, ed. Gloria T. Hull, Patricia Bell Scott, and Barbara Smith (Old Westbury, NY: Feminist Press, 1982), 62–65.

25. Somers-Willett, "A Music in Language," 77.

26. Alexia Clifton, in discussion with the author, July 26, 2004.

27. According to Clifton, Ira Zeff was a professor at the University of Maryland on the Eastern Shore. After Martin Luther King's assassination in 1968, Zeff put together a commemorative volume that Clifton was unable to locate during our interview of March 5, 2004.

28. Born in 1933, Yevgeny Aleksandrovich Yevtushenko is a Russian poet best known for his poems "The Heirs of Stalin" and "The Brastz Station" (1964–1965). See *The Concise Columbia Encyclopedia*, ed. Judith S. Levey and Agnes Greenhall (New York: Columbia University Press, 1983).

29. Hugh Downs hosted the *Today* show from 1962 to 1771. Frank McGhee was host from 1971 to 1974 and Bryant Gumbel from 1982 to 1997 (http://www.Today+show &page'18result-url'redir%3Dwebsearch).

30. Clifton is probably referring to a panel discussion about Shelley Fisher Fishkin's controversial book, *Was Huck Black?: Mark Twain and African-American Voices* (New York: Oxford University Press, 1993). See Shelley Fisher Fishkin, "Mark Twain's America," http://www.pbs.org/ newshour/authors_corner/jan_june97.

31. Lucille Clifton, "The Magic Mama," *Redbook* (November 1969): 88–89; "Christmas Is Something Else," *House & Garden* (December 1969): 70–71; and "The End of Love Is Death, The End of Death Is Love," *Atlantic* (March 1971): 65–67.

32. See Hilary Holladay's discussion of two of these stories in *Wild Blessings*, 143–145.

33. *Baltimore Sun*, 11, January 27, 1974.

34. Maxine Kumin's remarks at "A Tribute to Lucille Clifton," November 18, 2004. Kumin received the Pulitzer Prize in 1972 for *Up Country: Poems of New England* (New York: W. W. Norton, 1972). See also Holladay, "Chronology," in *Wild Blessings*, xii.

35. The Baltimore Feminist Project, *Sexism and Racism in Popular Basal Readers 1964–1976*, Postscript by Mary Jane Lupton, Afterword by the Racism and Sexism Resource Center for Educators (New York: Racism and Sexism Resource Center for Educators, 1976), 5.

36. The genre of children's books written for black readers is not new. In 1919 noted intellectual W.E.B. Du Bois co-edited a publication, *The Brownies' Book*, aimed at making black children more familiar with their heritage. Other early efforts included Paul Laurence Dunbar's *Little Brown Baby*, a book of children's verse (1905), and his anthology of children's poetry, *The Upward Path* (1920).

37. Toni Morrison and her son Slade co-authored an interactive children's book entitled *My Book of Mean People Journal*, with pictures by Pascal LeMaitre (New York: Hyperion Books for Children, 2002). A more conventional book by Toni and Slade Morrison is *The Big Box* (New York: Hyperion Books for Children, 1999). Maya Angelou is the author of four children's books, the best known being *Life Doesn't Frighten Me*, which is superbly illustrated by Jean-Michel Basquiat. The short text is composed of a series of negative images that the central character rejects. See Maya Angelou, *Life Doesn't Frighten Me* (New York: Stewart, 1993).

38. Eisa Davis, "Lucille Clifton and Sonia Sanchez: A Conversation," *Callaloo* 25, no. 4 (2002): 1060–1061.

39. Rowell, "An Interview with Lucille Clifton," 66.

40. For a survey of children's books by African-American writers, see Lisa Clayton Robinson, "Children's Literature, African American," in *Encarta Africana* CD-ROM (Microsoft Corporation, 1999).

41. Audrey T. Mc Cluskey, "Tell the Good News: A View of the Works of Lucille Clifton," in *Black Women Writers (1950–1980): A Critical Evaluation*, ed. Mari Evans (Garden City, NY: Anchor-Doubleday, 1984), 140.

42. See H. W. Fuller, "Review of *Some of the Days of Everett Anderson*," *New York Times Book Review*, 16, September 6, 1970; and Marjorie Lewis, "Review of *Some of the Days of Everett Anderson*," *Library Journal* 95 (May 15, 1970): 1928.

43. Dianne Johnson, "The Chronicling of an African-American Life and Consciousness: Lucille Clifton's Everett Anderson Series," *Children's Literature Association Quarterly* 14, no. 4 (Winter 1989): 177.

44. Lucille Clifton, in discussion with the author, March 5, 2004.

45. Mc Cluskey, "Tell the Good News," 141.

46. Holladay, *Wild Blessings*, 179.

47. Freeman Habrowski, in discussion with the author, November 17, 2004. See Freeman Habrowski, Kenneth I. Maton, and Geoffrey L. Grief, *Beating the Odds: Raising Academically Successful Black Males* (New York: Oxford University Press, 1998).

48. Marlo Thomas and Friends, *Free to Be ... You and Me* (Philadelphia: Running Press, 1974) and *Three Wishes,* illustrated by Stephanie Douglas (New York: Viking Press, 1976).

49. Elaine Philip, in discussion with the author, July 6, 2005.

50. *Sonora Beautiful* "represents a thematic departure for Clifton in that it features a white girl as the main character." Jocylyn K. Moody, "Clifton, Lucille," in *The Oxford Companion to African American Literature*, ed. William L. Andrews, Frances Smith Foster, and Trudier Harris (New York: Oxford University Press, 1997), 157.

51. Lucille once told Shirley M. Jordan that her experiences as a black American have given her a special knowledge about white people and that no white author could know a black character as well as she could know a white one. Referring to the plantation tradition in which black mammies nursed white babies, Clifton said, "We have suckled these children. Not a lot of white people have suckled black kids." Shirley M. Jordan, "Lucille Clifton," in *Broken Silences* (New Brunswick, NJ: Rutgers University Press, 1993), 43.

52. *The Lucky Stone,* illustrated by Dale Payson (New York: Delacorte Press, 1979), 62.

53. Pamela Woolford, "Interview with Lucille Clifton," *Jambalaya* (1993). From the collection of Professor Margaret Reid.

54. "The Singing Bones," in *Afro-American Folk Tales*, ed. Roger D. Abrams (New York: Random House, 1985), 105–107.

55. Susan Feldmann, ed., "The Storytelling Stone," in *The Storytelling Stone* (New York: Random House 1965), 258–263.

56. Lucille Clifton, in discussion with the author, June 21, 2005.

57. Gerda Lerner, ed., *Black Women in White America: A Documentary History* (New York: Random House, 1973).

58. Lucille Clifton, in discussion with the author, March 5, 2004.

CHAPTER 3

1. "Kwanzaa," the Official Kwanzaa Web Site, http://www.officialkwanzaawebsite.org.

2. Lucille Clifton, in discussion with the author, March 5, 2004.

3. "Jackson State May 1970," http://www.may41970.com/Jackson%20State/jackson_state_may_1970.htm.

4. "American Civil Rights Movement," Nationmaster.com, http://www.nationmaster.com/encyclopedia.

5. Ibid.

6. "The Black Panthers: H. Rap Brown/Stokely Carmichael," AFRO-Americ@: The Black History Museum, http://afro .com/history/Panthers/Brown/Brown.html.

7. *Webster's New World College Dictionary*, 3rd ed. (New York: Simon & Schuster Macmillan, 1997).

8. George Herbert, *The Complete English Poems*, ed. John Tobin (New York: Penguin, 1991).

9. Mary Jane Lupton, *Maya Angelou: A Critical Companion* (Westport, CT: Greenwood Press, 1998), 38.

10. Sherley Anne Williams, "Some Implications of Womanist Theory," in *Reading Black, Reading Feminist*, ed. Henry Louis Gates, Jr. (New York: Meridian, 1990), 74–75n.

11. The word "hyperpotent" is Sherley Anne Williams's. Cleaver died a Republican and a Christian in 1998. See his obituary, "He Was a Symbol: Eldridge Cleaver Dies at 62," *U. S. News Story Page*, http://www.cnn.com/US/9805/01/cleaver.late.obit.

12. "Bobby Seale," http://www.law.umkc.edu/faculty/projects/ftrials/Chicago7/Account.html.

13. "Angela Davis," About.com, Women's History: Profiles Index, http://womenshistory.about.com/od/aframerwriters/p/angela.

14. A year before *Good News about the Earth* appeared, Angela Davis was the general editor of *If They Come in the Morning*. The title refers to an open letter from James Baldwin to Angela Davis in which "Brother James" claims solidarity with the writers represented in the collection, among them Bobby Seale and Huey Newton: "For if they take you in the morning, they will be coming for us that night." The letter is dated November 19, 1970. James Baldwin, "An Open Letter to My Sister, Angela Y. Davis," in *If They Come in the Morning* (New York: Signet, 1971), 23.

15. "Little Richard," http://www.history-of-rock.com/richard.htm.

16. Lucille Clifton, in discussion with the author, March 5, 2004. Activist Stokely Carmichael was born in Trinidad and graduated in 1964 from Howard University. His work on voter registration in Mississippi led to the formation of the Black Panther Party. In 1973 he and his wife, singer Miriam Makeba, moved to Uganda. He died under the name of Kwame Ture in 1998. "Kwame Ture," http://free.freespeech.org/mv/Kwame.htm.

17. Lucille Clifton, in discussion with the author, March 5, 2004.

18. Ibid.

19. Spike Lee's mother was a white art teacher who died in 1997. Amiri Baraka, when he was still known by the name of LeRoi Jones, had married a woman named Hetty Cohen. In *How I Became Hetty Jones* (New York: Grove Press, 1990), Cohen writes about meeting her husband and other black artists during the 1950s. Film director Spike Lee was born in 1957 and went to college at Morehouse in Atlanta. One of his films, *School Daze* (1988), is a satire about the caste system existing on black campuses, an issue to which Clifton alludes in *Generations*, 268–269.

20. Lucille Clifton, in discussion with the author, March 5, 2005. Baraka was at Howard between 1952 and 1954. During the early 1970s he was a key organizer in several militant groups, including the National Black Political Convention. In 1979 Baraka joined the African Studies Department at the State University of New York at Stony Brook, where he was tenured in 1982. See William J. Harris, "Introduction," *LeRoi Jones/Amiri Baraka Reader* (New York: Thunder's Mouth Press, 1991).

21. Alexia Clifton, in discussion with the author, July 26, 2004.

22. Lucille Clifton in discussion with the author, March 5, 2004. See also Obituary, "Fred Clifton," *Baltimore Sun*. From the collection of Professor Margaret Reid.

23. Lucille Clifton, in discussion with the author, March 5, 2004.

24. Mark Bernard White, "Sharing the Living Light: Rhetorical, Poetic, and Social Identity in Lucille Clifton," *CLA Journal* 40, no. 3 (March 1997): 303.

25. Japan Visitor, "Relations—Japan/Korea," http://www.japanvisitor.com/jc/relations.html.

26. Charles H. Rowell, "An Interview with Lucille Clifton," *Callaloo* 22, no. 1 (Winter 1999): 69.

27. "Memphis, Egypt," Absoluteastronomy.com, http://www.absoluteastronomy.com/encyclopedia/M.

28. "Myrlie Evers-Williams," Africanamericans.com, http://www.africanamericans.com/MyrlieEversWilliams.htm.

29. Numerous Web sites attribute "Old Man River" to *Showboat*, words by Jerome Kern and music by Oscar Hammerstein II.

30. "Gautama Buddha," *Wikipedia*, http://en.wikipedia.org/wiki/Gautama_Buddha.

31. Nowamgabe Austin Omoigui, "Who Are the Edos?" http://www.edo-nation.net/edos.htm.

32. Ivor Moorish, *Obeah, Christ and Rastaman.* (Cambridge: James Clark and Co., 1987).

33. Lucille Clifton, cited by Hilary Holladay in *Wild Blessings: The Poetry of Lucille Clifton* (Baton Rouge: Louisiana State University Press, 2004), 114.

34. John Keats, "Ode to a Nightingale," in *The Norton Anthology of Poetry*, 4th ed., ed. Margaret Ferguson, Mary Jo Salter, and Jon Stallworthy (New York: Norton, 1996), 845–847.

35. The Miwok "occupied a wide band in central California from present-day Marin and Sonoma Counties north of San Francisco Bay and the Sacramento River, extending beyond the Yosemite Valley into eastern Nevada, as far north as present-day Tehama County and as far South as the San Joaquin Valley." "Miwok," *Encyclopedia of North American Indians*, Houghton Mifflin College Division. http://college.hmco.com/history/readerscomp/naiind/html.

36. "Pomo," *Encyclopedia of North American Indians.*

37. *A Native American Encyclopedia*, ed. Barry M. Pritzker (New York: Oxford University Press, 2000), 143–145.

38. Ibid., 123.

39. Lucille Clifton, in discussion with the author, March 5, 2004.

40. "Strange Fruit," University of San Diego History Department WW2Timeline, http://history.acusd.edu/gen/WW2Timeline/start.html.

41. Trudier Harris, *Exorcizing Blackness* (Bloomington: Indiana University Press, 1984), 195.

42. "Karma," *Wikipedia*, http://en.wikipedia.org/wiki/Karma.

43. Ibid.

44. "Gautama Buddha," *Wikipedia*, http://en.wikipedia.org/wiki/Gautama_Buddha.

45. Constance M. Carroll, "Three's a Crowd: The Dilemma of Black Women in Higher Education," in *All the Women Are White, All the Men Are Black, But Some of Us Are Brave* (Old Westbury, NY: The Feminist Press, 1992), 115.

46. *The Council Chronicle*, NCTE (September 2001).

47. Eugenia Collier, in discussion with the author, October 18, 2004. Cave Canem is a noncommercial poetry foundation dedicated to discovering new talents among black poets. "Cave Canem," http://www.cavecanempoets.org.

48. Hilary Holladay, "Furious Flower Interview with Lucille Clifton," transcript provided by Joanne Gabbin, May 24, 2005.

49. Lucille Clifton, in discussion with the author, March 5, 2004.

50. "Mathias de Sousa," *Exploring Maryland's Roots: Library*, http://mdroots.thinkport.org/library/mathiasdesousa.asp.

51. Mary Kay Ricks, "Escape on the Pearl," *Washington Post* (August 12, 1998), http://www.washingtonpost.com/wpsrv/national.

52. Ibid.

53. "Many historians consider Paynter's anecdotes to be unverifiable, apparently based on stories passed among family members and friends over the years. Actually, extremely few documented facts are known about how the enslaved Americans involved in the Pearl escape acted or felt." Ibid.

54. Lucille Clifton, in discussion with the author, March 5, 2004. A Google search conducted on March 23, 2005, revealed no A. J. Smitherton, either in Texas, Tulsa, or Buffalo. There were several references to the Tulsa riots, which occurred during the two days following May 31, 1921. Three hundred people, most of them black, were killed, and more than 1,000 homes and businesses were demolished. See Tim Madigan, *The Burning: Massacre, Destruction, and the Tulsa Race Riot of 1921* (New York: St. Martin's Press, 2001).

55. Pauline Kael, cited by Jim Emerson in his review of *Mississippi Burning*, http://www.cinepad.com/reviews/mississippi.htm.

56. Ibid.

57. "Beneath the Underground: The Flight for Freedom," http://mdslavery.net/index.html.

58. Lucille Clifton, in discussion with the author, March 5, 2004.

59. Ibid.

60. "Anthony Johnson," http://www.pbs.org/wgbh/aia/part1/1p265.html.

CHAPTER 4

1. Unless otherwise indicated, citations in this chapter are from *Generations* (New York: Random House, 1976), republished in *Good Woman: Poems and a Memoir 1969–1980* (BOA Editions, 1987).

2. Alex Haley, *Roots* (New York: Dell, 1976).

3. Mary Jane Lupton, *Maya Angelou: A Critical Companion* (Westport, CT: Greenwood Press, 1998), 154.

4. "Oprah in Africa," *People* 63, no. 25 (June 27, 2005): 20.

5. "Dahomey, Early Kingdom of," *Encarta Africana* CD-ROM (Microsoft Corporation, 1999).

6. Susan Feldmann, "Introduction," *African Myths and Tales* (New York: 1972).

7. See Frederick Douglass, *Narrative of the Life of Frederick Douglass, an American Slave, Written by Himself,* 1845, in *The Classic Slave Narratives,* ed. Henry Louis Gates, Jr. (New York: Signet, 1987); and Maya Angelou, *I Know Why the Caged Bird Sings* (New York: Random House, 1970).

8. Lupton, *Maya Angelou,* 43.

9. Ibid., 43.

10. Ibid., 43.

11. Hilary Holladay, *Wild Blessings: The Poetry of Lucille Clifton* (Baton Rouge: Louisiana State University Press, 2004), 162.

12. Ibid., 167.

13. See in particular the last section of Joanne M. Braxton's *Black Women Writing Autobiography* (Philadelphia: Temple University Press, 1989), 203–208.

14. Deborah E. McDowell, "In the First Place: Making Frederick Douglass and the Afro-American Tradition," in *African American Autobiography*, ed. William L. Andrews

(Englewood Cliffs, NJ: Prentice Hall, 1993), 36–58; summarized by Lupton, *Maya Angelou*, 46.

15. Henry Louis Gates, Jr., "Introduction," *The Classic Slave Narratives*, xiii. I thank Dolan Hubbard for this reference.

16. The word "begat" is my word, not Lucille's. I use it because it communicates the biblical, epic quality of Lucille's brief text.

17. Cheryl A Wall, "Sifting Legacies in Lucille Clifton's *Generations*," *Contemporary Literature* 40, no. 4 (Winter 1999): 554.

18. Ibid., 555.

19. Book of Job 1:1 to 42:7. *Oxford NIV Scofield Study Bible*, ed. C. I. Scofield et al. (New York: Oxford University Press, 1984).

20. These citations from Walt Whitman's *Song of Myself* appear in Generations. Other citations from *Song of Myself* are from the Representative Poetry Online Edition, http://eir.library.utoronto.ca/rpo/display'poem2288.html.

21. Wall, "Sifting Legacies," 557.

22. In his 1916 poem, "The Second Coming," Irish poet William Butler Yeats had predicted the collapse of Western culture: "things fall apart / the center cannot hold." Chinua Achebe's 1959 novel *Things Fall Apart*, a book that takes its title from Yeats' poem, documents the British conquest of the Igbo people of Nigeria during the same colonialist period in which Lucille's great-great-grandmother Caroline was forced into slavery.

23. Jerry Ward, "*Generations: A Memoir*," by Lucille Clifton," *New Orleans Review* 5, no. 4 (1999): 569.

24. Lucille Clifton, in discussion with the author, March 5, 2004.

25. Ibid.

26. Michael S. Glaser, "I'd Like Not to Be a Stranger in the World: A Conversation/ Interview with Lucille Clifton," *Antioch Review* 58, no. 3 (Summer 2000): 316.

27. "Canticle," http://www.thefreedictionary.com/canticle.

28. Lucille Clifton, in discussion with the author, March 5, 2004.

29. *King James Version of the Bible*, http://www.cforc.com/kjv/1_Corinthians/13.html.

30. *Webster's New World College Dictionary*, 3rd ed. (New York: Simon & Schuster Macmillan, 1997).

31. Akasha Hull, "Channeling the Ancestral Muse: Lucille Clifton and Dolores Kendrick," in *Female Subjects in Black and White: Race, Psychoanalysis, Feminism*, ed. Elizabeth Abel, Barbara Christian, and Helen Moglen (Berkeley: University of California Press, 1997), 341.

32. "Automatic Writing," About.com, Paranormal Phenomena, http://paranormal.about.com/od/automaticwriting.

33. Alexia Clifton, in discussion with the author, July 26, 2004. Fred Clifton died on November 10, 1984, two days before Alexia's nineteenth birthday. A memorial service was held at the Paul Laurence Dunbar Senior High School, a school he had helped create. Obituary, "Fred Clifton, 49, Activist Wed Poet Laureate," *Baltimore Sun*, November 1984. From the collection of Professor Margaret Reid.

34. "On Strength Gotten from Others," Lucille Clifton Biography and Bibliography, http://www.math.buffalo.edu/~sww/ clifton/clifton-biobib.html.

35. Lucille Clifton, in discussion with the author, March 5, 2004.

36. Ibid.

37. "A Letter to Fred," *Essence* (November, 1989). From the collection of Professor Margaret Reid.

38. "Bill Haley," http://www.billhaley.co.uk/lyrics.htm.

39. Lucille Clifton, in discussion with the author, March 5, 2004.

40. Ibid.

41. Hilary Holladay, "Furious Flower Interview with Lucille Clifton," transcript provided by Joanne Gabbin, May 24, 2005.

42. Lucille Clifton, in discussion with the author, March 5, 2004.

43. Alexia Clifton, in discussion with the author, July 26, 2004.

44. Lucille Clifton, in discussion with the author, March 5, 2004.

45. Ibid.

46. Ibid.

CHAPTER 5

1. James A. Miller, "Lucille Clifton," *The Heath Anthology of American Literature*, 3rd ed., vol. 2 (Boston: Houghton Mifflin, 1998).

2. Mark Bernard White, "Sharing the Living Light: Rhetorical, Poetic, and Social Identity in Lucille Clifton," *CLA Journal* 40, no. 3 (March 1997): 288–305; and Jeannine Thyreen-Mizingnou, "Grace and Ethics in Contemporary American Poetry: Resituating the Other, the World, and the Self," *Religion and Literature* 32. no. 1 (Spring 2000): 87. The most comprehensive analysis of Clifton's poetic forms is to be found in Hilary Holladay's *Wild Blessings: The Poetry of Lucille Clifton* (Baton Rouge: Louisiana State University Press, 2004).

3. Alicia Ostriker, "Kin and Kin: The Poetry of Lucille Clifton," *American Poetry Review* 22, no. 6 (November–December 1993): 1–14. For contemporary views on black vernacular see Bryan McLucas, "African American Vernacular English," http://arches.uga.edu/~bryan/AAVE/main.html.

4. Clifton, cited by Eisa Davis, "Lucille Clifton and Sonia Sanchez: A Conversation," *Callaloo* 25, no. 4 (2002): 1070.

5. Akasha Hull, "Channeling the Ancestral Muse: Lucille Clifton and Dolores Kendrick," in *Female Subjects in Black and White: Race, Psychoanalysis, Feminism*, ed. Elizabeth Abel, Barbara Christian, and Helen Moglen (Berkeley: University of California Press, 1997): 330–348.

6. Hilary Holladay, "Black Names in White Space: Lucille Clifton's South," *Southern Literary Journal* 34, no. 2 (Spring 2002): 121.

7. Ibid., 126.

8. Stephen Butterfield, *Black Autobiography in America* (Amherst: University of Massachusetts Press, 1974), 211.

9. Richard Stewart and T. J. Milling, "Funeral in Jasper Draws Hundreds," *Houston Chronicle* June 14, 1998.

10. "James Byrd, Jr.," Texas NAACP, September 17, 1999, http://www.texasnaacp.org/jasper.htm.

11. Ibid.

12. Stewart and Milling, "Funeral in Jasper Draws Hundreds."

13. Ibid.

14. "James Byrd, Jr." Texas NAACP, September 17, 1999.

15. Richard M. Dorson, *American Negro Folktales* (Greenwich, CT: Fawcett, 1967), 147, 235–236.

16. Almost identical stories carry over into African-American and Caribbean lore, in the tales of "The Singing Bones," "My Mother Killed Me, My Father Ate Me," and "The Woman Who Was a Bird." In these gruesome stories, many of which involve cannibalism, the buried bones and skulls of innocent victims take a voice, accusing the ones who killed them and arousing the community to punish the crime. See Dorson, *American Negro Folktales*, 147–148.

17. Richard Wright, "Between the World and Me," in *Black Voices*, ed. Abraham Chapman (New York: Penguin Books, 1968), 437–438.

18. Trudier Harris, *Exorcizing Blackness* (Bloomington: Indiana University Press, 1984), 104.

19. Ostriker, "Kin and Kin," 9.

20. Lucille Clifton, in discussion with the author, March 5, 2004.

21. Ronna C. Thompson, "Jordan, June," in *The Oxford Companion to African American Literature*, ed. William L. Andrews, Frances Smith Foster, and Trudier Harris (New York: Oxford University Press, 1997), 409–410. Jordan is the author of many militant poems, including "The New Pieta: For the Mothers and Children of Detroit" and "For Somebody to Start Singing," both written to immortalize the riots in Detroit and Newark following the assassination of Martin Luther King, Jr.

22. Clifton, cited by Hilary Holladay, "Furious Flower Interview with Lucille Clifton," transcript provided by Joanne Gabbin, May 24, 2005.

23. "White Hair," http://skyways.lib.ks.us/genweb/archives/1912/w/white.

24. See James Welch, *Killing Custer* (New York: Penguin, 1994).

25. *Black Elk Speaks,* as Told to John G. Neihardt (Lincoln: University of Nebraska Press, 1998), 130.

26. Ibid., 270.

27. Naomi Thiers, "Lucille Clifton," *Belles Lettres* 9, no. 4 (Summer 1994): 89–90.

28. The nomadic Plains Indians periodically shifted their camps during buffalo hunts, seasonal moves, and raids on other tribes. See Alvin M Josephy, Jr., *The Indian Heritage of America* (New York: Bantam Books, 1968), 109–129.

29. James Welch, "Magic Fox," in *Riding the Earthboy 40* (Pittsburgh: Carnegie Mellon University Press, 1997), 138.

30. Jamie Sams and David Carson, *Medicine Cards: The Discovery of Power through the Way of Animals,* 2 vols. (Santa Fe, NM: Bear and Company, 1988), 99–101.

31. Richard Erdoes and Alfonson Ortiz, *American Indian Trickster Tales* (New York: Penguin, 1999), xix.

32. Clifton, cited by Thiers, "Lucille Clifton," 90.

33. Barry M. Pritzker, *A Native American Encyclopedia* (New York: Oxford University Press, 2000).

34. Susan B. A. Somers-Willett, "'A Music in Language': A Conversation with Lucille Clifton," in *The American Voice* (Louisville: Kentucky Foundation for Women, 1999), 86.

35. James Wilson, *The Earth Shall Weep: A History of Native America* (New York: Atlantic Monthly Press, 1998), 204–205.

36. Lucille Clifton, in discussion with the author, March 5, 2004.

37. "Lakota—Culture and Spirituality," http://www.elexion.com/lakota/lakota2/htm.

38. Homer, *The Iliad,* trans. Richard Lattimore (Chicago: University of Chicago Press, 1951).

39. A. Grove Day, *The Sky Clears: Poetry of the American Indians* (Lincoln: University of Nebraska Press, 1964), 23, emphasis in the original.

40. Joseph Campbell, *The Hero with a Thousand Faces* (New York: Meridian Books, 1956).

41. Lucille Clifton, in discussion with the author, March 5, 2004. Clifton is referring to the "Five Nations," an Iroquois confederacy formed in New York State in the sixteenth century. The original five tribes were the Mohawks, the Oneidas, the Onondagas, the Cayugas, and the Senecas. See "Iroquois," http://www.angelfire.com/realm/shades/nativeamericans.

42. Lucille Clifton, in discussion with the author, March 5, 2004. Recent discoveries by William Katz and other historians trace the "hidden heritage" among what are called *Black Indians*, especially among the Seminoles. See William Loren Katz, *Black Indians* (New York: Aladdin Books, 1997).

43. Charles H. Rowell and other critics have made this observation: see Charles H. Rowell, "An Interview with Lucille Clifton," *Callaloo* 22, no. 1 (Winter 1999): 58.

44. Somers-Willett, "A Music in Language," 84.

45. "MOVE," *Wikipedia,* http://www.amswers.com/topic/move–10.

46. Clifton's ventriloquism clearly resembles that of her predecessor, Walt Whitman. She assumes the voice of Ramona Africa and later of Lorena Bobbitt; Whitman assumes the voices of the "mash'd fireman with breast-bone broken" (l. 847) or the "gurgle" of a general who is dying (l. 869). Walt Whitman, *Song of Myself, The Representative Poetry Online Edition.*

47. *The Color Purple*, a film directed by Steven Spielberg, 1985.

48. The "waters" would suggest the voyage from Africa to America, although none of the three figures is historically associated with the Middle Passage. Clifton may be suggesting that all bound people are in danger of drowning unless they free themselves.

49. "The Prophet Jeremiah and Jerusalem," http://jeru.huji.ac.il/eb35s.htm.

50. "Fannie Lou Hamer," *SNCC 1960–1966*, http://www.ibiblio.org/sncc/hamer.html. See also Clifton, "memo: to fannie lou hamer" (*Quilting* 16).

51. "Geronimo," http://www.indians.org/welker/geronimo.htm.

52. Clifton, cited by Thiers, "Lucille Clifton," 90.

53. Rowell, "An Interview with Lucille Clifton," 58, emphasis in the original.

54. Ajuan M. Mance, "Re-Locating the Black Female Subject: The Landscape of the Body in the Poems of Lucille Clifton," in *Recovering the Black Female Body: Self-Representations by African American Women*, ed. Michael Bennett and Vanessa D. Dickerson (New Brunswick, NJ: Rutgers University Press, 2001), 138, 5n.

55. Holladay, *Wild Blessings*, 108.

56. Clifton, cited by Thiers, "Lucille Clifton," 31.

57. Ibid., 32.

58. Clifton, cited by John Lewis, "Still standing," *Cameo*. From the collection of Professor Margaret Reid.

59. Michael S. Glaser, "A Poet for Our Time," Writers' Center, Bethesda, Maryland National Poetry Month, e-mail message to author, April 14, 2005.

60. Zora Neale Hurston, *Moses, Man of the Mountain* (Chatham, NJ: Chatham Bookseller, 1974).

61. Akasha Hull, "In Her Own Images: Lucille Clifton and the Bible," *Dwelling in Possibility: Women Poets and Critics on Poetry*, ed. Yopie Prins and Maeera Shreiber (Ithaca, NY: Cornell University Press, 1997), 293.

62. Holladay, *Wild Blessings*, 105–106.

63. Hull suggests this association between Joseph's cry and making love: see "In Her Own Images," 283.

64. Ostriker, "Kin and Kin," 12.

65. Holladay, *Wild Blessings*, 120.

66. This sequence was included in *Blessing the Boats*, 72–81.

67. William Harmon and C. Hugh Holman, *A Handbook to Literature*, 8th ed. (Upper Saddle Creek, NJ: Prentice Hall, 2000), 166.

68. Robert Browning, "The Bishop Orders his Tomb at Saint Praxed's Church," in *The Norton Anthology of Poetry*, 4th ed., ed. Margaret Ferguson, Mary Jo Salter, and Jon Stallworthy (New York: Norton, 1996), 915–918.

69. A native of Detroit, Carolyn Forché won the Yale Series of Younger Poets award in 1982. Her anthology, *Against Forgetting: Twentieth Century Poetry of Witness*, was published in 1993, the same year as *The Book of Light*: see Carolyn Forché, ed., *Against Forgetting: Twentieth-Century Poetry of Witness* (New York: W. W. Norton, 1993). Both Clifton and Forché are committed to the ideas of remembering, recollection, and history.

70. Holladay, 132.

71. Shirley M. Jordan, "Lucille Clifton," in *Broken Silences* (New Brunswick, NJ: Rutgers University Press, 1993), 45.

72. "Jerusalem," http://www.crystalinks.com/jerusalem.html.

73. Clifton, cited by Rowell, "An Interview with Lucille Clifton," 63.

74. 2 Samuel 18:1–6, *Oxford NIV Scofield Study Bible,* ed. C. I. Scofield et al. (New York: Oxford University Press, 1984), 328–329.

75. Melissa Weininger, "The Trials of Lorena Bobbitt," http://www.digitas.harvard .edu/~perspy/old/issues/2000/retro/lorena_bobbitt.html.

76. Daniel Donaghy, "Review of *Blessing the Boats*," *The Hollins Critic* (October 2000): 16–17.

77. "The Rodney King Trials," http://www.seeingisbelieving.ca/handicam/king.

78. Clifton, cited by Hilary Holladay in "Furious Flowering."

79. William Butler Yeats, "The Second Coming," 1921, in *The Norton Anthology of Poetry*, 4th edition, ed. Margaret Ferguson, Mary Jo Salter, and Jon Stallworthy (New York: Norton, 1996), 1091.

80. "Leda," http://www.answers.com/main/ntquery?tname+leda%2...%/31.

81. Holladay, *Wild Blessings*, 55–56.

82. Thiers, "Lucille Clifton," 32.

83. In the fox sequence the poet refers to "fuckless days and nights," in "leaving fox," *The Terrible Stories*, 113.

84. Scott Beatty, *Superman: The Ultimate Guide to the Man of Steel* (New York: DK Publishing, 1998).

85. John Shelton Lawrence and Robert Jewett, *The Myth of the American Superhero* (Cambridge, UK: Wm. B. Erdmans, 2002). Lawrence and Shelton include Superman, Clint Eastwood, and the policeman from *Jaws* as conforming to the pattern of the monomyth.

86. Lucille Clifton, in discussion with the author, June 21, 2005.

87. Elvis Presley (1935–1977) derived his musical style from black music; Marvin Gaye (1939–1984) had an early concept album, *What's Going On*. See "Marvin Gaye," http://www.history-of-rock.com/marvin_gaye.htm; and "Elvis Presley," http://www.elvis .com/elvisology/bio/elvis_overview.asp.

CHAPTER 6

1. From a poem by Anne Sexton, cited by Janice Delaney, Mary Jane Lupton, and Emily Toth in *The Curse: A Cultural History of Menstruation* (Urbana: University of Illinois Press, 1988), 192. See also the chapter on the menopause and literature, 224–239.

2. The hysterectomy was performed while Lucille was teaching in California in 1987. Information on the dates of Lucille Clifton's surgeries was verified by Alexia Clifton in a telephone discussion with the author, March 23, 2005.

3. "Abracadabra," http://www.worldwidewords.org/qa/qa/abr1.htm.

4. Lucille Clifton, in discussion with the author, March 5, 2004.

5. Christopher Bollas, "Cutting," paper written for the Group for the Research and Application of Psychoanalysis and the Psychoses, Paris, 1989, cited in Mary Jane Lupton, *Menstruation and Psychoanalysis* (Urbana: University of Illinois Press, 1998), 139–141. I thank Kenneth Reinhard for this reference.

6. Elaine Philip, in discussion with the author, July 6, 2005.

7. Michael S. Glaser, "I'd Like Not to Be a Stranger in the World: A Conversation/ Interview with Lucille Clifton," *Antioch Review* 58, no. 3 (Summer 2000): 322.

8. Lupton, *Menstruation and Psychoanalysis*, 137.

9. Hilary Holladay, *Wild Blessings: The Poetry of Lucille Clifton* (Baton Rouge: Louisiana State University Press, 2004), 32.

10. Lupton, *Menstruation and Psychoanalysis*, 137.

11. Alicia Ostriker, "Kin and Kin: The Poetry of Lucille Clifton," *American Poetry Review* 22, no. 6 (November–December 1993): 7.

12. Melissa Weininger, "The Trials of Lorena Bobbitt," http://www.digitas.harvard .edu/~perspy/old/issues/2000/retro/lorena_bobbitt.html.

13. Ibid.

14. Delaney, Lupton, and Toth, *The Curse*, 161–171; 186–200.

15. Mary Chadwick, *The Psychological Effects of Menstruation* (New York: Nervous and Mental Disease Publishing Company, 1932).

16. Julianne Fleenor, "The Change," *Broomstick* 8, no. 5 (September–October 1986): 3–8.

17. Langston Hughes, "The Negro Speaks of Rivers," in *The Norton Anthology of African American Literature*, ed. Henry Louis Gates, Jr. and Nellie Y. McKay (New York: W. W. Norton, 1997), 1254.

18. Julie London's "Cry Me a River" (1955) was recorded by other female artists, including Peggy Lee in 1957 (http://www.thissideofsanity.com/songs/songs/cr/ crymeariver).

19. Hilary Holladay also associates the delta with the vagina in *Wild Blessings*, 95.

20. Delaney, Lupton, and Toth, *The Curse*, 69–70.

21. The "red dress" should recall poet Sylvia Plath's image of the menses as "little bloodied skirts," in *Sylvia Plath: The Collected Poems*, ed. Ted Hughes (New York: Harper and Row, 1981), 203.

22. Lucille Clifton, in discussion with the author, March 5, 2005.

23. Millay's biographer claims that she "almost never" wrote to her husband "when she was not suffering from her periods," in Daniel Mark Epstein, *What Lips My Lips Have Kissed: The Loves and Love Poems of Edna St. Vincent Millay* (New York: Henry Holt, 2001), 237.

24. See Delaney, Lupton, and Toth, *The Curse*, 192–193.

25. Plath, *The Collected Poems*, 98.

26. Holladay, *Wild Blessings*, 95.

27. Ibid., 96.

28. Ibid., 93–96, 102.

29. Delaney, Lupton, and Toth, *The Curse*, 50. The authors claim that the word "menstruation" means "moon change," and in some cultures it is the moon that initiates the menarche. Like the lunar cycle, the menstrual cycle is regular.

30. William Butler Yeats, cited by Delaney, Lupton, and Toth, *The Curse*, 194–195.

31. David Larsen et al., ed., *Mayo Clinic Family Healthbook* (New York: William Morrow, 1990), 1067.

32. Delaney, Lupton, and Toth, *The Curse*, 262–264.

33. Klaus Theweleit, *Male Fantasies: Women, Floods, Bodies, Histories*, trans. Stephen Conway (Minneapolis: University of Minnesota Press, 1987), 411, cited by Lupton, *Menstruation and Psychoanalysis*, 137.

34. Stephen Crane, *The Red Badge of Courage*, hypertext, Project Gutenberg, http://www.cs.cmu.edu/~rgs/badge-table.html.

35. "Shapeshifting," *Wikipedia*, http://en.wikipedia.org.wiki/Shapeshifting.

36. Larsen et al., ed., *Mayo Clinic Family Healthbook*, 484.

37. Holladay, *Wild Blessings*, 156.

38. Greg Kuzma, cited by Holladay in *Wild Blessings*, 157.

39. Clifton, quoted by Sandra Crockett, "Lucille Clifton," *Baltimore Sun*, February 7, 2001. I am grateful to Alexia Clifton for confirming the dates for her mother's surgeries (in a telephone discussion with the author, March 23, 2006).

40. "Greek Mythology: Amazons," http://www.milica.com.au/greek_myths/others/amaz_t.htm.

41. "Dahomy Amazons," http://dahomy-amazons.biography.ms. See also "Amazon," Microsoft *Encarta Africana* CD-ROM (Microsoft Corporation, 1999).

42. The Dahomey Amazons were "the elite troops of the West African Kingdom of Dahomey in the eighteenth and nineteenth centuries. No other group of women warriors, including those the Greeks dubbed amazons for their alleged lack of one breast, has ever been more than a myth." Stanley B. Alpern, *Amazons of Black Sparta: The Women Warriors of Dahomey* (New York: New York University Press, 1999).

43. Audre Lorde was born in Harlem in February 1924 of Caribbean immigrants. Like Lucille Clifton, she began writing poetry at the age of twelve. In 1980 she published *Cancer Journals*, an autobiographical account of her mastectomy. *Cancer Journals* was "the first exploration by a black woman of her experience with breast cancer, published some ten years before the disease was acknowledged to be [an] epidemic among American women." Lorde refused to wear a prosthesis, and she chose a "noninvasive" treatment for her spreading cancer. Beverly Threatt Kulii, "Lorde, Audre," in *The Oxford Companion to African American Literature*, ed. William L. Andrews, Frances Smith Foster, and Trudier Harris (New York: Oxford University Press, 1997).

44. Holladay, *Wild Blessings*, 82. By "synecdochial" Holladay means that Clifton's single breast represents her whole body.

45. Helmut and Richard Wilhelm, *The Wilhelm Lectures on the Book of Changes* (Princeton, NJ: Princeton University Press, 1995).

46. Alexia Clifton, in discussion with the author, July 26, 2004. "Dialysis is an artificial means of removing the waste products from the blood when the kidneys are unable to do so on their own," Larsen et al., ed., *Mayo Clinic Family Healthbook*, 208–209.

47. Alexia Clifton, in discussion with the author, July 26, 2004.

48. Lucille Clifton, in discussion with the author, March 5, 2004.

49. Ibid.

50. Alexia Clifton, in discussion with the author, July 26, 2004.

51. Ibid.

52. Lucille Clifton, in discussion with the author, March 5, 2004.

53. Larsen et al., ed., *Mayo Clinic Family Healthbook*, 731–734.

54. Crockett, "Lucille Clifton."

55. Lucille Clifton, in discussion with the author, March 5, 2004.

56. Ibid.

57. Edgar Silex, e-mail message to author, June 12, 2005. Used with permission from the author.

58. Glaser, "I'd Like Not to Be a Stranger in the World," 312.

CHAPTER 7

1. Freeman Habrowski, in discussion with the author, November 17, 2004.

2. Clifton, cited by Eisa Davis in "Lucille Clifton and Sonia Sanchez: A Conversation," *Callaloo* 25, no. 4 (2002): 1071. The reading was sponsored by the New School of New York and by Cave Canem in 2002.

3. Michael S. Glaser, e-mail message to the author, April 14, 2005.

4. Eugenia Collier, in discussion with the author, October 18, 2004.

5. Lucille Clifton, in discussion with the author, March 5, 2004.

6. Marilyn Kallet, "Doing What You Will Do: An Interview with Lucille Clifton," in *Sleeping with One Eye Open: Women Writers and the Art of Survival*, ed. Marilyn Kallet and Judith O. Cofer (Athens: University of Georgia Press, 1999), 84.

7. Gloria Oden, formerly a professor at the University of Maryland at Baltimore County, now lives in The Charleston, a retirement home in West Baltimore. Oden, a 1944 graduate of Howard, received her J.D. degree from that institution in 1948. Since 1952 she has published at least three volumes of poetry.

8. Sharon Olds, *The Gold Cell* (New York: Alfred A. Knopf, 1993), 16, 19. See also *Strike Sparks: Selected Poems, 1980–2002* (New York: Alfred A. Knopf, 2004).

9. Among other honors, Oliver won the Pulitzer Prize for Poetry in 1983 for *American Primitive* and the National Book Award in 1992 for *New and Selected Poems*.

10. Lucille Clifton, in discussion with the author, March 5, 2004. Richard Wilbur is an established and widely anthologized American poet who was educated at Amherst College and Harvard University. His poems are collected in *Walking to Sleep: New Poems and Translations* (New York: Harcourt Brace, 1992).

11. "Celebrating Josephine Jacobsen," *The Writing Life Cable TV Series*, http:// www.hocopolitso.org/The_Writing_Life/Celebrating_Josephine_Jacobson2003.html. See Josephine Jacobsen, *In the Crevice of Time* (Baltimore: Johns Hopkins Press, 1995).

12. "Answering Crows," in *Poetry at the Angel*, ed. Kenneth Baldwin and Mary Jane Lupton (Baltimore: Bloomery Books, 1978), 38.

13. Anselm Hollo, *Outlying Districts: Poems* (Minneapolis, MN: Coffee House Press, 1990).

14. Lucille Clifton, in discussion with the author, October 21, 2005.

15.. Martin Meredith, *Nelson Mandela: A Biography* (New York: St. Martin's Press, 1998).

16. "The Mandala—Sacred Geometry and Art," *Exotic India*, http://www.exoticindia naret.com/article/mandala.

17. Lucille had written two other poems to the Buddha in *california lessons*, also published in *Next* (81, 85).

18. Clifton could not have anticipated Winnie Mandela's fate. In 1991 she was charged with the "assault and kidnapping" of a fourteen-year-old militant, Stompei Seipei, who was found murdered. The turmoil led to a divorce. "Winnie Mandela: Fallen Political Heir," *Truth and Reconciliation*, BBC News, October 28, 1998.

19. Lucille Clifton, in discussion with the author, March 5, 2004.

20. Ruth E. Fine, *The Art of Romare Bearden* (Washington, DC: The National Gallery of Art, 2003).

21. Clifton, "Blessing the Boats," in *Well Versed* (*The New Yorker*, June 13 and 20, 2005), attachment from AIG Insurance.

22. Lucille Clifton, untitled poem, *Baltimore* (September 2005): 152.

23. George Ciscle, "Is It a Gallery?" *Baltimore* (September 2005): 158.

24. Clifton, cited by Michael S. Glaser, "I'd Like Not to Be a Stranger in the World: A Conversation/Interview with Lucille Clifton," *Antioch Review* 58, no. 3 (Summer 2000): 311, emphasis in the original.

25. Kallet, "Doing What You Will Do," 84.

26. Michael Glaser's in-depth interview with Lucille did not go to press until the summer of 2000, whereas Frederica died in 2000 and Channing in 2004.

27 Lucille Clifton, in discussion with the author, March 5, 2004.

28. Other elegies to Rica and Chan are discussed in chapter 4, Generations Coming and Going.

29. Eugenia Collier, in discussion with the author, October 18, 2004.

30. Haki Madhubuti, "Lucille Clifton: Warm Water, Greased Legs, and Dangerous Poetry," in *Black Women Writers 1950–1980: A Critical Evaluation*, ed. Mari Evans (Garden City, NY: Anchor/Doubleday, 1984), 53.

31. In commenting on the poem "donor," Alexia remarked that Lucille likes to tease her. "She always says I'm stubborn. I do what I want anyway, and I was like that inside." Alexia Clifton, in discussion with the author, July 26, 2004.

32. Davis, "Lucille Clifton and Sonia Sanchez: A Conversation," 1044–1046.

33. "September Song," http://www.theguitarguy.com/septermb2.htm.

34. Estrin's review, "September Song," argues that instead of being innocent, Bush and his staff were complicit in the bizarre events of 9/11. Marc Estrin, "September Song," http://www.serendipity.li/wot/September-song.htm.

35. Teresa Ballard, "Review of *Mercy*," *The Cortland Review*, http://www.cortland review.com/features/05/spring.

36. "Pentecost (Whitsunday)," *Catholic Encyclopedia*, http://www.newadvent.org/cathen/15614b.htm.

37. Julia Reinhard Lupton, "On Rosh Hashanah-Yizkor Memorial Service for the Dead," e-mail message to author, July 31, 2005.

38. See *Bearing Witness: Selections from African-American Autobiography in the Twentieth Century*, ed. Henry Louis Gates, Jr. (New York: Random House, 1991); and *Bearing Witness: Stories of the Holocaust*, ed. Hazel Rochman and Darlene McCampbell (New York: Scholastic, 1995).

39. See http://www.TraditionsJewishGifts.com.

40. John Milton, *Paradise Lost*, in *Paradise Lost and Paradise Regained* (New York: Signet Classics, 2001).

41. Peggy Rosenthal, "In the Beginning," *Christian Century* (January 30, 2002): 2.

42. Erica L. Still, "Body Language," *The Iowa Review,* http://www.uiowa.edu/~iareview/reviews/erica-still.htm.

43. Edgar Silex, e-mail message to author, June 12, 2005. Used with permission from the author.

44. Lucille Clifton, in discussion with the author, October 21, 2005.

45. Ibid.

46. "St. Mary Magdalen," *Catholic Encyclopedia,* http://www.newadvent.org/cathen/09761a.htm.

47. Although Dan Brown briefly associates Mary Magdalen with Isis, the Egyptian goddess (317), he makes no reference to the many statues of Black Madonnas that have been discovered in churches throughout France. Dan Brown, *The Da Vinci Code* (New York: Doubleday, 2003).

48. Akasha Hull, "In Her Own Images: Lucille Clifton and the Bible," *Dwelling in Possibility: Women Poets and Critics on Poetry*, ed. Yopie Prins and Maeera Shreiber (Ithaca, NY: Cornell University Press, 1997), 280.

49. For a view of Mary Magdalen and the Black Madonna, see Cassandra Eason, "Black Madonnas: Women, Spirit, and Healing," http://www.casandraeason.co.uk/black_ madonnas.htm. See also *Black Saints, Mystics, and Holy Folk* (E-book, pdf; Apostle Dos Rosas Press, 2005).

50. "Sally Hemings (1773–1835)," About.com, Women's History: Profiles Index, http://womenshistory.about.com/ library/bio/blbio_hemings.

51. Lucille Clifton, in discussion with the author, October 21, 2005.

52. Paula Gunn Allen reveals the historical Pocahontas in her biography, *Pocahontas: Medicine Woman, Spy, Entrepreneur, Diplomat* (New York: HarperCollins, 2003).

53. "Nancy Green, the Original 'Aunt Jemima,'" *The African American Registry,* http://aaregistry.com/african-american-history.

54. Ibid.

55. Lucille Clifton, in discussion with the author, June 21, 2005.

56. http://www.brainyquote.com/quotes/quotes/l/lucilleclifton.

Selected Bibliography

WORKS BY LUCILLE CLIFTON

Children's Books

All Us Come Cross the Water. Pictures by John Steptoe. New York: Holt, Rinehart, and Winston, 1973.

Amifika. Illustrated by Thomas DiGrazia. New York: Dutton, 1977.

The Black BC's. Illustrated by Don Miller. New York: Dutton, 1970.

The Boy Who Didn't Believe in Spring. Pictures by Brinton Turkle. 1973. Reprint, New York: Dutton, 1988.

Dear Creator: A Week of Poems for Young People and Their Teachers. Illustrated by Gail Gordon Carter. New York: Doubleday Book for Young Readers, 1977.

Don't You Remember? Illustrated by Evaline Ness. New York: Dutton, 1973.

Everett Anderson's 1-2-3. Illustrated by Ann Grifalconi. 1977. Reprint, New York: Henry Holt, 1992.

Everett Anderson's Christmas Coming. Illustrated by Jan Spivey Gilchrist. New York: Henry Holt, 1991.

Everett Anderson's Christmas Coming. Illustrated by Evaline Ness. New York: Holt, Rinehart, and Winston, 1971.

Everett Anderson's Friend. Illustrated by Ann Grifalconi. 1976. Reprint, New York: Henry Holt, 1992.

Everett Anderson's Goodbye. Illustrated by Ann Grifalconi. New York: Holt, Rinehart, and Winston, 1983.

Everett Anderson's Nine Month Long. Illustrated by Ann Grifalconi. New York: Holt, Rinehart, and Winston, 1978.

Everett Anderson's Year. Illustrated by Ann Grifalconi. 1974. Reprint, New York: Henry Holt, 1992.

Good, Says Jerome. Illustrated by Stephanie Douglas. New York: Dutton, 1973.

Lucky Stone. Illustrated by Dale Payson. New York: Delacorte Press, 1979.

My Brother Fine With Me. Illustrated by Moneta Barnett. New York: Holt, Rinehart, and Winston, 1975.
My Friend Jacob. Illustrated by Thomas Di Grazia. New York: Dutton, 1980.
One of the Problems of Everett Anderson. Illustrated by Ann Grifalconi. New York: Henry Holt, 2001.
Some of the Days of Everett Anderson. Illustrated by Evaline Ness. New York: Holt, Reinhart, and Winston, 1969.
Sonora Beautiful. Drawings by Michael Garland. New York: Dutton, 1981.
Three Wishes. Illustrated by Michael Hays. New York: Doubleday Books for Young Readers, 1992.
Three Wishes. Illustrated by Stephanie Douglas. New York: Viking Press, 1976.
Times They Used to Be. Illustrated by Susan Jeschke. New York: Holt, Rinehart, and Winston, 1974. Reprint, Illustrated by E. B. Lewis. New York: Delacorte Press, 2000.

Memoir

Generations: A Memoir. New York: Random House, 1976.

Poetry

An Ordinary Woman. New York: Random House, 1974.
Blessing the Boats: New and Selected Poems, 1988–2000. Rochester, NY: BOA Editions, 2000.
The Book of Light. Port Townsend , WA: Copper Canyon Press, 1993.
Good News about the Earth: New Poems. New York: Random House, 1972.
Good Times: Poems. New York: Random House, 1969.
Good Woman: Poems and a Memoir, 1969–1980. Rochester, NY: BOA Editions, 1987.
Mercy. Rochester, NY: BOA Editions, 2004.
Next: New Poems. Rochester, NY: BOA Editions, 1987.
Quilting: Poems, 1987–1990. Rochester, NY: BOA Editions, 1991.
The Terrible Stories: Poems. Rochester, NY: BOA Editions, 1996. Reprint, London: Slow Dancer Press, 1998.
Two-Headed Woman. Amherst: University of Massachusetts Press, 1980.
"Untitled." *Baltimore,* September 2005, 152.

Other Publications

"Christmas Is Something Else." *House & Garden*, December 1969.
"The End of Love Is Death, the End of Death Is Love." *Atlantic*, March 1971.
"A Letter to Fred." *Essence,* November 1989. From the collection of Professor Margaret Reid.
"The Magic Mama." *Redbook*, November, 1969.
Sisters My Girls, No. 3. Lucille Clifton and Gwyneth Walker. Chapel Hill, NC: Treble Clef Music Press, 1999. From the collection of Professor Margaret Reid.
This Morning My Girls, No 1. Lucille Clifton and Gwyneth Walker. Chapel Hill, NC: Treble Clef Music Press, 1999. From the collection of Professor Margaret Reid.

"Three Wishes." In *Free to Be...You and Me*, edited by Marlo Thomas. Ms. Foundation, Inc. Philadelphia: Running Press, 1974.

To My Girls My Girls, No. 2. Lucille Clifton and Gwyneth Walker. Chapel Hill, NC: Treble Clef Music Press, 1999. From the collection of Professor Margaret Reid.

SELECTED INTERVIEWS WITH LUCILLE CLIFTON

Anaporte-Easton, Jean. "A Conversation with Lucille Clifton." *SAGE: A Scholarly Journal on Black Women* 2, no. 1 (Spring 1985): 52.

Crockett, Sandra. "Lucille Clifton." *Baltimore Sun,* February 7, 2001.

Davis, Eisa. "Lucille Clifton and Sonia Sanchez: A Conversation." *Callaloo* 25, no. 4 (2002): 1038–74.

Glaser, Michael S. "I'd Like Not to Be a Stranger in the World: A Conversation/Interview with Lucille Clifton." *Antioch Review* 58, no. 3 (Summer 2000): 310–39.

Holladay, Hilary. "Lucille Talks about Lucille: An Interview." In *Wild Blessings: The Poetry of Lucille Clifton,* 181–200. Baton Rouge: Louisiana State University Press, 2004.

———. "Furious Flower Interview with Lucille Clifton." Transcript provided by Joanne Gabbin. May 24, 2005.

Jordan, Shirley M. "Lucille Clifton." In *Broken Silences,* 38–49. New Brunswick, NJ: Rutgers University Press, 1993.

Kallet, Marilyn. "Doing What You Will Do: An Interview with Lucille Clifton." In *Sleeping with One Eye Open: Women Writers and the Art of Survival*, edited by Marilyn Kallet and Judith O. Cofer, 80–85. Athens: University of Georgia Press, 1999. Originally published as "Poetry Is a Human Art" in *New Millennium Writings* 3, no. 2 (1998–99).

Rowell, Charles H. "An Interview with Lucille Clifton." *Callaloo* 22, no. 1 (Winter 1999): 56–72.

Somers-Willett, Susan B. A. "'Music in Language': A Conversation with Lucille Clifton." *The American Voice,* Summer 1999, 73–92.

Thiers, Naomi. "Lucille Clifton." *Belles Lettres* 9, no. 4 (Summer 1994): 30–35, 88–90.

Woolford, Pamela. "Interview with Lucille Clifton." *Jambalaya,* 1993. From the collection of Professor Margaret Reid.

INTERVIEWS CONDUCTED BY MARY JANE LUPTON

Formal Interviews

Clifton, Alexia. Interview by Mary Jane Lupton. July 26, 2004.

Clifton, Lucille. Interview by Mary Jane Lupton. March 5, 2004.

———. Interview by Mary Jane Lupton. June 21, 2005.

Collier, Eugenia. Interview by Mary Jane Lupton. October 18, 2004.

Habrowski, Freeman. Interview by Mary Jane Lupton. November 17, 2004.

Reid, Margaret. Interview by Mary Jane Lupton. October 16, 2003.

Telephone Interviews

Clifton, Alexia. Telephone interview by Mary Jane Lupton. March 23, 2006.
Clifton, Lucille. Telephone interview by Mary Jane Lupton. October 21, 2005.
———. Telephone interview by Mary Jane Lupton. March 21, 2006.
———. Telephone interview by Mary Jane Lupton. April 7, 2006.
Dyer, Martin. Telephone interview by Mary Jane Lupton. December 23, 2004.
LeBlanc, Whitney. Telephone interview by Mary Jane Lupton. January 12, 2005.
Patterson, Donald. Telephone interview by Mary Jane Lupton. January 11, 2005.
Philip, Elaine. Telephone interview by Mary Jane Lupton. July 6, 2005.
Reeves, Iris. Telephone interview by Mary Jane Lupton. January 11, 2005.
Reid, Margaret. Telephone interview by Mary Jane Lupton. January 20, 2005.
Sullivan, William. Telephone interview by Mary Jane Lupton. January 11, 2005.

BOOKS ON LUCILLE CLIFTON

Holladay, Hilary. *Wild Blessings: The Poetry of Lucille Clifton*. Baton Rouge: Louisiana State University Press, 2004.

SELECTED CRITICISM, REVIEWS, AND OTHER SOURCES

"Abracadabra." http://www.worldwidewords.org/qa/qa/abr1.htm.
Abrahams, Roger D., ed. *Afro-American Folktales*. New York: Random House, 1985.
Achebe, Chinua. *Things Fall Apart*. London: William Heinemann Ltd., 1958.
AFRO-Americ@: The Black History Museum. "The Black Panthers: H. Rap Brown/ Stokely Carmichael." http://www.afro.com/history/Panthers/Brown/Brown.html.
Allen, Paula Gunn. *Pocahontas: Medicine Woman, Spy, Entrepreneur, Diplomat*. New York: HarperCollins, 2003.
Alpern, Stanley B. *Amazons of Black Sparta: The Women Warriors of Dahomey*. New York: New York University Press, 1999.
"Amazon." *Encarta Africana* CD-ROM. Microsoft Corporation, 1999.
American Booksellers Association. "Literary Award Winners: National Book Awards." http://www.bookweb.org/news/awards/1289.html.
"American Civil Rights Movement." Nationmaster.com. http://www.nationmaster.com/ encyclopedia.
Andrews, William L., Frances Smith Foster, and Trudier Harris, eds. *The Oxford Companion to African American Literature*. New York: Oxford University Press, 1997.
"Angela Davis." About.com, Women's History: Profiles Index. http://womenshistory .about.com/od/aframerwriters/p/angela_davis.htm.
Angelou, Maya. *Even the Stars Look Lonesome*. New York: Random House, 1997.
———. *I Know Why the Caged Bird Sings*. New York: Random House, 1970.
———. *Life Doesn't Frighten Me*. Illustrated by Jean-Michel Basquiat. New York: Stewart, 1993.
"Anthony Johnson." http://www.pbs.org/wgbh/aia/part1/1p265.html.
"Automatic Writing." About.com, Paranormal Phenomena. http://paranormal.about .com/od/automaticwriting/.

Bagby, George F. Review of *Blessing the Boats. Richmond Times-Dispatch,* February 4, 2001.

Baldwin, James. *Amen Corner.* Directed by Owen Dodson. 1955.

———. "An Open Letter to My Sister, Angela Y. Davis." In *If They Come in the Morning,* edited by The National United Committee to Free Angela Davis., Inc., 19–23. New York: Signet, 1971.

Baldwin, Kenneth, and Mary Jane Lupton, eds. *Poetry at the Angel.* Baltimore: Bloomery Books, 1978.

Ballard, Teresa. Review of *Mercy. The Cortland Review.* http://www.cortlandreview .com/features/05/spring/lucille_clifton.html.

Baraka, Amiri (LeRoi Jones). *"Dutchman," and "The Slave": Two Plays.* London: Faber and Faber, 1965.

———. *The LeRoi Jones/Amiri Baraka Reader.* New York: Thunder's Mouth Press, 1991.

Barksdale, Richard. The Papers of Richard Kenneth Barksdale. University of Illinois at Urbana-Champaign Archives, Record Series Number: 15/7/45. http://web.library.uiuc.edu/ahx/unaccard/UAControlCard.

Beatty, Scott. *Superman: The Ultimate Guide to the Man of Steel.* New York: DK Publishing, Inc., 1998.

"Beneath the Underground: The Flight for Freedom." http://mdslavery.net/ index.html.

Bierce, Ambrose. *The Devil's Dictionary.* New York: Oxford University Press, 1999.

"Bill Haley." http://www.billhaley.co.uk/lyrics.htm.

"The Black Panthers." Afro.com. http://afro.com/history/Panthers/Brown/Brown.html.

Black Saints, Mystics, and Holy Folk. E-book, pdf. Apostle Dos Rosas Press, 2005.

Blake, William. "Songs of Innocence." 1789. Reprint, in *The Poetry and Prose of William Blake,* edited by David V. Erdman and Harold Bloom. Garden City, NY: Doubleday Anchor, 1970.

"Bobby Seale." http://www.law.umkc.edu/faculty/projects/ftrials/Chicago7/Account .html.

Bollas, Christopher. "Cutting." Paper written for the Group for the Research and Application of Psychoanalysis and the Psychoses. Paris, 1989.

"Book of 1 Corinthians." *King James Version of the Bible.* http://www.cforc.com/kjv/1_ Corinthians/index.html.

Braxton, Joanne M. *Black Women Writing Autobiography.* Philadelphia: Temple University Press, 1989.

Brooks, Gwendolyn. "The Mother." In *Black Voices,* edited by Abraham Chapman, 461. New York, Penguin Books, 1968.

———. "We Real Cool." In *The Norton Anthology of African American Literature,* edited by Henry Louis Gates, Jr., and Nellie Y. McKay, 1591. New York: W. W. Norton & Company, Inc., 1997.

Brown, Dan. *The Da Vinci Code.* Special illustrated edition. New York: Doubleday, 2003.

"Brown v. Board of Education: About the Case." http://brownvboard.org/summary.

"Buffalo Soldiers." http://buffalosoldiers.net.

Butterfield, Stephen. *Black Autobiography in America.* Amherst: University of Massachusetts Press, 1974.

Campbell, Joseph. *The Hero with a Thousand Faces.* New York: Meridian Books, 1956.

Carroll, Constance M. "Three's a Crowd: The Dilemma of Black Women in Higher Education." In *All the Women Are White, All the Men Are Black, But Some of Us Are*

Brave, edited by Gloria T. Hull, Patricia Bell Scott, and Barbara Smith 115–28. Old Westbury, NY: The Feminist Press, 1992.

"Cave Canem." http://www.cavecanempoets.org.

"Celebrating Josephine Jacobsen." *The Writing Life Cable TV Series*. http://www.hocopolitso.org/The_Writing_Life/Celebrating_Josephine_Jacobson2003.html.

Chadwick, Mary. *The Psychological Effects of Menstruation*. New York: Nervous and Mental Disease Publishing Company, 1932.

"Chesapeake Bay History." Chesapeake Bay Program. http://chesapeakebay.net/info/aframer.cfm.

Ciscle, George. "Is It a Gallery?" *Baltimore,* September 2005, 158.

Clark, Keith. "*Amen Corner.*" In *The Oxford Companion to African American Literature*, edited by William L. Andrews, Frances Smith Foster, and Trudier Harris, 15. New York: Oxford University Press, 1997.

Cleaver, Eldridge. *Soul on Ice*. New York: McGraw-Hill, 1968.

Collier, Eugenia. *Breeder and Other Stories*. Baltimore: Black Classic Press, 1994.

The Color Purple. Directed by Steven Spielberg. 1985.

The Council Chronicle. NCTE. September 2001. http://www.ncte.org/chronicle/September2001/clifton.shtml

Crane, Stephen. *The Red Badge of Courage*. Hypertext, Project Gutenberg. http://www.cs.cmu.edu/~rgs/badge-table.html.

Crockett, Sandra. "Lucille Clifton." *Baltimore Sun,* February 7, 2001, 1–3.

"Dahomey, Early Kingdom of." *Encarta Africana* CD-ROM. Microsoft Corporation, 1999.

Davis, Angela. *Women, Race, and Class*. New York: Random House, 1981.

Dawson, Horace G. "The Legacy of Patricia Roberts Harris at Howard University." http://www.huarchivesnet.howard.edu/0005huarnet/harris1.htm.

Day, A. Grove. *The Sky Clears: Poetry of the American Indians*. Lincoln: University of Nebraska Press, 1964.

Delaney, Janice, Mary Jane Lupton, and Emily Toth. *The Curse: A Cultural History of Menstruation*. New York: E. P. Dutton, 1976. Reprinted and updated, Urbana: University of Illinois Press, 1988.

"Depew, New York, Detailed Profile." http://www.city-data.com/city/Depew-New-York.html.

Donaghy, Daniel. Review of *Blessing the Boats*. *The Hollins Critic,* October 2000, 16–17.

Dorson, Richard M. *American Negro Folktales*. Greenwich, CT: Fawcett, 1967.

Douglass, Frederick. *Narrative of the Life of Frederick Douglass, an American Slave, Written by Himself*. In *The Classic Slave Narratives*, edited by Henry Louis Gates, Jr. New York: Signet, 1987.

Eason, Cassandra. "Black Madonnas: Women, Spirit, and Healing." http://www.casandraeason.co.uk/black_madonnas.htm.

Elk, Black and John G. Neihardt. *Black Elk Speaks*. 1932. Reprint, Lincoln: University of Nebraska Press, 1998.

Ellis, Kimberly C. ("Dr. Goddess"). Review of the Furious Flower Conference, September 23–25, 2004. AFAM-Lit@Listserv.UIC.edu. 10/4/2004.

"Elvis Presley." http://www.elvis.com/elvisology/bio/elvis_overview.asp.

Emerson, Jim. Review of *Mississippi Burning*. http://www.cinepad.com/reviews/mississippi.htm.

Encyclopedia of North American Indians. Houghton Mifflin College Division. http://college.hmco.com/history/readerscomp/naiind/html.

Epstein, Daniel Mark. *What Lips My Lips Have Kissed: The Loves and Love Poems of Edna St. Vincent Millay*. New York: Henry Holt, 2001.

Erdoes, Richard, and Alfonson Ortiz. *American Indian Trickster Tales*. New York: Penguin, 1999.

Estrin, Marc. "September Song." Review of *The New Pearl Harbor*, by David Ray Griffin. *Counterpunch*. http:www.serendipity.li/wot/September-song.htm.

"Fannie Lou Hamer." *SNCC 1960–1966*. http://www.ibiblio.org/ sncc/hamer.html.

Feldmann, Susan, ed. Introduction to *African Myths and Tales*. 1963. Reprint, New York: Dell Publishing Co., Inc., 1972.

———, ed. *The Storytelling Stone*. New York: Random House, 1965.

Ferguson, Margaret, Mary Jo Salter, and Jon Stallworthy, eds. *The Norton Anthology of Poetry*. 4th ed. New York: Norton, 1996.

Fine, Ruth E., curator. *The Art of Romare Bearden*. Washington, DC: The National Gallery of Art, 2003.

Fishkin, Shelley Fisher. "Mark Twain's America." April 11, 1997. http://www.pbs.org/ newshour/authors_corner/jan_june97.

———. *Was Huck Black?: Mark Twain and African-American Voices*. New York: Oxford University Press, 1993.

Fleenor, Julianne. "The Change." *Broomstick* 8:5 (September–October 1986), 3–8.

Forché, Carolyn., ed. *Against Forgetting: Twentieth-Century Poetry of Witness*. New York: W. W. Norton & Company, Inc., 1993.

"Fred Clifton, 49, Activist Wed Poet Laureate." *Baltimore Sun* (November 1984). From the collection of Professor Margaret Reed.

"Frederica Clifton, 39, Graphics Designer." *Baltimore Sun* (2000). From the collection of Professor Margaret Reid.

Friedan, Betty. *The Feminine Mystique*. 1963. Reprint, New York: W. W. Norton and Company, Inc., 2001.

Frost, Robert. "Fire and Ice." *The Poetry of Robert Frost*, edited by Edward Connery Lathem. New York: Henry Holt and Company, Inc., 1979.

Fuller, H. W. Review of *Some of the Days of Everett Anderson*. *New York Times Book Review*, September 6, 1970, 16.

Gabbin, Joanne, ed. *The Furious Flowering of African American Poetry*. Charlottesville: University Press of Virginia, 1999.

Gates, Henry Louis, Jr., ed. *Bearing Witness: Selections from African-American Autobiography in the Twentieth Century*. New York: Random House, 1991.

Gates, Henry Louis, Jr., and Nellie Y. McKay, eds. *The Norton Anthology of African American Literature*. New York: W. W. Norton & Company, 1997.

"Guatama Buddha." *Wikipedia*. http://en.wikipedia.org/wiki/Gautama_Buddha.

"Geronimo." Indians.org. http://www.indians.org/welker/geronimo.htm.

Glaser, Michael S. "A Poet for Our Time." Writers' Center, Bethesda, Maryland. National Poetry Month, April 1999, updated. E-mail communication, April 14, 2005.

Gregory, Dick. *Nigger*. New York: E. P. Dutton, Inc., 1964.

Grimm, Jacob, and Wilhelm Grimm. "*Sleeping Beauty*." In *Grimm's Fairy Tales*. Illustrated by Trina Schart Hyman. Boston: Little, Brown, 1977.

Gwiazda, Piotr. "The Aesthetics of Politics/The Politics of Aesthetics: Amiri Baraka's 'Somebody Blew Up America.'" *Contemporary Literature* 43, no. 3 (2004): 460–85.

Habrowski, Freeman, Kenneth I. Maton, and Geoffrey L. Grief. *Beating the Odds: Raising Academically Successful Black Males*. New York: Oxford University Press, 1998.

———. "The Role of Youth in the Civil Rights Movement: Reflections on Birmingham." *African Americans and Civil Rights: A Reappraisal (1997 Black History Learning Resource Package)*. Washington, DC: The Association for the Study of Afro-American Life and History, Inc., and Associated Publishers, 1996.

Haley, Alex. *Roots*. New York: Dell, 1976.

Harmon, William, and C. Hugh Holman. *A Handbook to Literature*. 8th ed. Upper Saddle Creek, NJ: Prentice Hall, 2000.

Harris, Trudier. "Baldwin, James." In *The Oxford Companion to African American Literature*, edited by William L. Andrews, Frances Smith Foster, and Trudier Harris, 44–46. New York: Oxford University Press, 1997.

———. *Exorcizing Blackness*. Bloomington: Indiana University Press, 1984.

Harris, William J. "Introduction." *Le Roi Jones/Amiri Baraka Reader*. New York: Thunder's Mouth Press, 1991.

Harvey, Brett. *The Fifties*. New York: HarperCollins Publishers, 1993.

"He Was a Symbol: Eldridge Cleaver Dies at 62." *U.S. News Story Page*. http://www.cnn.com/US/9805/01/cleaver.late.obit.

Herbert, George. *The Complete English Poems*, edited by John Tobin. New York: Penguin, 1991.

Holladay, Hilary. "Black Names in White Space: Lucille Clifton's South." *Southern Literary Journal* 34, no. 2 (Spring 2002): 430–44.

———. "'I Am Not Grown Away from You': Lucille Clifton's Elegies for her Mother." *CLA Journal* 42, no. 4 (June 1999): 430–44.

———. "Song for Herself: Lucille Clifton's Poems about Womanhood." *The Furious Flowering of African American Poetry*, edited by Joanne Gabbin, 281–97. Charlottesville: University Press of Virginia, 1999.

Hollo, Anselm. *Outlying Districts: Poems*. Minneapolis, MN: Coffee House Press, 1990.

Homer. *The Iliad*. Trans. Richard Lattimore. Chicago: University of Chicago Press, 1951.

Howe, Florence, ed. *No More Masks!: An Anthology of Twentieth Century Women Poets*. New York: HarperCollins Publishers, Inc., 1993.

Hughes, Sheila Hassell. "Walker, Joseph A." In *The Oxford Companion to African American Literature*, edited by William L. Andrews, Frances Smith Foster, and Trudier Harris, 751–52. New York: Oxford University Press, 1997.

Hull, Akasha. "Channeling the Ancestral Muse: Lucille Clifton and Dolores Kendrick." In *Female Subjects in Black and White: Race, Psychoanalysis, Feminism*, edited by Elizabeth Abel, Barbara Christian, and Helen Moglen, 330–48. Berkeley: University of California Press, 1997.

———. "In Her Own Images: Lucille Clifton and the Bible." *Dwelling in Possibility: Women Poets and Critics on Poetry*, edited by Yopie Prins and Maeera Shreiber, 273–95. Ithaca, NY: Cornell University Press, 1997.

Hurston, Zora Neale. *Moses, Man of the Mountain*. 1939. Chatham, NJ: Chatham Bookseller, 1974.

"Inner Sanctum Mysteries." *Radio Hall of Fame*. http://www.radiohof.org/adventure drama/innersanctum.html.

"Iroquois." *Pages of Shades*. http://www.angelfire.com/realm/shades/nativeamericans/.

"Jackson State May 1970." Mike and Kendra's Kent State, May, 4, 1970, Web Site. http://www.may41970.com/Jackson%20State/jackson_state_may_1970.htm.

Jacobsen, Josephine. *In the Crevice of Time*. Baltimore: Johns Hopkins University Press, 1995.

"James Byrd, Jr." Texas NAACP. September 17, 1999. http://www.texasnaacp.org/jasper.htm.

Japan Visitor. "Relations—Japan/Korea." http://www.japanvisitor.com/jc/relations.html.

"Jerusalem." http://www.crystalinks.com/jerusalem.html.

Johnson, Dianne. "The Chronicling of an African-American Life and Consciousness: Lucille Clifton's Everett Anderson Series." *Children's Literature Association Quarterly* 14, no. 4 (Winter 1989): 174–78.

Jones, Hetty. *How I Became Hetty Jones*. New York: Grove Press, 1990.

Jones, Patricia Spears. Review of *The Terrible Stories*. *Quarterly Black Review*, November/December–January/February 1997, 30.

Jordan, June. *Naming Our Destiny: New and Selected Poems*. New York: Thunder's Mouth Press, 1989.

———. *Things I Do in the Dark*. 1967. Reprint, Boston: Beacon Press, 1977.

Josephy, Alvin M., Jr. *The Indian Heritage of America*. New York: Bantam Books, 1968.

"Karma." *Wikipedia*. http://en.wikipedia.org/wiki/Karma.

Katz, William Loren. *Black Indians*. 1986. Reprint, New York: Simon & Schuster, Aladdin Books, 1997.

Kelly, Frederic. "A Woman with Words." *Baltimore Sun Magazine*, January 27, 1974, 9, 11. From the collection of Professor Margaret Reid.

Kinnell, Galway. *Mortal Acts/Mortal Wounds*. Boston: Houghton Mifflin, 1980.

———. *What a Kingdom It Was*. Boston: Houghton Mifflin, 1960.

Kozol, Jonathan. *Free Schools*. 2nd printing. Boston: Houghton Mifflin, 1972.

Kulii, Bevery Threatt. "Lorde, Audre." In *The Oxford Companion to African American Literature*, edited by William L. Andrews, Frances Smith Foster, and Trudier Harris. New York: Oxford University Press, 1997.

Kumin. Maxine. *Selected Poems 1960–1990*. New York: W. W. Norton & Company, 1998.

———. *Up Country: Poems of New England*. New York: W. W. Norton, 1972.

"Kwame Ture." Cordley Coit. http://www.cordleycoit.com/FeeSpeach/free.freespeech.org/mw/Kwame.htm.

"Kwanzaa." Official Kwanzaa Web Site. http://www.officialkwanzaawebsite.org.

"Lakota—Culture and Spirituality." *Lakota Culture and Spirituality*. http://www.elexion.com/lakota/lakota2.htm.

Larson, David E., et al., eds. *Mayo Clinic Family Healthbook*. New York: William Morrow and Company, Inc., 1990.

Lawrence, John Shelton, and Robert Jewett. *The Myth of the American Superhero*. Cambridge, UK: Wm. B. Eerdmans Publishing Co., 2002.

Lazer, Hank. "Blackness Blessed: The Writing of Lucille Clifton." *Southern Review* 25, no. 3 (Summer 1989): 760–70.

"Leda." Answers.com. http://www.answers.com/main/ntquery?tname+leda%2...%/31/.

Lerner, Gerda, ed. *Black Women in White America: A Documentary History*. New York: Random House, 1973.

Levey, Judith S., and Agnes Greenhall, eds. *The Concise Columbia Encyclopedia*. New York: Columbia University Press, 1983.

Lewis, John. "Still standing." *Cameo*, n.d. From the collection of Professor Margaret Reid.

Lewis, Marjorie. Review of *Some of the Days of Everett Anderson*. *Library Journal* 95 (May 15, 1970): 1928.

"Little Richard." *The History of Rock and Roll*. http://www.history-of-rock.com/richard .htm.

Lorde, Audre. *The Cancer Journals*. Duluth, MN: Aunt Lute Foundation Book, 1980.

————. *Collected Poems*. New York: W. W. Norton & Company, Inc., 1997.

Lott, Clarinda Harris. "Answering Crows." In *Poetry at the Angel*, edited by Kenneth H. Baldwin and Mary Jane Lupton. Baltimore: Bloomery Books, 1978.

"Lucille Clifton." African American Publications. http://www.africanpubs.com/ Apps/bios/0366CliftonLucille.asp?pic=none.

Lupton, Julia Reinhard. "On Rosh Hashanah—Yizkor Memorial Service for the Dead." Detail from e-mail message to the author, July 31,2005.

Lupton, Mary Jane. *Maya Angelou: A Critical Companion*. Westport, CT: Greenwood Press, 1998.

————. *Menstruation and Psychoanalysis*. Urbana: University of Illinois Press, 1998.

————. "Remember My Name: Lucille Clifton's Crazy Horse Poems." *The Zora Neale Hurston Forum* 18 (2004): 77–83.

Madhubuti, Haki. "Lucille Clifton: Warm Water, Greased Legs, and Dangerous Poetry." In *Black Women Writers (1950–1980): A Critical Evaluation*, edited by Mari Evans, 150–60. Garden City, NY: Anchor-Doubleday, 1984.

Madigan, Tim. *The Burning: Massacre, Destruction, and the Tulsa Race Riot of 1921*. New York: St. Martin's Press, 2001.

Mance, Ajuan M. "Re-Locating the Black Female Subject: The Landscape of the Body in the Poems of Lucille Clifton." In *Recovering the Black Female Body: Self-Representations by African American Women*, edited by Michael Bennett and Vanessa D. Dickerson, 123–40. New Brunswick, NJ: Rutgers University Press, 2001.

"The Mandala—Sacred Geometry and Art." *Exotic India*. http://www.exoticindiaart .com/article/mandala/. 1–11.

"Marvin Gaye." *The History of Rock and Roll*. http://www.history-of-rock.com/marvin _gaye.htm.

Mathias de Sousa." *Exploring Maryland's Roots: Library*. http://mdroots.thinkport .org/library/mathiasdesousa.asp.

McCluskey, Audrey. T. "Tell the Good News: A View of the Works of Lucille Clifton." *Black Women Writers (1950–1980: A Critical Evaluation*, edited by Mari Evans. Garden City, NY: Anchor-Doubleday, 1984. 139–49.

McDowell, Deborah E. "In the First Place: Making Frederick Douglass and the Afro-American Tradition." In *African American Autobiography*, edited by William L. Andrews, 36–58. Englewood Cliffs, NJ: Prentice Hall, 1993.

McLucas, Bryan. "African American Vernacular English." http://arches.uga.edu/ ~bryan/AAVE/main.html.

"Memphis, Egypt." Absoluteastronomy.com. http://www.absoluteastronomy.com/ encyclopedia/M.

Meredith, Martin. *Nelson Mandela: A Biography*. New York: St. Martin's Press, 1998.

Miller, Arthur. *The Crucible*. 1952. New York: Penguin, 1982.

Miller, James. "Lucille Clifton." *The Heath Anthology of American Literature*. 3rd ed. Vol. 2. New York: Houghton Mifflin Company, 1998. http://college.hmco.com/English/heath/syllabuild/iguide/clifton.html.

Milton, John. *Paradise Lost*. In *Paradise Lost and Paradise Regained*. New York: Signet Classics, 2001.

Moody, Jocylyn K. "Clifton, Lucille." In *The Oxford Companion to African American Literature*, edited by William L. Andrews, Frances Smith Foster, and Trudier Harris, 157–58. New York: Oxford University Press, 1997.

Moore, Gerald, and Ulli Beier, eds. *The Penguin Book of Modern African Poetry*. 3rd ed. New York: Penguin Books, 1984.

Moorish, Ivor. *Obeah, Christ and Rastaman*. Cambridge: James Clark and Co., 1987.

"Morehouse." *Moorehouse College*. http://www.morehouse.edu/aboutmc/index.php.

Morrison, Toni. *My Book of Mean People*. Pictures by Pascal Lemaitre. New York: Hyperion Books for Children, 2002.

Morrison, Toni, and Slade Morrison. *The Big Box*. Illustrated by Giselle Potter. New York: Hyperion Books for Children, 1999.

"MOVE." *Wikipedia*. http://www.amswers.com/topic/move-10.

Ms. Magazine. "Her Story: 1971–Present." http://www.msmagazine.com/about.asp.

"My Lai Massacre." *Wikipedia*. http://en.wikipedia.org/wikiMy_Lai_massacre.

"Myrlie Evers." Africanamericans.com. http://www.africanamericans.com/MyrlieEversWilliams.htm.

"Nancy Green, the Original 'Aunt Jemima.'" *The African American Registry*. http://www.aaregistry.com/african_american_history/1287/Nancy_Green_the_original_Aunt_Jemima.

Oden, Gloria Catherine. *The Naked Frame: A Love Poem and Sonnets*. New York, Exposition Press, 1952.

———. *Resurrections*. Homestead, FL: Olivant Press, 1978.

———. *The Tie That Binds*. Homestead, FL: Olivant Press, 1980.

Olds, Sharon. *Strike Sparks: Selected Poems, 1980–2002*. New York: Alfred A. Knopf, 2004.

Oliver, Mary. *American Primitive*. Boston: Back Bay Books, 1983.

———. *Why I Wake Early*. Boston: Beacon Press, 2004.

Omoigui, Nowamgabe Austin. "Who Are the Edos?" *Edo Nation*. http://www.edo-nation.net/edos.htm.

"On Strength Gotten from Others." *Lucille Clifton Biography and Bibliography*. http://www.math.buffalo.edu/~sww/ clifton/clifton-biobib.html.

"Oprah in Africa," *People,* June 27, 2005, 20.

Ostriker, Alicia. "Kin and Kin: The Poetry of Lucille Clifton." *American Poetry Review* 22, no. 6 (November–December 1993): 1–14.

Parker, Alan (director). *Mississippi Burning*. MGM, 1988.

"Pentecost (Whitsunday)." *Catholic Encyclopedia*. http://www.newadvent.org/cathen/15614b.htm.

Plath, Sylvia. *The Collected Poems*, edited by Ted Hughes. New York: Harper and Row, 1981.

———. "Daddy." In *The Norton Anthology of Literature by Women*, edited by Sandra Gilbert and Susan Gubar, 2208–9. W. W. Norton and Company, 1985.

Pritzker, Barry M., ed. *A Native American Encyclopedia*. New York: Oxford University Press, 2000.

"The Prophet Jeremiah and Jerusalem." *The Jerusalem Mosaic.* http://jeru.huji.ac .il/eb35s.htm.

"Race Riot in Tulsa, Oklahoma." *The African American Registry.* http:// www.aareg-istry.com/african_american_history/21.

Reed, Ishmael. *Mumbo Jumbo.* New York: Scribner, 1996.

———. *The Reed Reader.* New York: Basic Books, 2000.

Reuben, Paul P. "Chapter 10: Late Twentieth Century, 1945 to the Present: (Lucille Clifton)." *PAL: Perspectives in American Literature: A Research and Reference Guide.* http:/www.csustan.edu/english/reuben/pal/chap10/clifton.html.

Ricks, Mary Kay. "Escape on the Pearl." *Washington Post,* August 12, 1998. http://www .washingtonpost.com/wp-srv/national/horizon/aug98/pearl.htm.

Robinson, Alonford James, Jr. "Howard University." *Encarta Africana CD-ROM.* Microsoft Corporation, 1999.

Robinson, Lisa Clayton. "Children's Literature, African American." *Encarta Africana CD-ROM.* Microsoft Corporation, 1999.

Rochman, Hazel, and Darlene McCampbell, eds. *Bearing Witness: Stories of the Holocaust.* New York: Scholastic, 1995.

"The Rodney King Trials." *Seeing Is Believing.* http://www.seeingisbelieving.ca/ handicam/king/.

Rosenthal, Peggy. "In the Beginning," *Christian Century* (January 30, 2002): 1–3.

Rushing, Andrea B. "Lucille Clifton: A Changing Voice for Changing Times." In *Coming to Light: American Women Poets in the Twentieth Century*, edited by Diane W. Middlebrook and Marilyn Yalom, 214–33. Ann Arbor: University of Michigan Press, 1985.

Salaam, Kalamu ya. "Historical Background of the Black Arts Movement." *The Magic of Juju: An Appreciation of the Black Arts Movement.* http://www.black-collegian.com/ african/bam1_200.shtml.

"Sally Hemings (1773–1835)." About.com, Women's History: Profiles Index. http:// womenshistory.about.com/library/bio/blbio_hemings_sally.htm.

Sams, Jamie and David Carson. *Medicine Cards: The Discovery of Power through the Way of Animals.* 2 vols. Santa Fe, NM: Bear and Company, 1988.

Sanchez, Sonia. *Shake Loose My Skin.* Boston: Beacon Press, 1999.

———. *We a BaddDDDPeople.* Detroit: Broadside Press, 1982.

Scofield, C. I., et al., eds. *Oxford NIV Scofield Study Bible.* New York: Oxford University Press, 1984.

"September Song." *Song Index.* http://www.theguitarguy.com/septemb2.htm.

Sexism and Racism in Popular Basal Readers 1964–1976. The Baltimore Feminist Project. Postscript by Mary Jane Lupton. Afterword by the Racism and Sexism Resource Center for Educators. New York: Racism and Sexism Resource Center for Educators, 1976.

Sexton, Anne. "The Abortion." In *The Complete Poems of Anne Sexton.* Foreword by Maxine Kumin. New York: Mariner Books, 1999.

"Shapeshifting." *Wikipedia.* http://en.wikipedia.org/wiki/Shapeshifting.

Silex, Edgar. *Acts of Love.* Willimantic, CT: Curbstone Press, 2004.

———. *Through All the Displacements.* Willimantic, CT: Curbstone Press, 1995.

"Spike Lee." Gale Research Inc. http://www.galegroup.com/ free_resources/bhm/bio/lee _s.htm.

"St. Mary Magdalen." *Catholic Encyclopedia*. http://www.newadvent.org/cathen/09761a.htm.

Stafford, William. "About William Stafford." *Modern American Poetry*. http://www.english.uiuc.edu/ maps/poets/s_z/stafford/about.htm.

"Statement for Peace." Letter. *The New York Review of Books* 50, no. 2 (February 13, 2003).

Stetson, Erlene. "Studying Slavery: Some Literary and Pedagogical Considerations on the Female Slave." In *All the Women Are White, All the Men Are Black, But Some of Us Are Brave*, edited by Gloria T. Hull, Patricia Bell Scott, and Barbara Smith. Old Westbury, NY: Feminist Press, 1982.

Stewart, Richard, and T. J. Milling. "Funeral in Jasper Draws Hundreds." *Houston Chronicle*, June 14, 1998. http://www.chron.com/disp/story.mpl/special/jasper/byrd/228093.html.

Still, Erica L. "Body Language." *The Iowa Review*. http://www.uiowa.edu/~iareview/reviews/erica-still.htm.

"Strange Fruit." University of San Diego History Department WW2Timeline. http://history.acusd.edu/gen/WW2Timeline/start.html.

"Students Keep Her Young." *The Council Chronicle* http:/www.ncte.org/chronicle/September2001/clifton.shtml.

Theweleit, Klaus. *Male Fantasies: Women, Floods, Bodies, Histories*. Trans. Stephen Conway. Minneapolis: University of Minnesota Press, 1987.

"Three-Time Pulitzer Prize Nominee, Lucille Clifton, Wins National Book Award." *Baltimore Times* (November 24–30, 2000). n.p. From the collection of Professor Margaret Reid.

Thompson, Ronna C. "Jordan, June." In *The Oxford Companion to African American Literature*, edited by William L. Andrews, Frances Smith Foster, and Trudier Harris. New York: Oxford University Press, 1997.

Thyreen-Mizingnou, Jeannine. "Grace and Ethics in Contemporary American Poetry: Resituating the Other, the World, and the Self." *Religion and Literature* 32, no. 1 (Spring 2000): 67–97.

"Trail of Tears." *Cherokee Messenger*. http://www.powersource.com/cherokee/history.html.

"A Tribute to Lucille Clifton." The Poetry Society of America. Hunter College, November 18, 2004.

Wall, Cheryl A. "Sifting Legacies in Lucille Clifton's *Generations*." *Contemporary Literature* 40, no. 4 (Winter 1999): 552–74.

Walsh, Chad. Review of *Good Times. Book World*, March 8, 1970, 7.

Ward, Jerry. "*Generations: A Memoir*, by Lucille Clifton." *New Orleans Review* 5, no. 4 (1999): 552–74.

Webster's New World College Dictionary. 3rd ed. New York: Simon & Schuster Macmillan Company, 1997.

Weeks, Linton. "Poetry's Persistent Listener." *Washington Post* (November 18, 2000): C1, C11. From the collection of Professor Margaret Reid.

Weininger, Melissa. "The Trials of Lorena Bobbitt." http://www.digitas.harvard.edu/~perspy/old/issues/2000/retro/lorena_bobbitt.html.

Welch, James, with Paul Stekler. *Killing Custer*. New York: Penguin, 1994.

———. *Riding the Earthboy 40*. Pittsburgh: Carnegie Mellon University Press, 1997.

"White Hair." *Blue Skyways, a Service of the Kansas State Library.* http://skyways.lib.ks .us/genweb/archives/1912/w/white_hair.html.

White, Mark Bernard. "Sharing the Living Light: Rhetorical, Poetic, and Social Identity in Lucille Clifton." *CLA Journal* 40, no. 3 (March 1997): 288–305.

Whitley, Edward. "Lucille Clifton (1936–)." In *African American Autobiographers: A Sourcebook*, edited by Emmanuel S. Nelson, 68–72. Westport, CT: Greenwood, 2002.

Whitman, Walt. *Song of Myself.* The Representative Poetry Online Edition. http:// eir.library.utoronto.ca/rpo/display'poem2288.html.

Wilbur, Richard. *Walking to Sleep: New Poems and Translations.* 1969. Reprint, New York: Harcourt Brace, 1992.

Wilhelm, Helmut, and Richard Wilhelm. *The Wilhelm Lectures on the Book of Changes.* Princeton, NJ: Princeton University Press, 1995.

Williams, Sherley Anne. "Some Implications of Womanist Theory." *Reading Black, Reading Feminist*, edited by Henry Louis Gates, Jr., 68–75. New York: Meridian, 1990.

Wilson, James. *The Earth Shall Weep: A History of Native America.* New York: Atlantic Monthly Press, 1998.

"Winnie Mandela: Fallen Political Heir." *Truth and Reconciliation.* BBC News, October 28, 1998. http://news.bbc.co.uk/1/hi/special_report/1998/10/98/truth_and_reconciliation/ 202516.stm.

Witmyer, Jannette J. "Poetry in the Key of Life: Lucille Clifton." *Jubilee*, April 2001, 26–27.

Worsham, Fabian C. "The Poetics of Matrilineage: Mothers and Daughters in the Poetry of African American Women, 1965–1985." In *Women of Color: Mother-Daughter Relationships in 20th Century Literature*, edited by Elizabeth Brown-Guillory, 177–231. Austin: University of Texas Press, 1996.

Wright, Richard. "Between the World and Me." 1935. Reprint, in *Black Voices*, edited by Abraham Chapman, 437–38. New York: Penguin Books, 1968.

Yeats, William Butler. "The Second Coming." In *The Norton Anthology of Poetry*, edited by Margaret Ferguson, Mary Jo Salter, and Jon Stallworthy, 1091. 4th ed. New York: Norton, 1996.

Index

About the Author

MARY JANE LUPTON is Professor Emeritus at Morgan State University. She is the author of numerous essays in the areas of feminism, Indian Studies, and Black Studies. She is the author of two Greenwood Critical Companions: *Maya Angelou* (1998) and *James Welch* (2004). Her book *Menstruation and Psychoanalysis* was published in 1993.